EXPLORATIONS IN LOCAL AND
REGIONAL HISTORY

Centre for Regional and Local History, University of Hertfordshire
and
Centre for English Local History, University of Leicester

SERIES EDITORS: NIGEL GOOSE AND RICHARD JONES

Portrait photograph of Alan Milner Everitt.

THE COUNTY COMMUNITY
IN SEVENTEENTH-CENTURY
ENGLAND AND WALES

EDITED BY JACQUELINE EALES
AND ANDREW HOPPER

UNIVERSITY OF HERTFORDSHIRE PRESS

Explorations in Local and Regional History
Volume 5

First published in Great Britain in 2012 by
University of Hertfordshire Press
College Lane
Hatfield
Hertfordshire
AL10 9AB

British Library Cataloguing in Publication Data
A catalogue record for this book is available from the British Library

ISBN 978-1-907396-70-0

Design by Mathew Lyons
Printed in Great Britain by Hobbs the Printers Ltd

Contents

Figures

Contributors

DAVID J. APPLEBY is lecturer in early modern British history at the University of Nottingham. He completed his PhD at Keele University and is the author of *Black Bartholomew's day: preaching, polemic and Restoration nonconformity* published by Manchester University Press in 2007.

LLOYD BOWEN is senior lecturer in early modern and Welsh history at the University of Cardiff and is the author of *The politics of the principality: Wales, c.1603–1642* published by the University of Wales Press in 2007.

JAN BROADWAY was technical director of the Centre for Editing Lives and Letters at Queen Mary, University of London. She completed her PhD at the University of Birmingham in 1997 and has recently finished a biography of Sir William Dugdale. Recent publications include *'No historie so meete': gentry culture and the development of local history in Elizabethan and early Stuart England* published by Manchester University Press in 2006.

JACQUELINE EALES is professor in early modern history at Canterbury Christ Church University. She is President of the Historical Association (2011–2014) and has published extensively on Kent during the English civil wars. She is the director of the John Hayes Canterbury 1641 Project which aims to reconstruct the allegiance and experience of the city's inhabitants during the civil war period. She is the author of *Puritans and roundheads: the Harleys of Brampton Bryan and the outbreak of the English civil war*, published by Cambridge University Press in 1990 and recently republished in 2002. Professor Eales is currently working on a book examining women in seventeenth-century English clerical families.

DAVID HEY is emeritus professor in local and family history at the University of Sheffield. He completed his PhD at the University of Leicester under the supervision of W.G. Hoskins and Alan Everitt. With a prolific record of publications, he is among the most well known local historians in Britain. Among his recent works is the second edition of *The Oxford companion to family and local history*, published in 2008.

ANDREW HOPPER is lecturer in English local history at the University of Leicester. He completed his PhD at the University of York examining parliamentarian allegiance in Yorkshire during the civil wars. He is the author of *Black Tom: Sir Thomas Fairfax and the English Revolution*, published by Manchester University Press in 2007. He is currently finishing a book entitled *Turncoats and renegadoes: changing sides during the English civil wars* for Oxford University Press.

STEPHEN K. ROBERTS is the editor of the House of Commons 1640–1660 section of the History of Parliament. He is the editor of the Worcestershire Historical Society and joint editor of *Midland History*. He is the author of *Recovery and Restoration in an English County: Devon local administration 1646–1670*, published by Exeter University Press in 1985 and is a vice-president of the Cromwell Association.

IAN WARREN is a former junior research fellow at Queen's College, Oxford. He completed his doctoral thesis entitled 'The gentry, the nobility, and London residence, c.1580–1680' at the University of Oxford in 2006.

Abbreviations

BL	British Library, London
Bodl.	Bodleian Library, Oxford
CCA	Canterbury Cathedral Archives
CJ	*Journals of the House of Commons*
CKS	Centre for Kentish Studies, Maidstone
ERO	Essex Record Office, Chelmsford
HALS	Hertfordshire Archives and Local Studies
HL	Parliamentary Archives, House of Lords
HMC	Historical Manuscripts Commission
HRO	Hampshire Record Office, Winchester
LJ	*Journals of the House of Lords*
NLW	National Library of Wales, Aberystwyth
NRO	Norfolk Record Office, Norwich
ODNB	*Oxford Dictionary of National Biography* online
SBT	Shakespeare Birthplace Trust Archive, Stratford-upon-Avon
TNA	The National Archives, Kew
WCRO	Warwickshire County Record Office, Warwick
WYAS	West Yorkshire Archive Service

Acknowledgements

The genesis of this book was a conference held at the Centre for English Local History at the University of Leicester on 12 December 2009. The original intention was to commemorate the passing away the year before of Professor Alan Everitt, a former director of Leicester's Department for English Local History. The conference re-examined his influential work *The community of Kent and the Great Rebellion*, and explored new avenues through which Everitt's ideas about the county community might be approached and reassessed. The editors would like to thank all who attended and participated at the conference, in particular Professor Christopher Dyer, and the organisation and administrative support of Lucy Byrne and Danielle Jackson. We are grateful to the staff of the University of Hertfordshire Press, in particular Jane Housham and Sarah Elvins for their unfailingly helpful assistance. We are also thankful to the Aurelius Trust, the Isobel Thornley bequest, London University and Canterbury Christ Church University, whose generous financial support has greatly aided in the publication of this volume.

Jacqueline Eales and Andrew Hopper

Series Editors' Preface

The series of *Explorations in Local and Regional History* is a continuation and development of the 'Occasional Papers' of the University of Leicester's Department of English Local History, a series started by Herbert Finberg in 1952. This succeeding series is published by the University of Hertfordshire Press, which has a strong profile in English local and regional history. The idea for the new series came from Harold Fox, who, with Nigel Goose, served as series editor in its first two years.

Explorations in Local and Regional History has three distinctive characteristics. First, the series is prepared to publish work on novel themes, to tackle fresh subjects – perhaps even unusual ones. We hope that it serves to open up new approaches, prompt the analysis of new sources or types of source, and foster new methodologies. This is not to suggest that more traditional scholarship in local and regional history are unrepresented, for it may well be distinctive in terms of its quality, and we also seek to offer an outlet for work of distinction that might be difficult to place elsewhere.

This brings us to the second feature of the series, which is the intention to publish mid-length studies, generally within the range of 40,000 to 60,000 words. Such studies are hard to place with existing publishers, for while there are current series that cater for mid-length overviews of particular historiographical topics or themes, there is none of which we are aware that offers similar outlets for original research. *Explorations*, therefore, intends to fill the publishing vacuum between research articles and full-length books (the latter, incidentally, might well be eligible for inclusion in the existing University of Hertfordshire Press series, *Studies in Regional and Local History*).

Third, while we expect this series to be required reading for both academics and students, it is also our intention to ensure that it is of interest and relevance to local historians operating outside an institutional framework. To this end we ensure that each volume is set at a price that individuals, and not only university libraries, can generally afford. Local and regional history is a subject taught at many levels, from schools to universities. Books, magazines, television and radio all testify to the vitality of research and writing outside universities, as well as to the sustained growth of popular interest. It is hoped that *Explorations in Local and Regional History* will make a contribution to the continued flourishing of our subject. We will ensure that books in the series are accessible to a wide readership, that they avoid technical language and jargon, and that they will usually be illustrated.

This preface, finally, serves as a call for proposals, and authors who are studying local themes in relation to particular places (rural or urban), regions, counties or provinces, whether their subject matter comprises social groups (or other groups), landscapes, interactions and movements between places, microhistory or total history should consider publication with this series. The editors can be consulted informally at the addresses given below, while a formal proposal form is available from the University of Hertfordshire Press at uhpress@herts.ac.uk.

Nigel Goose
Centre for Regional and Local History
Department of Humanities
University of Hertfordshire
College Lane
Hatfield AL10 9AB
N.Goose@herts.ac.uk

Richard Jones
Centre for English Local History
Marc Fitch Historical Institute
5 Salisbury Road
Leicester LE1 7QR
rlcj1@leicester.ac.uk

Preface
A personal memory of Alan Everitt

DAVID HEY

The portrait photograph of Alan that adorns this volume and the staircase at Marc Fitch House glowers at us, disapprovingly. He could be like that occasionally – I have a letter from him in which he describes the publisher of one of his books as 'a malicious oaf' – but that is not how I and other old friends remember him. He was a kind and gentle man, very supportive of his staff and students and always ready to take an interest in their work. I met him first in 1968 when I was doing a part-time PhD under William Hoskins at Leicester. Shortly afterwards, William retired and Alan became my supervisor. Then in 1969 I was his first appointment when he became head of department. I was a research fellow in agrarian history at Leicester until I moved to Sheffield University in 1973, but we remained in close contact and I have always thought of my time at Leicester under Alan's guidance as my formative years as a local historian.

But, of course, as I did not meet him until 1968, I can offer no insights into the origins of his book *The community of Kent and the Great Rebellion* that will be discussed in this volume. By the time that I first knew him he had moved on to other interests. He had finished his PhD on this subject in 1957, but in that year he was appointed as research assistant at Leicester, to Dr Joan Thirsk, working on volume four of *The agrarian history of England and Wales, 1500–1640*.[1] In 1960 he became research fellow in urban history at Leicester, and therefore the conversion of his thesis into a book was done in his leisure time and it was not published until 1966. Joan tells me that when Alan sent her a copy of his book, The community of Kent and the Great Rebellion, upon its publication he wrote that, thanks to her, he had become more interested in economic and social history and that the study of the probate inventories of ordinary Kent farmers had set him off on a new track. He also said that the underlying theme of his book had changed since the completion of his original thesis. It was now 'the close-woven fabric of Kentish family life', which was 'the only point that still interests me'.

---

1. J. Thirsk (ed.), *The agrarian history of England and Wales*, 4: 1500–1640 (Cambridge, 1967).

This probably explains why he never responded to the later debate about county communities stemming from his book. His interests had moved elsewhere. Another point that Joan makes is that, later on, he seems to have downgraded the traumatic effects on people of the civil wars when set against other crises such as acute food shortages resulting from harvest failure.[2]

My own memory is that 'the close-woven fabric of Kentish family life' was indeed a major and abiding interest of Alan's and one that stemmed from his childhood in Sevenoaks, which he remembered as 'a quiet, small market town'. He wrote a memoir of his younger days, which we hope will be published, and which he asked me to comment on some twenty years or so ago. I was impressed by his vivid, detailed memories of an environment that was totally different from my own upbringing on the edge of the Pennines. Two things in particular stand out in my memory. One is his love of the streets, houses and shops of Sevenoaks and particularly the wooded countryside around the town at a time when there was little traffic and plenty of freedom for a child to roam. This nourished his lifelong interest in woodlands and commons, culminating in his great book *Continuity and colonization: the evolution of Kentish settlement* and the research on commons and greens that occupied his later years, but which, alas, he never finished.[3] He had a sharp eye and a fondness for nature, as well as a deep feeling for the built environment and the history of the countryside. Any discussion of his work on Kent must start with the depth of his emotional attachment to and deep knowledge of his native county, which I noted at first hand when I went with his MA students on a field trip there one spring. An unresolved puzzle is why Alan continued to live in a south Leicestershire village when he took early retirement rather than move back to Kent. Perhaps he realised how much Sevenoaks had changed and preferred to rely on his memories as a continued source of emotional support for his later research? But this, of course, is just speculation.

The other thing that I remember vividly from his memoir is his upbringing in a family of fully committed members of the Exclusive Sect of the Plymouth Brethren. Although he broke away from the Brethren in 1963, after a period of great strain, his memories of his upbringing amongst them were happy ones. Alan was a deeply religious man, although he kept his beliefs private amongst his colleagues. His own background as a member of the Plymouth Brethren and his detailed knowledge of the Bible certainly informed his work on religious nonconformity, such as his essay on Philip Doddridge, the eighteenth-century

---

2.   J. Thirsk, 'Alan Milner Everitt (1926–2008)', *Proceedings of the British Academy*, 166 (2010), p. 187.

3.   A. Everitt, *Continuity and colonization: the evolution of Kentish settlement* (Leicester, 1986); A. Everitt, 'Common land', in J. Thirsk (ed.), *The English rural landscape* (Oxford, 2000), pp. 210–35, 339–40.

4.   A. Everitt, 'Springs of sensibility: Philip Doddridge of Northampton and the evangelical tradition', in A. Everitt (ed.), *Landscape and community in England* (London, 1985), pp. 209–45; A. Everitt, *The pattern of rural dissent, the nineteenth century*, Department of English Local History, occasional papers, second series, 4 (Leicester, 1972).

evangelical minister from Northampton, whose writings he came across during his tenure of the fellowship in urban history, and his occasional paper on The pattern of rural dissent: the nineteenth century, in the new series that he started when he became professor and head of department at Leicester in 1968.[4] As I shared an interest in nonconformist history, he asked me to comment on his paper. He was on study leave at the time and I have a closely written eight-page letter in which he replied in detail to the points I raised. In it, he taught me a valuable lesson in not being too hard on other historians with whom one disagreed, for in my reply I had criticised an influential article on which he had relied. He agreed with my criticisms but pointed out that the article was a pioneering one. Alan wrote, 'It is possible – not, I think, probable at all – that his theory is true in some areas. But I will leave the trouncing of the poor nitwit to you.' He ended his letter with a detailed explanation of the meaning of 'Jehovah Jireh', an inscription which I had seen on a Sheffield chapel and had asked him about, then perhaps smiling to himself he apologised for 'that little homily (which you asked for!)'.

In his memoir, Alan noted the strength of family life and the cohesion of the Brethren through their weekly meetings and their intermarriage. These memories reinforced his historical interest in the importance of family connections, starting with the diaries and letters of the Kentish gentry in the civil wars. His own experiences during the Second World War, when his home was destroyed by a bomb and families were torn apart, informed his work on the breakdown of family relationships and what he called 'Kent cousinages' during the 1640s. Three hundred years later, he himself was conscripted into the army as a non-combatant in 1944, serving until 1948.

When he became Joan Thirsk's research assistant for The agrarian history Alan's interests turned from the gentry to other social groups. He wrote an influential chapter on farm labourers for volume four. When I was a member of his department he was working on inns and country carriers and on decayed market towns, as well as on religious dissent.[5] That was an exciting time, in which the frontiers of the relatively new subject of local history were pushed out in all sorts of directions as Alan encouraged us to follow our interests. His own interests moved back in time to the origins of settlement in Kent and forward into the Victorian and Edwardian period. I was impressed by his tremendous knowledge of English literature. I learned later that he had read all the eighteenth- and nineteenth-century classical authors in English while he was still at school. Now the novels of George Eliot, Elizabeth Gaskell, Margaret Oliphant and Arnold Bennett, in particular, informed his work on the intense lives of dissenting families up and down the land.

5.   A. Everitt, 'Urban growth, 1570–1770', *The Local Historian*, 8 (1968), pp. 118–25; A. Everitt, 'County carriers in the nineteenth century', *Journal of Transport History*, 3 (1976), pp. 176–202.

Alan's interest in Kentish families and their inter-connections, first revealed in his work on the civil wars, underpinned his later research and writing. Two of his collected essays, published in 1985 as Landscape and community in England, are 'Kentish family portrait',[6] a study of the family of the great antiquarian Edward Hasted, and 'Dynasty and community since the seventeenth century', which dealt with 'entire networks of regional and dynastic connexion which extended beyond the limits of the individual community, and which developed largely outside the ranks of the aristocracy and squirearchy'. Here we see his interests extending beyond the county gentry and going much lower down the social scale. He described 'this principle of dynastic connexion' as 'an extraordinarily pervasive feature of English provincial society' which:

> not only shaped the structure of politics, where it has long been familiar: it influenced the course of regional trade; it facilitated the evolution of technical skills; it moulded the development of many professions; it channelled the diffusion of ideas; it bounded the society of town and country together. It affected farming; it affected industry, it affected retail trade, it affected craftsmanship. It affected the church, it affected nonconformity, it affected the army and the navy.

He went on to say that, 'in studying any provincial society, we need to identify the core of dominant families who for one reason or another came to form the focus of influence within it'. Leading on from this, 'we need to consider the origins of these central or focal families', most of which were drawn from 'the indigeneous families of the area in question'. He demonstrated this by a detailed study of what he called 'some 220 paramount dynasties', comprising 4,450 separately established families, virtually all of which were confined to Kent, with such distinctive local names as Blaxland, Denne, Hambrook, or Kingsnorth.[7] In such ways, his early interests persisted, but within the sphere of social and economic history rather than the political, and widening in their social and geographical compass.

I have three quick, unrelated memories of Alan to finish with. First, Alan came to speak at an extramural day-school that I organised at Sheffield in the 1970s. He was on after lunch, but I also had to see to the main speaker in the morning, Maurice Beresford. Maurice was a garrulous man who loved a good meal and the lunch went well over time, leaving me to race back to the lecture theatre to apologise for my bad manners in leaving Alan to fend for himself in setting up his slides. But I need not have feared, for he was sitting on the stage

---

6.   A. Everitt, 'Kentish family portrait: an aspect of the rise of the pseudo-gentry', first published in C.W. Chalklin, M.A. Havinden and M. Ashley (eds), *Rural change and urban growth, 1500–1800: essays in English regional history in honour of W.G. Hoskins* (London, 1974), pp. 169–99.

7.   A. Everitt, 'Dynasty and community since the seventeenth century', in Everitt (ed.), *Landscape and community in England*, pp. 311–12, 320–21.

serenely regarding the audience. 'There is a seriousness of purpose about a northern adult audience that I approve of,' he said. He put it down to the West Riding nonconformist tradition and thought that midland audiences were lacking in comparison.

Second, he stayed overnight on another occasion and at six o'clock in the morning I was woken by the sound of voices. To my dismay, I realised that my two young children were in his bedroom. I raced in to apologise, but found Alan sitting on the edge of his bed talking to my enthralled offspring about some old coins, which he had found on the window sill. He was not at all fazed about their intrusion at that early hour and always took an interest in my children as they grew older.

The third memory is rather a perplexing one. We all have our little quirks and Alan was able to laugh at his, but on this occasion I do not think that he intended to be funny. He lived alone with the company of a succession of cats. I have to confess to a certain indifference to cats, but they meant much to Alan. In 1999 he finished a long letter to me by writing: 'Must stop, as my cat Shadow has come for his tea. The history of cats needs looking into next – a most interesting topic is the changing attitudes to them. Did you know that windows were not invented to let light in, but for cats to look out of?' Alan did not joke about cats, but I do not think he pursued this particular line of research any further.

After the retirement of William Hoskins, Alan became the leading English local historian of his time. It is very fitting that this memorial volume should arise from a conference held in his old department, now the Centre for English Local History, at the University of Leicester.

Introduction
The impact of the county community hypothesis

ANDREW HOPPER

On 12 December 2009 a memorial conference for the late Alan Everitt was hosted by the Centre for English Local History at the University of Leicester. Its purpose was to re-examine Everitt's influential 'county community' hypothesis in the light of recent scholarship and signpost future directions for the topic. The papers indicated a recent reinvigoration of the topic that Everitt first pioneered in a series of publications during the 1960s and 1970s. Together, their revised versions form the basis for this volume. Rather than commenting upon these papers, this introduction seeks to contextualise them by summarising Everitt's notion of the 'county community' for a general readership unfamiliar with the minefields of Stuart historiography. It will then proceed to assess the impact of this hypothesis and the reactions it provoked. Even over 45 years on, this remains a delicate task because Everitt himself felt that his views were oversimplified and then misrepresented by his critics.

Published by Leicester University Press in 1966, Alan Everitt's *The community of Kent and the Great Rebellion* was an inspirational work that defined debate for a generation. It bestowed a new scholarly respectability onto county studies of the civil-war period by showing that wide-ranging conclusions could be drawn from the study of a particular county, and that counties were worth studying in their own right rather than merely to illustrate the national narrative. The book's conclusions were qualified and furthered by Everitt's Historical Association pamphlet of 1969, *The local community and the Great Rebellion*. This extended the geographical focus to include a brief comparative study of Leicestershire and Northamptonshire.

Everitt's approach anticipated aspects of the revisionist historiography of the 1970s and 1980s because it was written in reaction to the deterministic certainties of the national narratives of the civil wars offered by Whig and Marxist historiography. Whigs saw this period as the rise of parliamentary government, liberty and toleration. Marxists saw it as the rise of the bourgeoisie, entailing the replacement of feudalism with capitalism. Instead, by focusing on his native

Kent, Everitt emphasised the importance of local identities and allegiances, not as reflections of national concerns, but for their own sake.[1] This was so important, he argued, because in the late Tudor–early Stuart period the gentry of a county formed large, self-contained county communities. England was composed of these, and was 'a union of partially independent county-states or communities, each with its own distinct ethos and loyalty'.[2] Many revisionist historians were initially broadly sympathetic to Everitt's view of the provinces. Keen to refute that the outbreak of civil war had long-term causes, they argued for the gentry's lack of interest in and suspicion of national political developments. This perceived moderate consensus among the gentry was held to explain the accidental and contingent nature of the war's outbreak, the reluctance of the majority to take sides and the strength of neutralist feeling thereafter.[3]

Everitt depicted Kent as insular, or self-contained, the home of an ancient gentry, most of whom were long established in the county, and who therefore sought to preserve their county's stability and independence from the central government, as represented by Charles I, the Long Parliament or Oliver Cromwell. The book tended to a view that stressed polarity between national and local concerns, which Everitt characterised later as a 'conflict between loyalty to the local community and loyalty to the state'.[4] The recurring theme was the victory of the nation state, represented by the New Model Army and the puritan regime at Westminster, over the 'county-state' of Kent. He considered that throughout the 1640s and 1650s there was a yearning for a return to more traditional, and therefore more local, forms of government.[5]

The county community in Everitt's Kent was held together by three key factors. The first was intermarriage: the majority of gentry families married into local families and belonged to vast countywide kinship networks. Everitt considered these insular and 'excessively inbred'.[6] This was reflected in his observation of a nineteenth-century saying: 'in Kent, they are all first cousins.'[7] The result of this was that the leaders of Kentish society, the 20 or 30 leading county families, formed a particularly homogenous group. The second factor was long settlement: most gentry had resided on the same estate for generations and

1.   R.C. Richardson, *The debate on the English revolution* (London, 1977), pp. 119–20.
2.   A. Everitt, *The community of Kent and the Great Rebellion* (Leicester, 1966), p. 13.
3.   R. Cust and A. Hughes, 'Introduction: after Revisionism', in R. Cust and A. Hughes (eds), *Conflict in early Stuart England: studies in religion and politics, 1603–1642* (Harlow, 1989), pp. 5–7; G. Burgess, 'Revisionism, politics and political ideas in early Stuart England', *The Historical Journal*, 34 (1991), pp. 467–70.
4.   A. Everitt, *The local community and the Great Rebellion*, Historical Association, general series, 70 (London, 1969), p. 5.
5.   Everitt, *The community of Kent*, pp. 13, 16, 301, 325.
6.   *Ibid.*, pp. 14, 41.
7.   A. Everitt, 'Social mobility in early modern England', *Past and Present*, 33 (1966), p. 61.

had become embedded, rooted in the physical fabric of society. Most of Kent's gentry were considered such before the Tudor period and only one in eight had established themselves since the reign of Elizabeth.[8] The third factor was paternalism. Everitt considered that Kent's gentry had a sense of responsibility to protect the poor and their tenants, which was perhaps most particularly evident in open-field parishes.[9] Such was his conviction in the significance of this gentry network that Everitt depicted the assemblies of county elites at assizes or quarter sessions time as a kind of 'informal county parliament'. He considered that Kent's leading gentry were surprisingly withdrawn from national politics, and that for them local issues took precedence over national ones.[10] This was expressed by the way in which contemporaries used the term 'country'; they meant it to refer to their county, rather than the nation as a whole.[11]

The community of Kent and the Great Rebellion met with immediate critical acclaim: Christopher Hill declared it 'a model of its kind' and full of 'local observations with national reverberations', while R.C. Richardson hailed it as a 'refreshingly different and stimulating approach'.[12] With its conclusions broadened and reinforced by two further essays,[13] Everitt's book did much to inspire a series of county studies, many of which first appeared as doctoral theses. Like Everitt, they unearthed much new evidence by taking full advantage of the newly opened county record offices.[14] Scholars such as David Underdown for Somerset (1973), John Morrill for Cheshire (1974) and Anthony Fletcher for Sussex (1975), influenced by Everitt's concept of the 'county community', delivered a new body of local scholarship based on impeccable archival research. Underdown concurred that many of parliament's committee in Somerset 'were men who put the unity of their county above partisan considerations'.[15] Despite differing from Everitt on several points, Morrill's work on Cheshire uncovered a strong county identity among the gentry, who endeavoured to remain neutral or keep their county out of the civil war in 1642, when their previous moderate opposition to Charles I became no longer viable.[16] Of the three, Anthony Fletcher's book on Sussex lent Everitt the strongest support. He argued that, of the leading gentry families in Sussex, only

8.   Everitt, The community of Kent, pp. 35–7, 44.
9.   Ibid., p. 48.
10. Ibid., pp. 96n, 121.
11. Everitt, The local community, p. 6.
12. C. Hill, review of Everitt, The community of Kent, in Economic History Review, 20 (1967), p. 169; Richardson, Debate, p. 119.
13. Everitt, The local community; A. Everitt, Change in the provinces: the seventeenth century, University of Leicester, occasional papers, 2nd series, 1 (1972).
14. J.S. Morrill, Revolt in the provinces: the people of England and the tragedies of war, 1630–1648, 2nd edn (London, 1999), p. 10.
15. D. Underdown, Somerset in the civil war and Interregnum (Newton Abbot, 1973), p. 69.
16. J.S. Morrill, Cheshire 1630–1660: county government and society during the English revolution (Oxford, 1974).

ten were 'Tudor newcomers', and that the established county gentry constituted a source of social stability, with their shared pursuits of hunting, bowling, falconing and horse racing.[17] Fletcher saw the Sussex gentry's custom of marrying at home within their own county as generating a vast and intricate network of cousinage, which tended to limit their social contacts to those within their own shire. He also argued this was the case with Dorset, Lancashire, Leicestershire, Suffolk and Yorkshire. He saw kinship as the dominant principle in this community, which encouraged introversion and to some extent determined allegiances.[18] Everitt heartily approved of Fletcher's argument for 'the overriding sense of cohesion in Sussex society', suggesting that the continuity and stability of Sussex county administration was the key theme of Fletcher's book.[19] Although Fletcher and Morrill extended Everitt's chronology earlier and did not agree with all his findings, Morrill reminisced in 1999 that they worked 'within the paradigms created by Everitt'.[20] The subsequent highly successful careers embarked upon by these historians, along with the unit of the county appearing so conveniently suited to gentry studies of this nature, ensured that by the 1990s few counties were left uncovered.

Despite its influential and far-reaching impact, by the 1970s the county community hypothesis began to attract serious criticism. In 1972, Derek Hirst's study of Sir Edward Dering, Kent's knight of the shire in the Long Parliament, argued that by 1640 Kent's political polarisation suggested that Everitt's county community was exaggerated.[21] In 1977 Clive Holmes indicated his discomfort with Fletcher's 'infatuation with the nebulous "county community" concept', arguing that rather than being 'forged exclusively in the local arena' the Sussex gentry were capable of viewing 'political and religious controversies' in a 'national context'.[22] In a seminal article of 1980 Holmes depicted Everitt's hypothesis as having neglected contrary evidence while also underplaying popular politics and ideological divisions to engender a 'roseate aura of mutual love, charity and unity' in the Kentish community.[23] He considered that Everitt's patriarchal inclination to the 'politics of deference' was 'misleadingly elitist', and criticised his assumption that groups below the gentry shared their concerns.[24] In this Holmes has been

---

17. A. Fletcher, *A county community in peace and war: Sussex 1600–1660* (London, 1975), pp. 25, 29–30.

18. Ibid., pp. 44–8, 53.

19. A. Everitt, 'Downland and weald', *Times Literary Supplement*, 17 September 1976, p. 1180.

20. Morrill, *Revolt*, p. 12.

21. D. Hirst, 'The defection of Sir Edward Dering', *Historical Journal*, 15 (1972), p. 195.

22. C. Holmes, review of A. Fletcher, *A county community in peace and war: Sussex 1600–1660*, in *American Historical Review*, 82 (1977), pp. 632–3.

23. C. Holmes, 'The county community in Stuart historiography', *Journal of British Studies*, 19 (1980), pp. 55, 68.

24. Ibid., pp. 71–2.

supported by subsequent studies of civil-war allegiance that have argued the gentry could not automatically rely upon the mobilisation of their tenants.[25]

Holmes attacked the heart of Everitt's argument, suggesting that his linkage of ancient lineage with local sentiment was unproven. Composing a forthright and systematic rebuttal, Holmes argued that the county gentry were far from insular in forging political contacts from other counties at university and the Inns of Court, and through marriage, kinship networks and meetings of parliament. He contended that many more gentry and clergy attended university by the early 1600s and that there they learnt that their county was part of a nation state, rather than a unit opposed to it. Although some colleges at Oxford and Cambridge admittedly had strong connections with particular counties, they remained arenas where future local governors would mix with their counterparts from across the kingdom. Some colleges had a religious rather than a county identity, such as Emmanuel at Cambridge, with its reputation for Godly religion. Many gentry followed their time at university with a year or two at one of London's Inns of Court for a rudimentary grounding in the law.[26] England was an increasingly litigious society with a common law enforced in all counties, and an understanding of how the central law courts at Westminster operated would be critical for the future of many gentlemen. Many would later seek to bring in contacts from London, the court or parliament to arbitrate or intervene in local disputes. Other wealthy gentlemen emulated the peerage by travelling abroad for a tour of European cities to learn foreign languages and culture. Some learned French, Europe's international military language, or even Dutch, which could be heard spoken by immigrant populations on the streets of London, Norwich and Colchester. Many more received a military education in Dutch service in the Low Countries or Germany, while Roman Catholic gentry often served in the Spanish Army of Flanders. Holmes contested that these educational experiences did much to produce 'a common language of intellectual discourse, and, thus, a common gentry culture'.[27]

In matters of local government, Holmes pointed out that quarter sessions were rarely county-wide events with all the justices present. Rather, they administered divisions within a county, and when justices referred to their 'country' they often meant their hundred, wapentake or local neighbourhood rather than the entire county.[28] In the West Riding of Yorkshire during the 1640s

---

25. A. Hopper, 'Black Tom': Sir Thomas Fairfax and the English revolution (Manchester, 2007), p. 93; M. Stoyle, Loyalty and locality: popular allegiance in Devon during the English civil war (Exeter, 1994), p. 143; J. Walter, 'The English people and the English Revolution revisited', History Workshop Journal, 61 (2006), p. 178; A. Wood, 'Beyond post-revisionism? The civil war allegiances of the miners of the Derbyshire "Peak Country"', Historical Journal, 40 (1997), pp. 32–3, 39.
26. Holmes, 'The county community', pp. 56–9.
27. Ibid., p. 60.
28. Ibid., p. 62.

and 1650s the quarter sessions met in nine locations at Barnsley, Bradford, Doncaster, Leeds, Pontefract, Rotherham, Skipton, Wakefield and Wetherby.[29] Instead, the assizes were the occasions where collective county sentiment could be voiced, but Holmes reminds us that the assizes also represented the apparatus of central government. He argued that in several counties the traditional court–country framework better explained local politics than did the gentry community hypothesis, and that an effective understanding of county administration was not possible without an awareness of the changing concerns of central government.[30] Holmes's conclusions were strengthened by his book on Lincolnshire that appeared the same year and repositioned the gentry as 'brokers', engaged in 'channelling the products of the national culture into the localities'.[31]

These arguments found support in an article by Ann Hughes two years later, attacking the relevance of Everitt's hypothesis to Warwickshire. Hughes pointed to important geographical contrasts such as the Arden–fielden divide outlined by John Leland, arguing that metalworking Birmingham, for instance, had far more in common with Dudley and Wolverhampton in neighbouring Staffordshire than it did with the settled arable agricultural region south of the river Avon.[32] Hughes followed up this article by developing her doctoral thesis into a book on Warwickshire which became the new benchmark for county studies.[33] She depicted a county with great contrasts to Everitt's Kent, arguing that the Warwickshire gentry were less cohesive and that their county was 'undergoing rapid economic change'. Unlike the situation in Kent, many of the 288 families classed by Hughes as gentry were relative newcomers, around one-quarter establishing themselves after 1600. Others were wealthy upstarts who had bought monastic land in the sixteenth century.[34] Over half, even among the minor gentry, married outside the county, while Hughes reflected that marriage links did not always lead to harmonious ties between families. Many of the justices of the peace were unrelated and held residences or estates outside the county.[35] Hughes considered that these factors widened their horizons and she placed a new stress on religious and political conflict in the localities that properly addressed the significance of non-gentry activism. She concluded that parochial gentry and middling sorts from the populous and more unruly Arden sided with

29. WYAS, Wakefield, QS 4/2 and QS 4/3.
30. Holmes, 'The county community', pp. 63–4, 66.
31. C. Holmes, *Seventeenth-century Lincolnshire* (Lincoln, 1980), p. 5.
32. A. Hughes, 'Warwickshire on the eve of civil war: a "county community"?', *Midland History*, 7 (1982), pp. 43–4.
33. A. Hughes, *Politics, society and civil war in Warwickshire, 1620–1660* (Cambridge, 1987).
34. *Ibid.*, pp. 27–9, 37.
35. *Ibid.*, pp. 38–41.

parliament, inclining the leading Arden families and established squirearchy of the fielden south of the Avon to adopt a more authoritarian politics in supporting the king.[36]

Although wording her arguments more modestly than Holmes, Hughes strongly contended that county boundaries did not dictate local communities and were 'no guides to social and economic characteristics'.[37] She also pointed to the multiple ecclesiastical jurisdictions within Warwickshire, split between the dioceses of Worcester and Lichfield. There were clearly deep ideological divisions between the puritan lectureships of Birmingham and Coventry, the latter dubbed by Richard Montagu as 'a second Geneva', and the Roman Catholic gentry of Barlichway hundred in south-west Warwickshire. Religious differences endowed a wider identity for which national politics, not county boundaries, were more important.[38] This religious plurality reflected a significant part of Warwickshire opinion during the 1630s, which was that Charles I's court had forsaken them, leading to an ideological disapproval of a 'popishly affected' court and a desire for reform through parliament, not a localist desire to be free from the centre.[39] Later, Hughes extended this argument to claim that, once civil war broke out, parliamentarians were generally more flexible and effective than the royalists were at accommodating and harnessing such local feeling, even successfully integrating it into parliament's war effort.[40]

From an economic perspective, the question of a county community in Warwickshire appeared even more questionable. The needs of commerce crossed county borders, while those close to a boundary might have closer market towns in adjacent counties. England's premier manufacturing industry, the cloth trade, operated along road and river links to ports such as London, Great Yarmouth, Bristol and Hull for export, thereby encouraging links, integration and cooperation between people of different counties. The coalfields outside Coventry and Nuneaton had a national market. Bedworth coal furnished Oxford, Leicester and Northampton. Birmingham's ironmongers, nailmakers and cutlers had strong Staffordshire connections and trade links extending to London and East Anglia, so its urban society tended to be based not on manorial ties but on commercial ones that stretched well outside the area.[41]

36. Hughes, 'Warwickshire', pp. 63–4; A. Hughes, *The causes of the English civil war*, 2nd edn (Basingstoke, 1998), p. 140.
37. Hughes, *Politics, society*, p. 1.
38. Hughes, 'Warwickshire', p. 51; P. Marshall and G. Scott (eds), *Catholic gentry in English society: the Throckmortons of Coughton from Reformation to emancipation* (Aldershot, 2009).
39. Hughes, 'Warwickshire', pp. 58–9.
40. A. Hughes, 'The king, the parliament and the localities during the English civil war', *Journal of British Studies*, 24 (1985), p. 241.
41. Hughes, *Politics, society*, pp. 9–20.

Hughes also fundamentally challenged Everitt's identification of political moderation with localism and radical parliamentarian politics with a creeping and unwelcome centralisation. She depicted the county committee of Warwickshire as champions of localism, yet also radical parliamentarian militants.[42] This questioned notions that county government was traditionally about resenting or moderating the demands of central government. Rather, as officeholders at parish, hundredal and county level, the gentry had to balance local interests, harmony and good neighbourliness with the effective exercise of state power. As such, they circulated in multiple overlapping arenas, acting not just as defenders of local interests but more as arbiters between the government and provinces.[43] Recently, Clive Holmes has stressed again this dialogue and cooperation between local interests and central authority to discredit Everitt's idea that some localities were isolated from and by their very nature suspicious of Westminster.[44]

The mental world of such gentry is illuminated in their diaries, journals and commonplace books, into which they noted politically topical material such as news, corantoes, gossip, libels, satirical ballads and parliamentary speeches, much of which nurtured an interest in national events.[45] The last entry in the diurnal of Adam Eyre, a minor gentleman from a remote Pennine township, noted how on 26 January 1649 he intended to go to London. This was just four days before Charles I's execution, so he may well have arrived in time to witness it.[46] Historians of print culture have established how the English provinces exhibited an insatiable thirst for news in the early seventeenth century, and identified an explosion of cheap print that inflamed the political crisis of 1641.[47] This helped forge a national culture of literacy as the market became flooded with tens of thousands of cheap pamphlets spreading and shaping awareness of national

42. A. Hughes, 'Militancy and localism: Warwickshire politics and Westminster politics, 1643–1647', *Transactions of the Royal Historical Society*, 5th series, 31 (1981), pp. 51–68.

43. Hughes, *Politics, society*, p. 50.

44. C. Holmes, 'Centre and locality in civil-war England', in J. Adamson (ed.), *The English civil war: conflict and contexts, 1640–1649* (Basingstoke, 2009), pp. 153–4, 165.

45. Holmes, 'The county community', p. 61; an excellent example is the commonplace book of Ralph Assheton of Kirkby Grange, near Wakefield, held by the Beinecke Rare Book and Manuscript Library, Yale University, Osborn shelves b101, but also available on microfilm in the British Library, R.P. 57.

46. H.J. Morehouse (ed.), 'A dyurnall or catalogue of all my accions and expences from the 1st of January 1646–7, by Adam Eyre', in C. Jackson (ed.), *Yorkshire diaries and autobiographies in the seventeenth and eighteenth centuries*, Surtees Society, 65 (1875), p. 117; WYAS, Kirklees, KC312/5/3: The diary of Adam Eyre, 1647–1649, fo. 38v.

47. J. Peacey, *Politicians and pamphleteers: propaganda during the English civil wars and revolution* (Aldershot, 2004); J. Raymond, *The invention of the newspaper: English newsbooks, 1641–1649* (Oxford, 1996); R. Cust, 'News and politics in early seventeenth-century England', *Past and Present*, 112 (1986), pp. 60–90.

political issues even in places as far flung as Pennine Halifax, where, in 1642, another minor gentleman noted how 'papers flew up and down in every place'.[48]

The work of Richard Cust has uncovered a variety of concepts of honour collectively upheld by gentry across England, found among all their native counties. Attachment to blood, lineage and martial valour jostled for position among more recent notions of civic humanism, godliness, restraint and service to the state.[49] Yet such competing notions of honour were not mutually exclusive and Barbara Donagan has demonstrated that a code of military honour emerged, commonly adhered to by the gentry on both sides during the civil wars, that 'ameliorated relations between enemies' and 'helped to prevent irrevocable social divisions'.[50] Yet such was the corrosive competition for honour among the English gentry that the ties of kinship, marriage and neighbourliness, rather than promoting harmony as stressed by proponents of the 'county community', might be undermined by violence or litigation over status contests before tribunals such as Star Chamber or the Court of Chivalry.[51]

Some counties were just too large for a single county community to become possible. For example, Yorkshire had almost 700 well-established county gentry families in 1642, in addition to even larger numbers of minor gentry in the West Riding alone.[52] Many of Yorkshire's greater gentry were well travelled and educated, some individuals among them holding estates in up to seven other counties.[53] The contrasts of regions within the county were so great that cloth towns such as Halifax and Bradford had far more in common in religious, cultural, and socio-economic terms with adjacent areas of Lancashire than they did with the vale of York. Bradford, Bingley, Huddersfield, Bolton and Manchester all lay within the social sphere of clothing district parishes such as Almondbury, while Salford hundred in east Lancashire shared neighbouring Calderdale's inclination towards Godly reformation.[54]

48. J.H. Turner (ed.), *The autobiography of Captain John Hodgson of Coley, near Halifax* (Brighouse, 1882), p. 21.

49. R. Cust, 'Honour and politics in early Stuart England: the case of Beaumont v. Hastings', *Past and Present*, 149 (1995), pp. 60, 79–80, 91; R. Cust, 'Catholicism, antiquarianism and gentry honour: the writings of Sir Thomas Shirley', *Midland History*, 23 (1998), p. 48.

50. B. Donagan, 'The web of honour: soldiers, Christians, and gentlemen in the English civil war', *Historical Journal*, 44 (2001), p. 365.

51. R.P. Cust and A.J. Hopper (eds), *Cases in the Court of Chivalry, 1634–1640*, Publications of the Harleian Society, new series, 18 (2006), pp. 3, 38, 51–4, 60, 68, 84, 90, 185, 217–18, 305.

52. J.T. Cliffe, *The Yorkshire gentry from the Reformation to the civil war* (London, 1969), p. 338.

53. J. Binns, *Yorkshire in the civil wars: origins, impact and outcome* (Pickering, 2004), pp. 4–7.

54. R.C. Richardson, *Puritanism in north west England: a regional study of the diocese of Chester to 1642* (Manchester, 1972), pp. 3–10; M. Spufford, 'The importance of religion in the sixteenth and seventeenth centuries', in M. Spufford (ed.), *The world of rural dissenters, 1520–1725* (Cambridge, 1995), pp. 42n, 48; W. Coster, 'Kinship and community in Yorkshire, 1500–1700', DPhil thesis (York University, 1992), pp. 74–5.

Yet, despite the persuasiveness of its critics, the concept of a county community has enjoyed a measure of continued recognition. Despite acknowledging that in most English counties 'county communitarian sentiment was surprisingly weak', Mark Stoyle has argued for an early modern Cornish particularism based on ethnicity and the 'Kernowok' language that permeated society below that county's gentry. Focusing on popular allegiance, he identified a rebellious spirit among the Cornish commons in defending their cultural identity from the encroachments of the English state. After Cornwall, he significantly identified Everitt's Kent as the next 'most culturally distinctive shire in England', pointing out that a comparable record of early modern insurrections began in Kent.[55]

There is also an increased acceptance that contemporaries maintained a more forceful emotional connection to their counties than some of the criticism of the 'county community' initially recognised: Ronald Hutton has uncovered cases of the respectful observation of county boundaries by civil-war soldiers, while Jan Broadway has done much to reveal the depth of the gentry's attachment to their county identities through the increasing fashion for antiquities, cartography and county histories.[56] It was native gentry families that funded the series of county histories published in the seventeenth century, hoping thereby to gain honour and status by establishing their ancient pedigrees and long-standing connection to their lands. This antiquarianism could become a tool to cement newcomer families into the establishment, but the arena and pecking order for this competition over status was invariably the county. Books such as Sir William Dugdale's *Antiquities of Warwickshire* reflected the gentry's concerns of family, manor and county, and did much to communicate the claims of a county's elite to the nation as a whole. The first county maps by Christopher Saxton and John Speed were often adorned with heraldic devices and it was the English gentry who bought them. In this way the county community came to acquire a powerful symbolic importance to the gentry and their self-image, even if it had little socio-economic reality.

In retrospect, Everitt's attachment to his native Kent may have inclined him to take gentry words and rhetoric too much at face value. His picture of central government as unshifting, interfering, malign and monolithic has been dated by

---

55. Stoyle drew his inspiration much more from David Underdown than Alan Everitt, but his doctoral thesis retained 'county community' in its title: M. Stoyle, *West Britons: Cornish identities and the early modern British state* (Exeter, 2002), pp. 27, 219; Stoyle, *Loyalty and locality*, pp. 3–6, 319; M.J. Stoyle, 'Divisions within the Devonshire "county community", c.1600–46', DPhil thesis (Oxford University, 1992).

56. R. Hutton, short notice of Holmes, *Seventeenth-century Lincolnshire*, in *English Historical Review*, 93 (1983), p. 871; J. Broadway, *'No historie so meete': gentry culture and the development of local history in Elizabethan and early Stuart England* (Manchester, 2006).

the influential works of Keith Wrightson, Mark Goldie and others that stress a vast unpaid network of local officeholders mediating the impact of that state upon the localities.[57] Everitt's hypothesis was very top-down in approach; because he so strongly focused on the gentry, he scarcely examined sub-gentry groups to consider how they might influence the gentry. Everitt made little attempt to defend himself from these criticisms. In 1996 he wrote a postscript to a reprint of his 1969 essay The local community and the Great Rebellion. It showed his dismay at how he felt he had been misrepresented by his critics. He pointed out that he had never suggested Kent was typical of the whole kingdom, and that he had never denied the importance of idealism behind the events of the 1640s.[58] He shied away from responding to criticism by pointing out his research had moved in other directions. Yet he expressed satisfaction that his idea of the county community had influenced the research of scholars writing on earlier periods. The idea was extended back into the sixteenth century by Hassell Smith and Diarmaid MacCulloch and into the fourteenth century by J.R. Maddicott.[59] Indeed, a great many medieval historians writing in the 1980s and 1990s assumed the existence of county communities, producing a series of county studies tackling the concept from the fourteenth to the sixteenth centuries. Some of this historiography presupposed the existence of seventeenth-century county communities, and then endeavoured to trace their emergence and development in earlier periods.[60]

The works of Michael Bennett and Nigel Saul argued that the late medieval period witnessed the emergence of a landed gentry community in the counties of Cheshire and Gloucestershire respectively, providing skilled officeholders for county and regional administration.[61] Their conclusions were challenged by A.J.

57. K. Wrightson, 'The politics of the parish in early modern England', in P. Griffiths, A. Fox and S. Hindle (eds), The experience of authority in early modern England (Basingstoke, 1996), pp. 10–46; M. Goldie, 'The unacknowledged republic: officeholding in early modern England', in T. Harris (ed.), The politics of the excluded, c.1500–1850 (Basingstoke, 2001), pp. 153–94.

58. Ronald Hutton agreed that Holmes had 'slightly exaggerated the obscurantism of his predecessors': A. Everitt, 'The local community and the Great Rebellion', in R.C. Richardson (ed.), The English civil wars: local aspects (Stroud, 1997), p. 34; Hutton, short notice of Holmes, Seventeenth-century Lincolnshire, p. 871.

59. A.H. Smith, County and court: government and politics in Norfolk 1558–1603 (Oxford, 1974); J.R. Maddicott, 'The county community and the making of public opinion in fourteenth-century England', Transactions of the Royal Historical Society, 5th series, 28 (1978), pp. 27–43.

60. C. Carpenter, 'Gentry and community in medieval England', Journal of British Studies, 33 (1994), pp. 342, 356–7, 380.

61. M.J. Bennett, 'A county community: social cohesion among the Cheshire gentry, 1400–25', Northern History, 8 (1973), pp. 24–44; M.J. Bennett, Community, class and careerism: Cheshire and Lancashire society in the age of Gawain and the Green Knight (Cambridge, 1983); N. Saul, Knights and esquires: the Gloucestershire gentry in the fourteenth century (Oxford, 1981).

Pollard and Christine Carpenter in their respective studies of Richmondshire and Warwickshire.[62] Pollard argued that the influence of great noble affinities in the north precluded the possibility of emerging gentry communities while Carpenter pointed to problems in applying criteria for membership of county elites. She considered that the gentry's intense competition for the patronage of the Beauchamp earls of Warwick stifled any spirit of cooperation, arguing that: 'Noble rule is therefore inimical to the idea of a county community.'[63] Carpenter made similar criticisms of proponents of the medieval county community to the ones raised by Holmes and Hughes against Everitt, such as the tendency to see national politics as external and divorced from county affairs:

> As with many of the early modern studies, an a priori acceptance of the existence of a community, an overconcentration on the greater gentry, and reluctance to consider not only other types of identity, but also the incorporation of the county within the body politic, have left the subject with more questions than answers.[64]

Carpenter criticised also what she saw as the unthinking use of the word 'community' by historians adopting 'the Leicester approach', arguing that the term, derived from anthropology and sociology, has been misapplied to something the size of a county. Aside from these theoretical shortcomings and the lack of a definition of 'community', she viewed what she termed the 'cosy parochialism' of Everitt as reactionary for a mythical and roseate past, considering the county as 'no more than the village writ large'. Carpenter has therefore called for a complete abandonment of the term 'community', instead advocating an investigation into 'how the gentry saw both themselves and their role within the polity and how others saw them'.[65]

Despite these powerful criticisms, questions over the validity of the 'county community' framework have continued to dominate discussion of medieval landed society for the past 20 years, and the concept has been exported to address the politics of landed society in the Pale. With a striking similarity to Everitt's concerns, Brendan Smith has argued that the gentry of Louth sought to dominate the political institutions of their county and resist outside interference:

> The primacy of the county in the hearts and minds of the English gentry in Louth by the 1330s at the latest cannot seriously be doubted. A powerful county

62. C. Carpenter, *Locality and polity: a study of Warwickshire landed society, 1401–1499* (Cambridge, 1992); A.J. Pollard, 'The Richmondshire community of gentry in the Wars of the Roses', in C.D. Ross (ed.), *Patronage, pedigree and power in later medieval England* (Gloucester, 1979), pp. 37–59; A.J. Pollard, *North-eastern England during the War of the Roses: lay society, war and politics, 1450–1500* (Oxford, 1990).
63. Carpenter, 'Gentry and community', p. 356.
64. Ibid., p. 365.
65. Ibid., pp. 342–3, 380.

community had emerged through the prompting of the Crown, the removal of its traditional magnate families and the demands of war.[66]

In England, the debate among medievalists continues but there has been a shift towards arguments of much greater complexity and an increased acceptance of the variety of local experience. Mark Arvanigian has recently argued for a rethinking rather than discarding of the 'community' concept. His research contested that although county boundaries made little practical difference to gentry careers in Durham, baronial service was not necessarily erosive of co-operation and community among the county's gentry. He has argued for a regional rather than a county framework, seeing Durham's gentry engaged across the whole north-east in crown service, baronial affinities and the administration of the Palatinate's bishops.[67]

In contrast, discussion of the seventeenth-century 'county community' has remained relatively muted. Therefore this volume intends both to reignite this debate among early modernists and to awaken an appreciation of the new directions arguments might take over the 'county community', its absence, or what new form it might take. While this volume is intended to honour the memory of Professor Everitt, the editors do not seek to endorse his interpretation or advance any one particular or exclusive approach. Rather, it is hoped that these essays will offer up-to-date and innovative interpretations of the concept of the 'county community' that reflect the variety of approaches, methods and theories generated by Everitt's legacy. Through all the criticism and debate provoked by this hypothesis, one certainty emerges. It is quite rare and remarkable for a historical monograph written 45 years ago to have such a long life, wide readership and prolonged impact beyond its own period. Even Everitt's strongest critics recognised that he was the 'most influential of modern local historians'.[68] Indeed, much of the subsequent criticism was unthinkable when *The community of Kent* was first published. In inspiring both its supporters and critics, the concept of the 'county community' has undoubtedly enriched the field of local history. Above all, it shows how the best local history, although determined by place, ought to remain driven by wider questions and concepts.

66. B. Smith, 'A county community in early fourteenth-century Ireland: the case of Louth', *English Historical Review*, 108 (1993), pp. 586–7.
67. M. Arvanigian, 'A county community or the politics of the nation? Border service and baronial influence in the palatinate of Durham, 1377–1413', *Historical Research*, 82 (2009), pp. 42, 44, 60.
68. Hughes, *Politics, society*, p. 20.

1

Alan Everitt and The community of Kent revisited

JACQUELINE EALES

The publication of Alan Everitt's *The community of Kent and the Great Rebellion, 1640–60* in 1966 was a major landmark in the historiography of the English civil wars. Everitt noted in his introduction that 'we have tended too much to look at the period through the eyes of the government, and especially of parliament'. He focused instead on the county gentry – the community of his title – and described the 'most striking political feature' of the county as its insularity. Kent was moderately royalist and sympathised more with Charles I than parliament, while the committed royalists and parliamentarians were extremist minorities. Yet it fell into the 'vice-like grip of parliamentary control' because of its strategic importance: parliament 'simply could not afford to countenance rebellion so close at hand', as he phrased it. He saw parliamentarianism as an outside imposition from the centre, whose unpopular leading adherents such as Sir Michael Livesey, the regicide and military commander, and Sir Anthony Weldon, the chairman of the parliamentarian county committee (Figure 1.1), maintained control through force and violence.[1]

The community of Kent was the first history of Kent during the civil wars to be published since Henry Abell's *Kent and the great civil war* in 1901, and it became a model for the study of other counties for a decade and a half.[2] A spate of printed monographs and doctoral dissertations investigated the gentry in civil-war Cheshire, Worcestershire, Sussex, Shropshire and Berkshire, among others.[3] While some of these studies observed differences to Kent, it was not until 1980 that a full-scale critique was launched in a seminal article by Clive Holmes, who argued that

1.   I am grateful to Norah Carlin, Catharina Clement, Lorraine Flisher, Andrew Hopper, Valerie Newill, Mary Jane Pamphilon and Stephen Rowlstone for the help and advice they provided. I would like to thank John Hills for cartography. I am also grateful to Penelope Corfield and Richard Eales for their comments on a previous draft and to those present at the Alan Everitt Memorial Day Conference at Leicester on 12 December 2009 for their comments on the paper upon which this is based. A. Everitt, *The community of Kent and the Great Rebellion, 1640–60* (Leicester, 1966), pp. 13–14.
2.   H. Abell, *Kent and the great civil war* (Ashford, 1901).
3.   J.S. Morrill, *Cheshire, 1630–1660: county government and society during the English revolution* (Oxford, 1974); R.H. Silcock, 'County government in Worcestershire, 1603–1660', PhD thesis (University

Sᴿ Antʸ. Welden.

From an Original Drawing in the
Collection of the Right Honᵇˡᵉ Lord
C A R D I F F.

Pubᵈ April 1ˢᵗ 1779. by Richᵈ Godfrey Nᵒ 120 Long Acre.

Figure 1.1 Sir Anthony Weldon (1583–1648). Special Collections of the University of Leicester, Fairclough Collection, EP42B/7.

Everitt had overemphasised the insularity of the county, overlooked ideological differences among the gentry and assumed that their views represented those of the entire population of the shire. Holmes countered this narrow model by emphasising that the views of groups of peasants and craftsmen, who formed political opinions and expressed them, also had to be recognised in order to explain the events of the civil wars. The concept of the county community was also reassessed by Ann Hughes in her study of Warwickshire, in which she emphasised the economic, regional, religious and social connections that transcended county borders.4 Their insights coincided with the publication of another important article by David Underdown on popular allegiance during the civil wars and together these historians had a major impact on subsequent research.5 Studies of civil-war Devon and Gloucestershire, among others, reflected this shift of emphasis by investigating the political engagement of other social groups and even embraced gender by considering the role of women.6 Work on Herefordshire also analysed how the gentry collaborated with the clergy to influence local opinion during the civil wars.7 Nearly half a century after the publication of Alan Everitt's influential work how then should these wide-ranging revisions be applied to the history of Kent?

We should start by considering whether the concept of the county community remains a meaningful category, if it is no longer to be seen simply as an alternative term for the gentry. Traditionally the county has been regarded as a clearly defined political unit with sheriffs, deputy lieutenants and justices of the peace all being chosen to govern and maintain order within its borders.8 This use of the county as a focus for the collection of taxation, raising of conscripts and dispensation of justice was maintained throughout the 1640s and 1650s. During this period the

of London, 1974); A. Fletcher, *A county community in peace and war: Sussex 1600–1660* (London, 1975); M. Wanklyn, 'Landed society and allegiance in Cheshire and Shropshire in the first civil war', PhD thesis (Manchester University, 1976); C. Durston, 'Berkshire and its county gentry, 1625–1649', PhD thesis (Reading University, 1977).

4.   C. Holmes, 'The county community in Stuart historiography', *Journal of British Studies*, 19 (1980), pp. 54–73; A. Hughes, 'Politics, society and civil war in Warwickshire, 1620–1650', PhD thesis (Liverpool University, 1980).

5.   D. Underdown, 'The problem of popular allegiance in the English civil war', *Transactions of the Royal Historical Society*, 5th series, 31 (1981), pp. 69–94.

6.   S.K. Roberts, *Recovery and Restoration in an English county: Devon local administration, 1646–1670* (Exeter, 1985); M. Stoyle, *Devon and the civil war* (Exeter, 2001); A.R. Warmington, *Civil war, Interregnum and Restoration in Gloucestershire 1640–1672* (Woodbridge, 1997); A. Hughes, *Women, men and politics in the English civil war* (Keele, 1997). See also A. Hughes, *Politics, society and civil war in Warwickshire, 1620–1660* (Cambridge, 1987); J.S. Morrill, *Revolt in the provinces: the people of England and the tragedies of war, 1630–1648*, 2nd edn (London, 1999).

7.   J. Eales, *Puritans and roundheads: the Harleys of Brampton Bryan and the outbreak of the English civil war* (Cambridge, 1990).

8.   The classic account is contained in T.G. Barnes, *Somerset, 1625–1640: a county's government during the 'personal rule'* (Cambridge, MA, 1961).

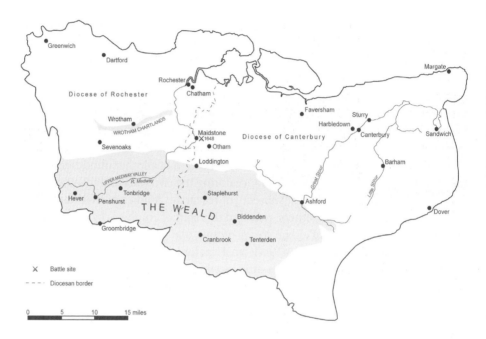

Figure 1.2 Map of Kent. © Canterbury Christ Church University, cartography John Hills.

committee system was extended from Westminster to the counties and Kent was governed by a central county committee and its sub-committees.[9] In early seventeenth-century Kent there were also some notable internal administrative divisions, as the quarter sessions for the west of the county were held at Maidstone and those for the east were held at Canterbury. Kent also contained two entire dioceses within its borders in the sees of Rochester and Canterbury (Figure 1.2). Despite this fragmentation, the assembly of the gentry, the clergy and the grand jury (chosen largely from minor gentry and freemen) at the biannual assize meetings was regarded as representative of the county as a whole.[10] The famous royalist Kentish Petition of 1642, devised in Maidstone at the March assizes of that year, was thus couched as the 'humble petition of the Gentry, Ministers and Commonalty for the County of Kent agreed upon at the General Assizes for the County'. The emphasis on the approval of the clergy in this and other petitions is significant and will be investigated more fully below.

The petition was drawn up by the recently expelled MP for Kent, Sir Edward Dering (Figure 1.3), and other gentlemen, and here we can see Everitt's notion of the opinions of the royalist gentry as representative of 'county' sentiment in

9.   A.M. Everitt, *The county committee of Kent in the civil war*, University of Leicester, Department of English Local History, occasional papers, 9 (Leicester, 1957).

10. J.H. Gleason, *The justices of the peace in England, 1558–1640* (Oxford, 1969), p. 103; J.S. Cockburn, *A history of English assizes to 1714* (Cambridge, 1972), p. 29.

Figure 1.3 Sir Edward Dering (1598–1644). Special Collections of the University of Leicester, Fairclough Collection, EP41B – Box 1.

action.[11] Parliament had just passed an ordinance without the consent of Charles I, which transferred the control of the militia from the king into its own hands. Dering's petition thus called for a militia bill and emphasised that 'the precious liberties of the subject' should be preserved by ensuring that no order was to be enforced until it had been fully enacted by both the king and parliament. It also supported the bishops and the established liturgy of the Church as set out in the Book of common prayer, attacked the 'schismaticall and seditious Sermons' of parliament's clerical supporters and demanded a law against lay preachers.[12] Everitt erroneously regarded the Kentish Petition as 'mildly royalist', but S.R. Gardiner, the great Victorian historian of the early Stuart period, thought that it was central to the royalist political platform. He concluded that the petition embodied 'the spirit which was soon to animate the King's supporters in the Civil War'. This included a 'newly awakened zeal' for the king's prerogative, which the royalists believed should be used to destroy the puritan opposition to the established Church.[13] The House of Commons did not regard the petition as a mild document: it ordered the common hangman to burn copies and threatened Dering with impeachment.[14]

The promotion of the Kentish petition at the county assizes was an important gesture: it was in this public arena that the grievances of the county were traditionally presented by the grand jurymen and this gave Dering's petition a further air of legitimacy. In 1648 petitioners from Kent stated that the grand jury 'are and ought to be the representers of the sence of our County'.[15] In the divisive months leading up to the declaration of war in August 1642, however, it was no longer possible for any group to represent the views of the whole county. A parliamentarian counter-petition was, therefore, rapidly launched at the Maidstone quarter sessions in late April by the parliamentarian magistrate Thomas Blount, who delivered it to Parliament on 5 May. Blount was appointed as colonel to a Kent regiment at the start of the war and remained anti-royalist during the civil wars and Interregnum. He was appointed as one of the commissioners to try Charles I, but he did not participate in the trial.[16] The newly discovered signatures on this petition, which are now in the parliamentary archives, were not

11. T.P.S. Woods, *Prelude to civil war, 1642: Mr justice Malet and the Kentish petitions* (Salisbury, 1980), in which Dering's petition is printed on pp. 140–44.
12. Ibid., pp. 140–44.
13. Everitt, *The community of Kent*, p. 96; S.R. Gardiner, *History of England, 1603–1642*, 10 (London, 1904), pp. 179–80.
14. Woods, *Prelude to civil war 1642*, pp. 66, 69–75.
15. BL, E441(25), *The humble petition of the knights, gentry, clergy, and commonalty of the county of Kent, subscribed by the grand iury, the 11th of May 1648* (London, 1648), p. 6.
16. For Blount see Woods, *Prelude to civil war*, pp. 32–42, 77–84, 171–9, J. Nickolls, *Original letters and papers of state addressed to Oliver Cromwell ... found among the political collections of John Milton* (London, 1743), pp. 94–6 and ODNB. I am also grateful to Stephen Roberts for allowing me to see the History of Parliament Trust biography of Blount in advance of publication as well as the biographies of John Nutt, William Kenwricke and Daniel Shatterden.

examined by Everitt and have never previously been analysed. They will, therefore, be considered at greater length below. Blount's petition did not claim to come from the whole of the county, but it used more inclusive language than did Dering's to describe its subscribers. It was thus presented in the name of 'many of the Gentry, Ministers, freeholders & other inhabitants of the County of Kent, the Cities of Canterbury, Rochester & the County of Canterbury, the Cinque Ports & their Members & other corporations w[i]thin the said County'.[17]

The different language used by the two groups of petitioners is of some significance. While Dering's petition clung to the patriarchal idea that the small groups gathered at the assizes represented the opinions of the county, Blount's petition was more individualistic. It was based on a wider constituency, while at the same time acknowledging that it represented the views of 'many' of the people of Kent and not all of them. It included the inhabitants of the towns, liberties and corporations, which traditionally were not a part of the administrative jurisdiction of the county. It might be objected that this was typical of parliament's approach to county government, in which the committee system was used to overcome opposition from a variety of local interests. Yet these differences also alert us to the fact that, even before the committee system got underway in Kent, there were at least two competing views of how communal opinions should be formed and expressed. By early 1649 the radical grouping in the county calling for the trial of Charles I and the execution of the royalist leaders described themselves simply as 'the well-affected in the county of Kent', without any social distinctions, perhaps because no major gentry signed their petition. In all of the major petitions examined in this essay there is, however, a clearly expressed view that the county was the focus for the expression of the political and religious opinions of its inhabitants. For the petitioners, there was indeed a community of Kent, even though that community was divided in its opinions and allegiances.[18]

By widening Everitt's definition of the county community to include the clergy, townsmen, freeholders and other inhabitants of Kent, it becomes possible to find evidence of all shades of political and religious opinion in the county during the civil wars. In particular, the existence of strong parliamentarian allegiances in the county demonstrates that the early acceptance of parliamentarian rule there was not achieved simply through force, as Everitt believed. Instead there was considerable support in Kent for the parliamentarian cause, which was often, but not always, associated with areas of long-standing nonconformity. A number of Wealden towns in west Kent, such as Cranbrook and Goudhurst, had puritan traditions which stretched back to Elizabeth's reign.

---

17.   HL, PO/JO/10/1/121, 5 May 1642, petition from Kent.
18.   For the two copies of the 1649 petition that survive see: Bodl., Tanner MS 57b; Bodl., Rawlinson MS A298, 1r. For a discussion of this petition see below.

It is thus not surprising that at the beginning of December 1640 the inhabitants of the Kentish Weald promoted a 'root and branch' petition to parliament which demanded the abolition of episcopacy and was subscribed by 2,500 people in the county, since east Kent also had its share of nonconformist groups in towns such as Ashford, Dover and Sandwich.[19] Ashford, Canterbury and Cranbrook, along with its surrounding parishes, all raised volunteer forces for parliament in 1642 even before war had broken out. Religious dissenters saw the conflict as a chance to achieve further Church reforms and the godly parliamentarian officer Sir William Springate described himself in his will, drawn up in May 1643 because of the 'danger in these times', as employed for 'Christ and his Church'. He also raised a force of 800 men from Kent, who enlisted with him because, according to his wife, they too were puritans.[20] Parliament later resorted to conscripting men from Kent, thus making it impossible to use their military service as a test of allegiance. In addition, the dominance of parliament made it difficult for the royalists to recruit men inside the county, similarly making it hard to assess the numbers who volunteered there to fight for the king. Nevertheless, 22 royalist colonels from Kent fought in the first civil war, 3 of whom died in the conflict.[21]

During the first civil war of 1642–6 Kent was not exposed to the movements of the main field armies, but there were two occasions when some of the population rebelled against parliamentarian hegemony in the county. In 1643 about 4,000–6,000 armed men set up three camps between Sevenoaks and Faversham. George Hornby has demonstrated that the rebels were not gentry-led, but were yeomen, husbandmen and craftsmen from the Upper Medway Valley around Tonbridge, the Wrotham Chartlands, Maidstone and Greenwich. Among their demands was a refusal to take the Vow and Covenant to support parliament against the king imposed in the wake of Waller's plot in London. The rebels were dispersed by troops commanded by Colonel Richard Browne after a 'hot fight' at Tonbridge, where the parliamentarians were in the minority among the

---

19. R. Acheson, 'The development of religious separatism in the diocese of Canterbury, 1590–1660', PhD thesis (University of Kent, 1983); J. Eales, '"So many sects and schisms": religious diversity in revolutionary Kent, 1640–1660', in C. Durston and J. Maltby (eds), *Religion in revolutionary England* (Manchester, 2006), pp. 226–48; L.B. Larking (ed.), *Proceedings, principally in the county of Kent, in connection with the parliaments called in 1640 and especially with the committee of religion appointed in that year*, Camden Society, 80 (1862), pp. 25–38.

20. C. Russell, *The causes of the English civil war* (Oxford, 1990), p. 226; CJ, 2, p. 714; CKS, PRC 31/125/371; H. Dixon, 'Original account of the Springett family', *Gentleman's Magazine* (October, 1851), p. 367.

21. F.D. Johns, 'The royalist rising and parliamentary mutinies of 1645 in west Kent', *Archaeologia Cantiana*, 110 (1992), pp. 1–15; J. Eales, 'Kent in the civil wars and commonwealth, 1642–1660', in T. Lawson and D. Killingray (eds), *An historical atlas of Kent* (Chichester, 2004), pp. 88–90; P.R. Newman, *The old service: royalist regimental colonels and the civil war, 1642–1646* (Manchester, 1993), pp. 282–5.

inhabitants.[22] Four years later the Christmas riots at Canterbury saw a sustained revolt against parliamentarian rule in the city which preceded the outbreak of the second civil war in Kent and Essex. By the summer of 1648 11,000 royalists and disillusioned former supporters of parliament were in arms in the county. They occupied strategic strongholds along the coast including Dover Castle, but were overcome in early June at Maidstone and Canterbury by the forces of the New Model Army under the command of Thomas, Lord Fairfax (Figure 1.4).[23] In the 1650s there were rumours of royalist conspiracies and uprisings in Kent led by Sir Thomas Peyton and Richard Thornhill, but no serious armed opposition to the commonwealth or the Protectorate ever emerged.[24]

The investigation of the views of social groups below the elite as petitioners and combatants leads in turn to questions about how people in Kent received information about the debates at Westminster and about the course of the war. How well informed were they and how did they respond to the news that they read or heard? The activities of the provincial clergy as spin doctors are particularly relevant here, as many of them used sermons and petitions to try to influence the allegiances of the laity. During the last 25 years there has been considerable research into the circulation of news and propaganda, both orally and in print, by Richard Cust, Alastair Fox, Joad Raymond and Jason Peacey, among others. This has demonstrated that there was a large market for news in the counties and that people of all social levels were interested in reading or hearing about the news. There was an overlap between oral and printed information and both could be relayed rapidly from London to the provinces and vice versa.[25] Trade and other communications between London and Kent were frequent in the period and letters, printed pamphlets, newsbooks and other sources of news could be sent into the county by a variety of means. In 1642 carriers from Kent towns came to Southwark on a weekly basis, and communities in the Weald, such as Biddenden, Cranbrook and Tenterden, were served in this way, as were other places, including Sevenoaks, Staplehurst, Penshurst, and Tonbridge in west Kent, and Canterbury, Dover, and Sandwich in the east. Hoys

22. I am grateful to Mr Hornby for allowing me to make use of his unpublished research on 'Allegiance in west Kent during the first civil war, 1642–1646'; HMC, Fifth report, part 1 (London 1876), p. 97; CJ, 3, p. 181; R. Almack (ed.), *Papers relating to proceedings in the county of Kent, A.D. 1642–A.D. 1646*, Camden Society, 61 (1855), pp. 26–35.
23. R. Ashton, *Counter revolution: the second civil war and its origins, 1646–8* (New Haven, CT, 1994).
24. J. Eales, 'Kent and the English civil wars, 1640–1660', in F. Lansberry (ed.), *Government and politics in Kent, 1640–1914* (Woodbridge, 2001), pp. 1–32.
25. R. Cust, 'News and politics in early seventeenth-century England', *Past and Present*, 112 (1986), pp. 60–90; A. Fox, *Oral and literate culture in England, 1500–1700* (Oxford, 2000); J. Raymond, *Pamphlets and pamphleteering in early modern Britain* (Cambridge, 2003) and J. Peacey, *Politicians and pamphleteers: propaganda during the English civil wars and Interregnum* (Aldershot, 2004).

Figure 1.4 Thomas, third Baron Fairfax (1612–1671). Special Collections of the University of Leicester, Fairclough Collection, EP101, p. 182.

and other ships from Sandwich and Dover landed in Sibbs docks and those from Faversham, Maidstone, Margate, and Rochester at St Katherine's docks. Additionally, a weekly foot post left Canterbury for Southwark every Wednesday and Saturday. The carriers, crews and postmen, who visited London so frequently, were also the bearers of gossip and news.[26]

The circulation of political news among the Kent gentry during the civil wars is well documented. Sheila Hingley has demonstrated, for example, the systematic way in which Henry Oxinden of Barham, near Canterbury in east Kent, obtained pamphlets and news from his correspondents in London.[27] Oxinden was a parliamentarian in the early stages of the war, but he shared information with a wide circle of local correspondents of varying political allegiances, including the royalist Sir Thomas Peyton and his cousin Henry Oxinden of Deane. Peyton was the MP for Sandwich in the Long Parliament, but he deserted the House in 1644 and during the 1650s, when he suffered repeated arrest, was one of the most influential royalist agents in the county. Henry Oxinden of Deane was a member of the parliamentarian county committee and represented Kent in the Protectorate parliaments of 1654 and 1656.[28] It was not only the gentry who read the newsbooks. John Franklyn, a Canterbury draper, was enthused by the news in May 1642 in a 'book printed by parliament' that the English had beaten the Irish rebels three times. In late 1644, as William Chandler, a shoemaker, was reading a book 'wherein there was men[n]con of the Scotch' in his shop in Sandwich, another man declared the Scots, who had recently helped the English to win the battle of Marston Moor, to be 'all Rogues and theeves and that all that tooke their p[ar]ts were knaves', which suggests that Chandler was reading aloud.[29] Pamphlets and written newsletters were produced in relatively small numbers and much information was conveyed orally, often among informal groups such as the men gathered in Chandler's shop. Those who were unable to read could also hear manifestoes from king and parliament read out both in market places and in churches during the 'paper war' before the outbreak of hostilities in the summer of 1642.[30]

Sermons were another vehicle for political comment and the clergy provided an

26. J. Taylor, *A brief director for those that would send their letters to any parts of England, Scotland or Ireland* (London, 1642).

27. S. Hingley, 'The Oxindens, Warlys and Elham parish library: a family library and its place in print culture in east Kent', PhD thesis (University of Kent, 2004).

28. D. Gardiner (ed.), *The Oxinden letters, 1607–1642* (London, 1933), p. 312; D. Underdown, *Royalist conspiracy in England, 1649–1660* (New Haven, CT, 1960), pp. 37, 47, 109–11; D. Underdown, *Pride's purge: politics in the puritan revolution* (Oxford, 1971), p. 197.

29. HL, PO/JO/10/1/126. 27 June 1642, Annexe 3, deposition of John Francklyn; BL, Additional MS 29,624 fo. 174r.

30. I am grateful to Lloyd Bowen for sharing with me his forthcoming paper 'Proclaiming the king's word: royalism, print and the clergy, 1639–1642'.

important point of contact between their parishioners and central politics. As members of a national institution, their religious and political concerns in the 1640s and 1650s drew issues of central debate into the local arena. Their beliefs about such issues as Church government and the divine right of bishops also informed their views about the extent and nature of royal power. Until the start of the first civil war royalist preaching could be heard in Kent at the two cathedrals of Rochester and Canterbury and at the county assizes, which were usually held at Maidstone. The royalist clergy actively preached about issues of obedience, rebellion and divine right in relation to the Scottish bishops' wars and the English civil wars. Thus when Charles I and his queen were briefly in Canterbury in mid-February 1642 they heard a sermon in the cathedral in favour of episcopacy, which was a calculated response to parliament's demands for the 'root and branch' abolition of bishops or their removal from the House of Lords.[31] The cathedral clergy were keen to refute any suggestions that they were Roman Catholic sympathisers and, in his will drawn up in April 1642, the Canterbury prebendary Thomas Jackson declared that he disclaimed all heterodox, novel, and curious tenets as by 'Papists, Arminians and Sectaries have been most unhappily broached, preached and printed' to the great trouble of the church. In late 1646 after episcopacy had been abolished the archdeacon of Canterbury, William Kingsley, affirmed in his will that he was resolved to live and die a firm and constant professor of the 'faith, doctrine and discipline' established by law in the Church of England.[32]

Yet historians have hugely underplayed the influence of the provincial clergy during the civil wars. The clergy do not always fit neatly into the model of county history, because their relationship to the county and its borders was very different from that of the gentry. Clerics might not be local men, and their professional lives were focused on the parish and diocese rather than the county. The failure to integrate the clergy into county histories of the civil wars also arises from the fact that very few of their sermons delivered in the parishes or cathedrals were printed or have survived in manuscript form.[33] Moreover, many of the accounts that survive of preaching or of the reading of political manifestoes by individual clerics were written by their opponents, who wanted to discredit them. For this reason historians have been reluctant to give too much credence to such hostile reports. Yet it is in these very areas of disagreement and opposition that we can see civil-war parties emerging in the counties and for this

31. BL, E52(10), R. Culmer, *Cathedrall newes from Canterbury* (London, 1644), pp. 10–12.
32. TNA, Probate 11/201, fo. 205v; Probate 11/204, fo. 109r.
33. For political sermons during the civil wars see W. Sheils, 'Provincial preaching on the eve of the civil war: some West Riding fast sermons', in A. Fletcher and P. Roberts (eds), *Religion, culture and society in early modern Britain: essays in honour of Patrick Collinson* (Cambridge, 1994), pp. 290–312; J. Eales, 'Provincial preaching and allegiance in the first English civil war, 1640–6', in T. Cogswell, R. Cust and P. Lake (eds), *Politics, religion and popularity in early Stuart Britain: essays in honour of Conrad Russell* (Cambridge, 2002), pp. 185–207.

reason they are tremendously valuable sources.

Both parliament and the king placed great weight on the allegiance of the clergy. According to Everitt just over half of the 450 benefices and canonries in Kent were forcibly vacated between 1642 and 1660 by a rolling purge of their incumbents.[34] As royalist preachers were ejected from their livings they were replaced by men with Presbyterian or Independent sympathies, who were more likely to support parliament. Thus, during the mid-1640s, the deans and chapters at Rochester and Canterbury were replaced with parliamentarian nominees.[35] Although there were Presbyterian clerics in Kent parishes, a fully fledged Presbyterian system never operated in the county, even after the abolition of episcopacy in 1646. Independency and the religious sects were also evident in Kent and by the early 1650s there were at least 19 Independent church congregations in Dartford and Ashford, in Cranbrook and other Wealden parishes, and in Canterbury and its environs.[36] The catalyst for the ejections was the parliamentary committee for scandalous ministers, chaired initially by Dering and then by John White, the MP for Southwark. In response to an order of December 1640 from the Commons for MPs to investigate the state of preaching in their counties, Sir Edward Dering received information and petitions from 58 communities, which Everitt dismissed as 'unimportant'.[37] Kent and Herefordshire are, however, the only counties where the original reports and petitions have survived in any quantity from 1640–41, making the Kent evidence unique for the south-east. This material reveals that while some parishioners were satisfied with the regular and careful preaching of their ministers, others were concerned that stipends were so low that educated and painstaking men were not attracted to the posts. The laity expressed concerns about pluralist clergy who employed negligent curates at low rates of pay or who refused to pay for a substitute when they were unable or unwilling to visit their parishes regularly. Some complained that their minister had adopted the Laudian 'innovations' of the 1630s with enthusiasm and in several parishes they made a connection between the excessive ceremonialism of their minister and the widely held fear that such changes heralded a return to Roman Catholic practices.[38]

At Sturry, just outside Canterbury, 20 parishioners complained that their

34. Everitt, *The community of Kent*, p. 299. See also A.G. Matthews (ed.), *Walker revised: being a revision of John Walker's sufferings of the clergy during the grand rebellion, 1642–1660* (Oxford, 1988).
35. *CJ*, 3, pp. 299, 359; *LJ*, 7, p. 10.
36. Nickolls, *Original letters and papers*, pp. 95–7.
37. I. Green, 'The persecution of "scandalous" and "malignant" parish clergy during the English civil war', *English Historical Review*, 94 (1979), pp. 507–31; the information sent to Dering is printed in Larking, *Proceedings*; Everitt, *The community of Kent*, p. 86.
38. Larking, *Proceedings*, pp. 101–240. For the Herefordshire material see Eales, *Puritans and roundheads*, pp. 109–10.

minister was 'famouslie noted for a forward Agent in superstitious and Popish innovations'. At Tonbridge two men claimed that several of the 'best minded' families there had been driven to live elsewhere or even emigrated because their minister was 'a great Innovator'.[39] The belief that there was a 'Popish Plot' at court to undermine the Protestant state and Church was widely held among parliament's supporters. It was grounded partly on the policy of reintroducing the railed altar in churches, which had been promoted during the Personal Rule by both Charles I and Archbishop Laud. Charles's marriage to the French Roman Catholic, Henrietta Maria, and the subsequent fashionable conversion to Catholicism by some members of the royal court served only to reinforce these fears. The belief that Catholicism would be extended from Ireland into Charles I's other kingdoms was compounded by his bishops' wars against the Scots in 1639 and 1640.[40] Some petitioners thus complained that their minister was excessively anti-Scottish and the curate at Chatham, Thomas Vaughan, was accused by 22 men of preaching against the Scots as invading rebels with the words 'putt a hoock into their nostrils, and turne them back by the waie they came'.[41]

The first cleric to be ejected in Kent was, however, John Marston, the rector of the parish of St Mary Magdalen in Canterbury, and he was removed from his livings in July 1642 by the House of Lords for speaking 'scandalous words' against parliament. The allegations against him included his prejudiced gloss of two rival manifestoes. A month earlier he had read to his congregation His majesties answer to a printed book entitled a remonstrance or the declaration of the Lords and Commons assembled in Parliament May the 26 1642. In this tract, Charles I had adamantly denied the charge that he intended to wage a civil war and instead accused parliament of aiming to be 'perpetual dictators over the king and people'. Before allowing the parish constable to read another 'roll' of papers from parliament, Marston had reportedly stated that they would take five or six hours to read and that anyone who wished to leave could do so. He had also challenged those who stayed to place their hands on their hearts, take up their bibles and find a text there which justified rebellion against the king. Marston later apologised to the Lords for having acted through his 'seduced iudgm[en]t, or troubled brayne'.[42] By the time that John White published a tract in 1643 listing the first hundred clerics ejected from their livings by his committee, 'malignancy' or royalism had been added to their shortcomings. Among the 15

39. Larking, *Proceedings*, pp. 185–8, 192–3.
40. C. Hibbard, *Charles I and the popish plot* (Chapel Hill, NC, 1983). See also K. Fincham and N. Tyacke, *Altars restored: the changing face of English religious worship, 1547–c.1700* (Oxford, 2007).
41. Larking, *Proceedings*, p. 227, see also pp. 149, 175.
42. LJ, 5, p. 243; HL, PO/JO/10/1/126, 130. 27 June 1642, Annex 1, letter from William Bridge and others, dated 28 June 1642, and 6 August 1642, petition from John Marston. See also J. Eales, 'The clergy and allegiance at the outbreak of the English civil wars: the case of John Marston of Canterbury', *Archaeologia Cantiana* (forthcoming).

men from Kent listed in the tract, John Jefferys stood accused of preaching that the king could take 'the whole of the subjects estates, if it please him'. Jefferys was one of a group of at least seven ministers whose livings were sequestered for their support for the 1643 revolt in the county against parliament.[43]

Through print, oral dissemination and the interventions of the clergy, then, the inhabitants of Kent at all social levels could be informed about the news and debates of the civil-war period. Yet did their potential awareness translate into political engagement? One source that has been vastly undervalued in Kent is the rare survival of the names of the men who endorsed two pro-parliamentarian petitions in May 1642 and January 1649. As a result of the great fire of 1834, which destroyed much of the palace of Westminster and the records of the House of Commons, many of the original signatures and endorsements of civil-war petitions to parliament have not survived, which makes these documents all the more valuable. Everitt's work traced the fortunes of the royalist gentry in Kent, but he regarded the parliamentarian leaders there as unrepresentative and personally unpleasant – in other words, both 'wrong and repulsive'. For these reasons he did not investigate the support that they commanded in any detail. Yet their activities were undoubtedly representative of certain bodies of opinion at two crucial points in time: just before the outbreak of civil war and on the eve of the king's execution. The 1640s was a period when the nature of collective petitioning changed significantly. David Zaret has argued that petitioning moved from being a closed process, in which representative groups such as those gathered at assizes articulated grievances directly to the political centre, to becoming an open process, which appealed directly to wider public opinion. This was reflected in the mass county petitions which were delivered to king and parliament from the counties and in the use of print to publicise their contents and gain more support. Petitions also became vehicles of political response and comment as rival groups vied in their claims to be representative of the 'true' opinions of their county.[44] Zaret thus locates the 'invention' of public opinion during the civil wars in these 'innovative' uses of petitions.[45]

The use of petitions to demonstrate the strength of public opinion on particular issues is, however, highly problematic. Civil-war allegiances were extremely fluid, but the survival of the signatures on the Kent petitions from 1642 and 1649 does allow a meaningful comparison to be made between the two groups of petitioners. In particular, it provides evidence about the commitment of individuals to parliamentarianism throughout the 1640s. The arrangement of the signatures on

43. BL, E76(21), J. White, *The first century of scandalous, malignant priests* (London, 1643), p. 10, see also pp. 2, 4–5, 11, 19, 21, 23–4, 30, 33, 36–7, 39–40, 43–4, 46–8.
44. D. Zaret, *Origins of democratic culture: printing, petitions, and the public sphere in early modern England* (Princeton, 2000), pp. 217–65.
45. Ibid., pp. 220–21.

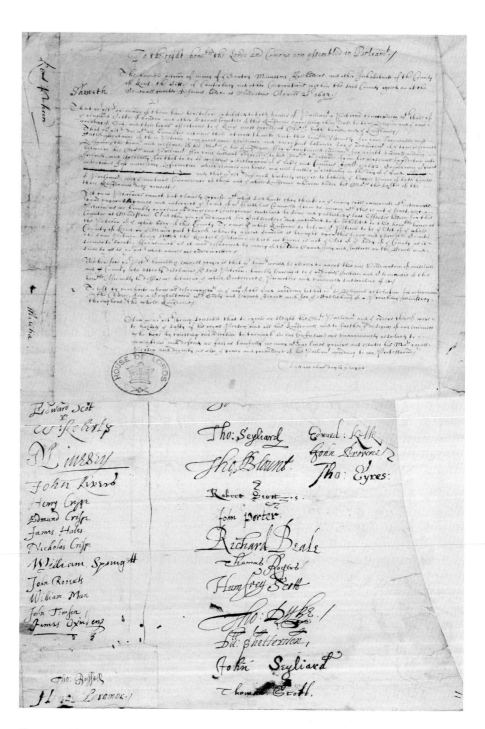

Figure 1.5 Blount's Kent petition to the Lords and Commons in Parliament, 5 May 1642. By permission of the Parliamentary Archives, London, HL, PO/JO/10/1/121.

the petitions also provides an insight into the social mechanisms at work in encouraging people to endorse them. The first of these petitions to be considered is Thomas Blount's petition, which was said to have attracted between 6,000 and 8,000 names in just over a fortnight, although the surviving signatures number just over 4,000.[46] Everitt argued that the 'parrot-like' phrases of this petition give scant insight into county opinion, while the 'burning issues of the day ... were simply ignored'. Far from giving little impression of their opinions, though, the petitioners started by reminding the Lords and Commons that many of them had previously endorsed the 'root and branch' petition against episcopacy from Kent of December 1640, in which they had agreed with 'the renowned Citty of London' and several other counties in expressing their zeal to 'true Religion & the pure Worship of God'. Now they supported parliament's intentions to summon an Assembly of Divines to consider reform of both the Church hierarchy and the prayer book. They roundly repudiated Dering's petition as unrepresentative, as it had been 'disavowed' at the assizes by many of the grand jury and magistrates, as well as by 'all us ye Petitioners, whose names are hereunder written'.[47]

The newly discovered signatures and marks of the petition's supporters reveal that Blount, Livesey and Springett were among the first to sign and they were followed by some of the gentry, freeholders, other inhabitants and clergy in Kent (Figure 1.5). In some communities the gentry or the clergy took the lead in signing the petition before others did so. The subscriptions of staunch parliamentarian gentry include those of Thomas Plumer, Andrew Broughton and Daniel Shatterden. Plumer was responsible for training the volunteer forces raised in Cranbrook and in other neighbouring parishes in August 1642. The Maidstone lawyer Broughton was later clerk to the court which tried Charles I in 1649 and read the charges and death sentence to the king. At the Restoration he was regarded as a regicide and fled to Switzerland, where he died in 1687. The puritan, Daniel Shatterden, was later elected as MP for Kent in the two Protectorate parliaments, but was excluded from taking his seat as an opponent of Cromwell in 1656.[48] It should be noted that none of the petitioners were women, which was also the case with the 1649 petition. Numerous copies of Blount's petition were circulated to different communities, some of which are clearly named, including

46. HL, PO/JO/10/1/121, 5 May 1642, petition from Kent, which claims to have 6,000 names; *To the right honourable the Lords and Commons assembled in Parliament. The humble petition of many of the gentry, ministers, free-holders, and other inhabitants of the county of Kent,* printed for William Larnar (1642), which claims 8,000 names. I am grateful to the following students on my third-year undergraduate course on the civil war for helping to count the 4,176 signatures: John Heron, Matthew Jackson, Gary Jephcote, Ricky Jones, Declan Lynch, Roseanne Powell and Olivia White.
47. Everitt, *The community of Kent*, p. 104; for the Kent root and branch petition, see Larking, *Proceedings*, pp. 26–38.
48. See above note 16, for Broughton see ODNB.

Figure 1.6 Canterbury signatures from Blount's Kent petition, 5 May 1642. By permission of the Parliamentary Archives, London, HL, PO/JO/10/1/121.

Canterbury, Dartford, Hever and Loddington, while parishes such as Chatham and Groombridge, among others, can be identified from the names of the subscribers. Canterbury and its locality supplied 185 signatures or marks, including those of the mayor and 11 of the 12 aldermen (Figure 1.6).[49] Many of the city governors of Canterbury would remain loyal to parliament throughout the 1640s and 1650s. Their support in 1642 was based partly on their experiences as intermediaries between the crown and the local population during Charles I's Personal Rule, as well as on their long-running disputes with the archbishop and the cathedral about the extent of ecclesiastical jurisdiction.[50] Of the Canterbury petitioners, 19 can be identified as parishioners of John Marston who also petitioned for his removal by the House of Lords during the following June. These men were largely freemen and artisans, who were now demonstrating their political engagement through the process of multiple petitioning.[51]

The sheet of names from Canterbury also bears a distinct central column reserved for the signatures of the clergy, but Edward Aldey, the puritan minister of St Andrews in Canterbury, was the only cleric from the 14 parishes within the city to sign. This starkly emphasises the dominance of the crown and the dean and chapter over appointments to these parishes. A further six clerics from nearby parishes signed in the same column, including Archbishop Laud's troublesome curate of Harbledown, Richard Culmer, who had been suspended from his livings in the 1630s for refusing to read the Book of sports to his congregation. In 1641 he had promoted a petition from Canterbury against bishops and in 1643 was responsible for destroying stained glass images in the cathedral in response to an ordinance from parliament.[52] Elsewhere the signature of the Presbyterian cleric, Thomas Wilson of Otham, can be found. He had been investigated by the ecclesiastical authorities for refusing to read the prayer against the Scots in his church during the bishops' wars. Later, in September 1642, he preached before the House of Commons in favour of abolishing episcopacy and argued that there was no divine right for bishops. By 1643 he had been chosen as a representative from Kent to the Westminster Assembly of Divines and soon replaced the Laudian cleric, Robert Barrell, at Maidstone. Here he engaged in a spiritual revival in the town, which the local godly described as previously prophane.[53] Neither Culmer nor Wilson would sign the 1649 petition for the trial of the king.

Many of the 1642 signatories would support parliament in the first and second

49. HL, PO/JO/10/1/121, 5 May 1642, petition from Kent; CJ, 2, p. 714; for Livesey and Broughton see ODNB.
50. CCA, AC4, fos 122r, 159r.
51. Eales, 'The clergy and allegiance'.
52. BL, E52(10), Culmer, *Cathedrall newes from Canterbury*; see also ODNB.
53. BL, E124(37), T. Wilson, *Jerichoes down-fall: as it was presented in a sermon preached in St. Margarets Westminster, before the honourable House of Commons at the late solemne fast, Septemb. 28. 1642* (London, 1643); G. Swinnock, *The life and death of Mr Thomas Wilson minister of Maidstone in the county of Kent MA* (1672); see also ODNB.

civil wars, but in Kent, as elsewhere, the crisis of the second civil war in 1648 saw a distinct split in the opposition to the king. The spectre of renewed civil war led to a hardening of anti-royalist feeling among both soldiers and civilians in the county. In December 1648 and January 1649 a resolute minority in Kent petitioned the commander-in-chief of the New Model Army, Thomas, Lord Fairfax, and parliament to bring Charles I to trial. Those who signed the 1649 petition were thus hardliners who rejected the moderation of the political Presbyterians, who wanted further negotiations with the king. Norah Carlin has traced five petitions from the county produced during this period, two of which were addressed to Fairfax from the officers of the forces under the command of Sir Michael Livesey and the officers of horse and foot in and 'about' Dover Castle. In both cases the petitioners also claimed to represent the views of their soldiers.[54] On 23 December 1648 some 'gentlemen' of Kent presented a petition to parliament from 'diverse well-affected' in the county, Canterbury and the Cinque Ports 'in the behalfe of themselves and others'. In response the speaker of the Commons, William Lenthall, commented that the 'most Part of that County have always stood very well affected to the Parliament'. Simultaneously the same group presented a petition to Fairfax and the 'generall Councell of Warre'.[55]

There has been a recent reassessment of the intentions of the army leadership in instigating the trial of Charles I. The king's execution was not necessarily a foregone conclusion and the trial was seen by many of his opponents as a final attempt to bring him to terms. A new constitution limiting the powers of the monarch or even Charles I's deposition were both actively debated as alternative outcomes to regicide. The refusal of moderates such as Lord Fairfax to participate in the trial, however, and the king's failure to negotiate the terms on which his life could be saved meant that his death remained the only solution to the political impasse.[56] While the four Kent petitions discussed thus far do not directly call for the king's death, all four of them supported the recent Remonstrance of the army of 16 November 1648, which called for the 'capital punishment' of the 'principal

54. 'The humble representation of the officers of horse and foot in and about Dover castle', in BL, E477(4), *The moderate, impartially communicating martial affaires to the kingdome of England*, no. 23, 12–19 December (London, 1648), pp. 211–12; BL, E536(15), *The declaration and engagement of the commanders, officers and seamen in the shippes, under the command of the right honourable the earle of Warwicke in the Downes* (London, 1648), pp. 7–8. I am grateful to Norah Carlin for sharing her unpublished paper 'Petitions and revolution in England, September 1648–January 1649' with me.

55. *CJ*, 6, p. 103; 'The humble proposals of the well affected in the county of Kent', in BL, E536(2), *The moderate, impartially communicating martial affaires to the kingdome of England*, no. 24, 19–26 December (London, 1648), pp. 223–4; BL, 669.f.13(64), *The Kentish petition to the honourable, the commons now sitting in parliament: the humble petition of diverse well-affected in the county of Kent* (London, 1648).

56. J. Adamson, 'The frightened junto, perceptions of Ireland and the last attempts at settlement with Charles I', and S. Kelsey, 'Staging the trial of Charles I', both in J. Peacey (ed.), *The regicides and the execution of Charles I* (Basingstoke, 2001), pp. 36–70, 71–93; S. Kelsey, 'The trial of Charles I', *English Historical Review*, 118 (2003), pp. 583–616.

To the Supreme Authority of y'e nation y'e Commons of England, in Parliament assembled,

The humble Petition of y'e well affected in y'e County of Kent

Humbly Sheweth,

That y'e Petitioners cannot but in all gratitude declare, how much their Spirits are refresh'd and heightned upon y'e Observation, especially, of y'e late imparalleld Actings of this honourable house, far above all other formerly, insomuch as y'e Petitioners are encourag'd to believe, y't y'e year of this nation's freedom (thro' God's blessing upon y'e Endeavours) is begun; and in order hereunto, we cannot but Express our hearty and highest acknowledgem't of thanks to this honourable house, for their vindicating and preserving of y'e just pow'r of y'e people in y'e late votes y't declare, y't y'e Legislative pow'r Originally, was in y'e people, and derivatively in y'e house of Commons as their representative; and also for y'e forwardness of this honourable house to satisfy y'e just and Earnest desires of this and other Countyes, for y'e bringing of y'e person of y'e King, w'th y'e rest of y'e grand delinquents, to a speedy tryal.

And forasmuch as we are not ignorant of y'e plottings and practices of those, y't are ill affected, to retard (and if possible) make void y'e proceedings of this honourable house, and y'e high Court of Justice in y'e s'd instance; and also to foment and raise (as much as in them lies) another war, we are forced, omitting other great and necessary particulars for y'e present, in all Earnestness and submission, to propose these two Ensuing particulars to y'r serious and speedy Considerations.

1. That notwithstanding all suggestions to y'e Contrary, y'e Tryal of Charles Stewart King &c may be vigorously prosecuted, and y't no pretence or overtures w'tsoever may cause this honourable house, and y'e high Court of Justice to be satisfied for y'e blood of three States, w'th less than y'e blood of those persons, who have been y'e principall Authors of its Effusion: forasmuch as God himself hath said, y't _who sheddeth man's blood, by man shall his blood be shed._

2. That, for y'e prevention of future insurrections and rebellions, this honourable house will be pleased to commit y'e Militia of this and other Counties, to his Excellency, y'e Lord ffairfax General &c: so to be new modelled as y't y'e Commissionating and Arming of all forces w'tsoever may by mediate pow'r and Authority from him, be deputed and put into y'e hands of such, and none but such, as adhere unto y'e Parliament and Army, in their present proceedings.

And y'e Petitioners, as ready to stand to you w'th their lives and fortunes, shall ever pray, &c

W'm Kenwricke	John Nordon	Peter Croshole	Thomas Hoare
Rich: Brown	Barth: May	Jehosaphat Sturr	Francis Young
John Rabson	Rich: Hope	Thomas Weller	John Pollings
Arthur Rolfe	Rich: Goodhue	John Bodsham	Andrew Ampleton
Alex: Riveringham	Thomas ffenn	Mich: Gilbert	Robert Silly
John Wilding	George Humphrey	W'm Steed	John Weller
James Woodley	W'm Onirum	Walter Streeter	Stephen Osborne
W'm Green	Thomas Sale	James Granton	Walter Woollle
Thomas fferrall	Alex: March		
Thomas Charton	W'm Foster		
	Tho: Chittenden		

Figure 1.7 Kent petition presented to the House of Commons, 2 February 1649. By permission of the Bodleian Library, University of Oxford. Rawlinson MS A298 fo. 1r.

author and some prime instruments in our late wars'. As Michael Braddick has argued, the Remonstrance was ambiguous on this point and also left the path open for a pardon and an agreement with the king, if he were to show remorse for his crimes.[57] The offer of mercy may well have been designed as a means of placating Fairfax and other moderates, since the Remonstrance was issued in his name along with the imprimatur of his general council of officers.[58]

The fifth petition, also from 'the well affected in the County of Kent', was more open in demanding the death penalty for the royalist leaders 'without distinction of persons' (Figure 1.7). It called for the trial of the king to be 'vigorously prosecuted' and demanded the blood of 'those persons who have been the principall Authors' of the wars. It thus referred to the Old Testament concept of 'blood guilt' and claimed that 'whosoe sheddeth mans blood by man shall his blood be shed'.[59] It was drawn up after the House of Commons had passed a resolution on 4 January 1649 declaring that the people 'under God' were the origins of all 'just power' and that the Commons, as the people's representative body, have 'the supreme power in this nation'. It was thus addressed to the House of Commons as the 'supreame Authority' assembled in parliament and, curiously, was presented on 2 February 1649, three days after the execution of Charles I.[60] Two copies of the petition have survived bearing the names of 1,135 petitioners, one of which was prepared for the speaker of the House of Commons, William Lenthall, but Everitt dismissed this valuable evidence by claiming that it was doubtful that the signatures are genuine. His conclusion was based on the fact that the original endorsements do not survive and all of the names on the petitions are copied in the hands of scribes. Admittedly, this makes it more difficult to verify the petitioners with complete accuracy, but many of them can be identified. The first to sign was William Kenwricke of Boughton under Blean, who was a parliamentarian colonel and commander of auxiliary forces in Kent, where he was also a prominent member of the county committee. He was an Independent in religion and in 1653 he was one of the five MPs from Kent in the Barebones Parliament, having been successfully nominated by representatives of 19 Independent congregations in the county along with Thomas Blount.[61] Kenwricke represents a new breed of politician, who became more influential as a result of the exclusion of royalists

---

57. M. Braddick, *God's fury, England's fire: a new history of the English civil wars* (London, 2008), p. 556.
58. BL, E473(11), *A remonstrance of his excellency Thomas, lord Fairfax, lord generall of the Parliament's forces. And of the general councell of officers held at St. Albans, the 16 of November* (London, 1648).
59. P. Crawford, 'Charles Stuart, that man of blood', *Journal of British Studies*, 16 (1977), pp. 41–61.
60. *CJ*, 6, pp. 110–11.
61. 'Humble petition of the well-affected in the county of Kent', in *A perfect collection of exact passages*, 2, pp. 15–16; for the two manuscript copies of this petition see Bodl., Tanner MS 57b (Lenthall's copy), and Bodl., Rawlinson MS A298; Everitt, *The community of Kent*, pp. 271–2; Nickolls, *Original letters and papers*, pp. 95–7. See also above, note 16.

and moderate parliamentarians from the parliaments of the 1650s.

The petition was presented to the House by a group of four soldiers and two civilians and the subscribers included men who had risen to prominence in the oligarchies of the east Kent towns of Canterbury, Hythe and Sandwich during the 1640s.[62] They were overwhelmingly Independents in religion and some of them, such as Jehosaphat Starr of Canterbury, had also signed Blount's petition of 1642, thus demonstrating a commitment to parliament from the outbreak of the civil wars.[63] Leading council members from Canterbury who signed both petitions included three former mayors, Daniel Masterson, John Pollen and William Bridge, the last of whom had been mayor during the 1647 Christmas riots. Among those who signed only the 1649 petition were Josias Nicholls and Zachariah Lee, who were founder members of the Independent congregation formed in 1645 in Canterbury, and John Nutt, the MP for Canterbury since the start of the Long Parliament. Nutt was named as one of the commissioners for the trial of the king, but did not take part in the trial proceedings.[64] In Sandwich a minister, the jurats and other town officers who signed are clearly identified on Speaker Lenthall's copy of the petition. They include Thomas Browne, Thomas Wilkes, Thomas Foxten, the town serjeant John Hammond, the collector of customs John Farwar and the minister Francis Prentice.[65]

The evidence provided by the names on the two petitions discussed above demonstrates how the political and religious issues had changed between the spring of 1642, when civil war was about to break out, and January 1649, when the trial of the king had become a near certainty. While Blount's petition commanded the support of Presbyterian ministers such as Culmer and Wilson, the later petition was overwhelmingly endorsed by religious and political radicals, who had become influential as the political landscape had changed. There is no doubt that such men were in the minority in 1649, a fact that is underscored by the relatively small number of signatures on the January petition of that year. Nevertheless, as Zaret has argued, the act of petitioning provided an avenue for the expression of informed local opinion about national political and religious debates. The use of petitions to demonstrate this process is greatly enhanced by the survival of these contemporary endorsements. They reveal the penetration of political debates beyond the circles of the gentry elite, as ministers, freeholders and other inhabitants of the county became involved in the local political process of petitioning. The role of the clergy in trying to influence the allegiance of their parishioners was particularly evident in the early stages of the war, but, as the purges of their ranks took place, the voices of

---

62. 'Humble petition of the well-affected in the county of Kent', in *A perfect collection of exact passages,* 2, pp. 15–16.
63. For Starr's will, see CKS, PRC32/53/32.
64. CCA, U37. See also above, note 43.
65. Bodl., Tanner MS 57b.

royalist clergy in particular were silenced in Kent.

Alan Everitt's work on the county provided an invaluable correction in its time to the over-emphasis on central political debates and processes, and his study of Kent influenced civil war studies for a generation. He had a finely tuned sense for the local evidence and for the position adopted by moderates and neutrals, who did not wish to engage with the extreme political positions of civil war. His emphasis on the central role of the royalist gentry in Kent during the civil wars also provided important evidence about the stance of the traditional governors of county society during the crisis of 1640–60. By 1980, however, Everitt's work had been overtaken by the new interest in social history in county studies, which meant that historians were increasingly investigating the agency of groups below the elites. Everitt's dismissal of the evidence illustrating the spread of parliamentarian allegiance below the gentry as either unimportant or unrepresentative led him to underestimate the strength of support for parliament in the county in 1642. By the time that Charles I was put on trial that support had been greatly eroded and it is through the evidence of the 1649 petition that this weakening of support for parliament is best demonstrated. It is only by extending the analysis of county society to include groups below the gentry that the full extent of the divisions in the county community can be examined. The concerted pressure from Kent for the trial of the king in 1648–9 can also be placed within the context of continued support from the radicals in the county for the *de facto* governments of the 1650s. The county, though, remained the arena for local political administration throughout the period of civil war and interregnum, and it thus presents us with a valid focus of study, even if the community itself was severely divided.

2

A convenient fiction? The county community and county history in the 1650s

JAN BROADWAY

Among other virtues it was for 'the generall coniunction and association of your minds, and your selfes in good amitie, and familiaritie, one toward an other' that Thomas Wotton was glad to call himself 'a member of this Countie' in the preface to William Lambarde's *Perambulation of Kent* (1576).[1] My work on the Elizabethan and early Stuart gentry has led me to conclude that the county community retained a symbolic importance, even when it had little social, economic or political reality. That is to say, the county gentry belonged to an imagined community, as defined by Benedict Anderson, which grew out of a perceived affinity based on shared values.[2] When the Roman Catholic antiquary Thomas Habington dedicated his history of Worcestershire to its gentry, and wrote of 'our Shyre' when addressing those he termed their nobility in 1642, he clearly saw himself as a member of such a county community. He believed that the values shared by the gentry community transcended religious differences.[3] The early county histories reflected the gentry community's ideal qualities of antiquity, continuity, piety, charity and unity within the spatial boundaries of the county, newly given visual form in the maps produced by Christopher Saxton and John Speed. This was a weak version of the county community as expounded by Alan Everitt, excluding all classes below the gentry, or rather below those gentry families who claimed the right to use a coat of arms. Significantly, however, it extended back in time to incorporate the medieval ancestors of contemporary gentlemen. It was perhaps largely an illusion, ignoring religious and political divisions and masking the true extent of social mobility and redistribution of land in the sixteenth century. Yet this weak version of the county community was

1. W. Lambarde, *Perambulation of Kent* (London, 1576), sig. a2–a3.
2. B. Anderson, *Imagined communities* (London, 1983).
3. T. Habington, *A survey of Worcestershire*, ed. J. Amphlett, Worcestershire Historical Society (Worcester, 1895), vol. 1, pp. 32–5; J. Broadway, '"To equall their virtues": Thomas Habington, recusancy and the gentry of early Stuart Worcestershire', *Midland History*, 29 (2004), pp. 1–24. The nobility Habington identified were Lord Coventry, the Earl of Shrewsbury, Lord Windsor, Sir Walter Devereux and Sir Robert Berkeley.

no more of an illusion than other imagined communities, such as the English nation or Christendom.

Hardly had the ink dried on Thomas Habington's dedication than his house was ransacked by soldiers.4 It seems incredible that even the illusion of the community of county gentry could survive the realities of the civil war. Any belief in local autonomy and the primacy of local allegiances was effectively destroyed by a conflict in which neutrality proved to be an unworkable strategy and no county managed to repel the war at its borders. And yet, as we shall see, the county histories that were published during the Interregnum continued to embody this apparently bankrupt ideal. A detailed analysis of two of these works will demonstrate that they were not simply produced within an existing idiom that had no relationship to contemporary reality; the ideal of the county community provided a convenient fiction by which the authors, their contributors and their readers could seek to build a bulwark against contemporary threats of social, religious and political radicalism.

Four county histories were published during the Interregnum: William Dugdale's *Antiquities of Warwickshire* and Daniel King's *Vale-royall of England*, on Cheshire, in 1656 and Richard Kilburne's *Survey of Kent* and Thomas Phillipot's *Villare Cantianum*, also on Kent, in 1659. This may seem an unimpressive total until we consider that the two decades preceding the civil war had witnessed the appearance of only William Burton's *Description of Leicestershire*, in 1622. It seems that the appetite for county history could largely be satisfied by the circulation of manuscripts and that they were rarely a commercial success on publication. It has long been recognised that Kent was in many ways an atypical county, and this was certainly so in the case of county history. William Lambarde's *Perambulation of Kent* was the first county study published in England and Lambarde was the only county historian in this period to see a second edition appear during his lifetime. A further edition of Lambarde's work was published in 1656 and was presumably sufficiently successful to encourage the publication of Kilburne's and Phillipot's books three years later. Since Kent represents a special case, this paper will concentrate predominantly on the works of Dugdale and King.

The two counties that concern us here have both been the subject of major studies influenced by Alan Everitt's pioneering work. In *Cheshire 1630–1660*, John Morrill showed that the gentry community presented a model of continuity and stability. A high proportion of families could trace their pedigrees back to the thirteenth century or beyond and there was a high incidence of marriage within the county boundaries, while the majority of manors changed hands by inheritance. Although topographically divided into diverse regions, the

---

4.   SBT, DR37/2/87/103. The letter is dated 27 November 1642. It is probable that the soldiers were part of the Earl of Essex's parliamentarian army that occupied nearby Worcester after the battle of Powick Bridge in September 1642.

jurisdictional distinction of being a county palatine distinguished Cheshire as a whole from its neighbours.[5] In contrast, Ann Hughes showed in *Politics, society and civil war in Warwickshire, 1620–1660* that the gentry there were largely of comparatively recent origin, that they tended to marry outside the county and that manors frequently changed hands by purchase rather than inheritance. The geographical division of Warwickshire between the forested Arden region to the north and the fielden in the south was reflected socially and politically among the gentry.[6] One characteristic both Cheshire and Warwickshire shared was the lack of a dominant aristocrat to act as a focus within the county hierarchy. Both counties were also drawn rapidly into the war in 1642. Warwickshire was the arena for skirmishes between the parliamentarian Lord Brooke and the royalist Earl of Northampton that summer, and it witnessed the first major battle of the war at Edgehill on 23 October 1642. Cheshire was strategically important because of its position on the routes to and from north Wales and Ireland. Consequently, the king moved to occupy Chester immediately after raising his standard at Nottingham. In December 1642 the active royalists and parliamentarians in Cheshire signed a neutrality treaty in an attempt to demilitarise the county, but this collapsed within months as both sides stepped up the war effort.[7] However much they might have been inclined to neutralism and localism, most of the gentry of both counties were obliged to take sides and to become embroiled in the national conflict.

The histories of these two counties that appeared in 1656 had very different evolutions. Dugdale's work arose out of his research into the history of Warwickshire conducted in collaboration with Sir Simon Archer during the 1630s. In 1638 Dugdale had assumed responsibility for the work and a draft was in existence by 1640. It was thus, in its first manifestation, a work that was written before the civil war. A substantial part of this initial draft appeared in the published version without significant alterations. The distractions of other research projects and Dugdale's duties as a herald, followed by the outbreak of the civil war, meant that the manuscript was neglected for much of the succeeding decade. In the summer of 1650, however, Dugdale described himself as 'hard at work upon my Warwickshire discourse', and four months later described how he intended to lay out certain details 'if ever my booke have the fortune to be printed'.[8] This period of renewed interest in county history coincided with Dugdale being unable to travel to London and was in part due to his working on the material available to him when he was confined in the

5. J.S. Morrill, *Cheshire 1630–1660: county government and society during the English revolution* (Oxford, 1974), pp. 2–4.
6. A. Hughes, *Politics, society and civil war in Warwickshire, 1620–1660* (Cambridge, 1987), pp. 1–50.
7. Morrill, *Cheshire*, pp. 54–9.
8. BL, Harleian MS 1,967, fos 78–9; SBT, DR422/165.

country. The support he received from members of the gentry at this time, particularly from some of those who had not opened their muniment rooms in the 1630s, encouraged him to continue. If Dugdale had not perceived that there was support for a county history of Warwickshire, it is unlikely that the work would have been completed once the restrictions on his travel were removed. Work on the *Antiquities of Warwickshire* continued to be interrupted by other concerns, notably Dugdale's work with the Yorkshire antiquary Roger Dodsworth on a collection of monastic charters published as *Monasticon Anglicanum* in 1655. The beginning of 1654 saw the production of the first engravings for the *Antiquities of Warwickshire*, although the printing of the text did not begin for a further year.[9] It was the financial support of a substantial proportion of the Warwickshire gentry for Dugdale's work through sponsorship of its many illustrations that was critical to its publication. The final additions to the text, the prefatory materials and index, were completed by Easter 1656 and the book was ready for distribution at the beginning of May.[10] There was no bookseller involved in the publication of the *Antiquities of Warwickshire*; Dugdale financed and managed the printing and distribution of the copies himself. Although he drew on the research and support of Archer and others, the work was very much Dugdale's own personal achievement.

By contrast, the *Vale-royall of England* was a compendium of existing manuscripts, of which little beyond the dedication and some of the engravings was Daniel King's own work.[11] It too had a lengthy gestation. In November 1653 Archer wrote to Dugdale: 'If it would be any benefitt to you, I could wish you would print the Discription of Staffordshyre, and that of Cheshyre, which I have; or any other manuscript that may yeld you profit.'[12] The description of Staffordshire was the work of Sampson Erdeswicke, who had died in 1603, and had been copied by Dugdale in the 1630s. In the preface to the *Antiquities of Warwickshire* Dugdale expressed the hope that Erdeswicke's work would soon appear in print, and it is probable that he intended to publish an expanded version himself. He certainly enlarged the account of Wolverhampton, which he knew well, as his wife's family came from that neighbourhood. The second manuscript mentioned by Archer was an account of Cheshire by William Webb.

9. BL, Additional MS 6,396, fo. 17; W. Hamper (ed.), *The life, diary and correspondence of Sir William Dugdale* (London, 1827), p. 285.
10. Hamper, *Dugdale*, p. 304; Merevale Hall Manuscripts, Merevale, near Atherstone, Warwickshire, HT4/10/8; WCRO, Z13/8.
11. D. King, *The vale-royall of England, or, the county palatine of Chester illustrated* (London, 1656), comprising: W. Smith, *The vale-royall of England*; W. Webb, *The vale royall of England*; S. Lee, *Chronicon Cestrensis*; J. Chaloner, *A short treatise of the Isle of Man*. The individual texts are separately paginated.
12. Hamper, *Dugdale*, p. 273.

This work, written in the 1620s, had its origins in a survey of the city of Chester inspired by John Stow's *Survey of London* (1598), but had subsequently been extended to include the whole county. It lacked the attention to manorial descents and documentary evidence that were the hallmarks of Dugdale's own work, and to have been directly associated with its publication would have done little for his scholarly reputation. So, rather than make use of the manuscript himself, Dugdale passed it on to Daniel King. King had been born in Chester and apprenticed to the Holme family of herald painters there. Dugdale had come to know him as an engraver, who produced views of English cathedrals and conventual churches for the *Monasticon Anglicanum*. Unlike Dugdale, King was not hampered by concerns for his scholarly reputation, being more interested in publishing for profit. In addition to the Webb manuscript, King also acquired a copy of the description of Chester written by William Smith, a Jacobean herald. This had been given to the judge Sir Ranulph Crewe and passed to his grandson, also Ranulph, who made it available to King. It is possible that King, the engraver, had become aware of the existence of Smith's manuscript through the survival of copperplates that had been prepared for an intended publication by the author 40 years before. One of the title pages that appear in King's work was clearly originally engraved at that time, bearing as it does the arms of Henry, Prince of Wales as Earl of Chester (Figure 2.1). The county map that was included in the *Vale-royall* was based on a map prepared by Smith, which presumably also already existed as a copperplate to which King gained access.

In February 1654 Dugdale mentioned King's intention to publish these existing accounts of Cheshire in a letter to John Crewe of Utkinton, the eldest son of Sir Ranulph Crewe. He sought Crewe's opinion as to how the Cheshire antiquaries William Vernon and Peter Leycester would react to the idea. The two men were working on a history of Cheshire, which Vernon had begun before the civil war. Dugdale acknowledged that their work would surpass the earlier attempts, if it was ever published. Given the doubts that surrounded it, however, he hoped it might prove acceptable to publish the existing texts in the short term. By this stage the extent of the support among the Warwickshire gentry for Dugdale's own work was becoming apparent and the first engravings were being produced. Clearly King hoped that his project would inspire similar enthusiasm among the Cheshire gentry. In this letter Dugdale mentioned a stationer 'your countryman also' who was 'trucking' with King to publish the texts.[13] It is unclear who this Cheshire stationer might have been, since the book was eventually entered in the stationers' register in February 1656 by Giles Calvert, a stationer from Somerset, and John Streater, a printer from Sussex.[14] Both these men were

13.   BL, Additional MS 6,396, fo. 17.
14.   *A transcript of the registers of the worshipful company of stationers*, vol. 2 (London, 1913), p. 30.

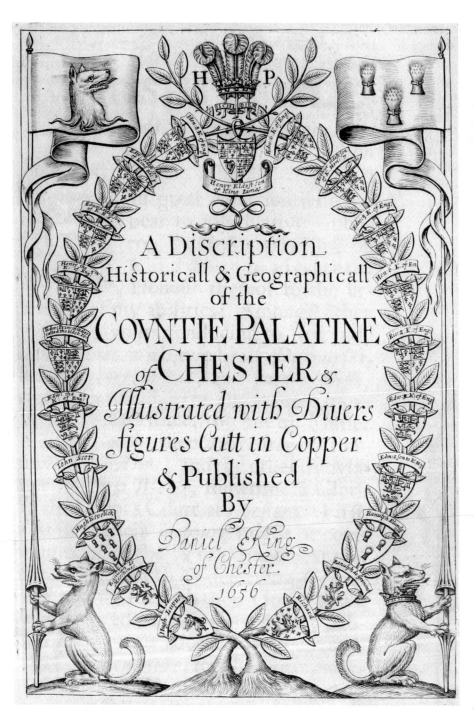

A Discription
Historicall & Geographicall
of the
COVNTIE PALATINE
of CHESTER &
Illustrated with Diuers
figures Cutt in Copper
& Published
By
Daniel King
of Chester.
1656

Figure 2.1 Title page from Daniel King, *The vale-royall of England, or, the county palatine of Chester illustrated* (London, 1656), showing the arms of Prince Henry (d. 1612).

radicals. Streater was a prolific pamphleteer in favour of a republic, while Calvert was associated with the publication of radical and particularly Quaker literature.[15] These were unlikely collaborators for the royalist Dugdale and it is probable that he was not involved in the publication of the work beyond the initial proposal. The approach to Crewe was successful in securing King sponsorship for his engravings and some access, possibly indirect, to Vernon's collections.[16] However, the project did not gain much obvious support among the Cheshire gentry. It is likely that King was unable to replicate in Cheshire the success Dugdale had in Warwickshire because he was not a member of the community whose support he sought.

As with Dugdale's *Antiquities of Warwickshire*, the slow progress of King's book towards publication was probably due largely to the time it took to produce the engravings that would attract a higher price and encourage greater sales. These included 11 plates of the arms of the Cheshire gentry, which were sponsored by Peter Venables, member for Cheshire in the Long Parliament, a leading royalist and supporter of the established church.[17] Although King was an engraver, there were far fewer illustrations in the *Vale-royall* than in the *Antiquities of Warwickshire*. King had secured the support of only a handful of sponsors to finance new engravings and some of the illustrations involved the reuse of existing copperplates. The view of Chester cathedral sponsored by Sir Orlando Bridgeman, for example, had been engraved by King for the *Monasticon Anglicanum*. During its evolution the *Vale-royall* acquired two further texts. The first was *Chronicon Cestrense* by Samuel Lee, which provided an account of the Roman history of the county and of its temporal and spiritual rulers. It added little that was new. The identity of Samuel Lee is uncertain. He appears to have lived in London, but his social status is unclear. In his introductory epistle he described himself as having Cheshire ancestors and distant relations still in the county. From his text we know that he visited Chester in 1653, which is probably also when he excavated a hypocaust at a Roman fort in north Wales.[18] Lee's work was not mentioned in King's preface to the reader and, as his epistle is dated May 1656, it is likely that it was a last-minute addition. The second extra text was James Chaloner's account of the Isle of Man. This was an extended version of a report on the island that Chaloner had originally

15. J. Raymond, 'John Streater and *The Grand Politick Informer*', *Historical Journal*, 41 (1998), pp. 567–74; M. Carrichio, 'News from the New Jerusalem: Giles Calvert and the radical experience', in A. Hessayon and D. Finnegan (eds), *Varieties of seventeenth- and early eighteenth-century English radicalism in context* (Farnham, 2011), pp. 69–96.

16. Copies of documents belonging to Vernon are interpolated into Webb's text: Webb, *Vale-royall*, in King, *The vale-royall of England*, pp. 75, 122.

17. M.F. Keeler, *The Long Parliament, 1640–1641: a biographical study of its members* (Philadelphia, 1954), p. 372; Venables was also elected to the Cavalier parliament: B.D. Henning (ed.), *The House of Commons, 1660–1690* (London, 1983), vol. 3, p. 633.

18. Lee, *Chronicon Cestrensis*, in King, *The vale-royall of England*, pp. 4 and 6.

written for Thomas, Lord Fairfax. The parliamentary general had been granted lordship of the Isle of Man on 15 October 1651 and the text is dedicated to him.[19] The dedication was written in December 1653. Its title page suggests that Chaloner's work was initially intended to be published separately and was incorporated into the *Vale-royall* at the last moment. It included a map of the island, surrounded by vignettes and a further four plates, none of which were sponsored.[20] The page numbering of the *Antiquities of Warwickshire* includes large gaps, reflecting the asynchronous way in which its different sections were printed. The *Vale-royall* avoided this problem by independently numbering each of its sections, thus increasing the sense of the book as an unconsidered compendium rather than a synthesis of the available material.

In concluding his preface to the *Antiquities of Warwickshire*, Dugdale wrote that his was an undertaking that 'would have been more proper for such a one whose Ancestors had enjoyed a long succession in this Countie, whereunto I cannot pretend'.[21] He had been born in the county, but his father was from Lancashire and it was Dugdale himself who had bought the manor of Blyth Hall as recently as 1625. Still, he was able to dedicate the work 'to my honoured friends the gentrie of Warwickshire' as a member of that community, albeit a recent recruit, and to address them as 'my Noble Countriemen'.[22] Similarly, the Kentish gentlemen Phillipot and Kilburne dedicated their works to the nobility and gentry of Kent, although, with an unusual touch of egalitarianism, Kilburne also included the commonalty in his dedication. By contrast, although King was born in Cheshire and Lee claimed ancestral ties, neither was a member of the gentry community of the county. Nor did King dedicate his work to that community or a member thereof. The *Vale-royall* was dedicated to Sir Orlando Bridgeman, who was born in Devon, although he had strong ties to Chester, where his father had been bishop.[23] Bridgeman's role in the royalist defence of Chester during the civil war had not made him a particularly popular figure among the county gentry. It is doubtful that King's description of him as one of the 'Principall Ornaments' of Cheshire would have met with general agreement.[24] However, in the 1650s Bridgeman was living and practising law in London and was for King a more useful potential patron than a provincial gentleman. Moreover, to single out a single Cheshire

19. A. Hopper, *'Black Tom': Sir Thomas Fairfax and the English revolution* (Manchester, 2007), p. 116.
20. Chaloner, *A short treatise of the Isle of Man*, dedication, in King, *The vale-royall of England*. It is probable that Chaloner commissioned the plates from King.
21. W. Dugdale, *The antiquities of Warwickshire* (London, 1656), sig. b4.
22. Ibid., sig. a3. For Dugdale's family background and status within Warwickshire society, see J. Broadway, *William Dugdale: a life of the Warwickshire historian and herald* (Gloucester, 2011), chapters 1 and 2.
23. The plan of Chester cathedral marks the burial place of the bishop, his wife and their son Dove Bridgeman: Webb, *Vale-royall*, in King, *The vale-royall of England*, p. 26.
24. King, *The vale-royall of England*, sig. Av.

gentleman might have been considered impolitic, while King could not address the entire gentry community on equal terms. According to Ormerod, in some copies of the *Vale-royall* the dedication to Bridgeman was cancelled and another to Peter Venables substituted.[25] Through his sponsorship of the engravings of the arms of the Cheshire gentry, Venables had provided the *Vale-royall* with a visual representation of the county community. Such a substitution of the dedicatee might suggest an appropriation of the work by that community.

Through their solicitation of sponsorship for the engravings both Dugdale and King invited the gentry to shape the visual appearance of their books. It is the engravings of funeral monuments and coats of arms in the Antiquities of Warwickshire that most effectively portray the Warwickshire gentry as a community linked through generations of intermarriage. A close perusal of the printed pedigrees conveys a similar impression through the repetition of surnames, but it is one less powerful than that created by the engravings. In what has been described as a 'petulant section' of the preface, Dugdale listed four monuments that had been omitted because the heirs refused to pay and three more that would have been had he realised that no money would be forthcoming.[26] For the researcher this list is useful, since it identifies precisely who was not prepared to subscribe to this attempt at community myth-making.[27] Of the seven families named only two, Ferrers of Baddesley Clinton and Beaufoe of Emscote, had a primary ancestral and enduring link to Warwickshire. Both these families had provided assistance to Dugdale in his research and might have hoped that their reluctance or inability to pay for the engravings would be overlooked.[28] The brevity of Dugdale's list emphasises that the vast majority of county families paid up, although there may have been a fair amount of persuasion involved. This reinforces the impression created by the engravings themselves of a community to which the gentry wanted to be seen to belong. In this respect King's work, which drew on very few gentry sponsors, was far less able to manifest a sense of community. Rather than innumerable illustrations of coats of arms and funeral monuments, the *Vale-royall* included a select collection of engravings of personal

25. G. Ormerod, *The history of the county palatine and city of Chester* (London, 1819), vol. 1, p. 92. Dugdale also dedicated *The antiquities of Warwickshire* to Christopher, Lord Hatton. Hatton was associated with Northamptonshire, but he had been Dugdale's patron for several years before the civil war and had supported his research for the book.

26. A. Hughes, 'Warwickshire on the eve of the civil war: a "county community"?', *Midland History*, 7 (1982), p. 53; Dugdale, *Warwickshire*, sig. b3.

27. The sponsors of the engravings are only indicated by the inclusion of their coat of arms, where they are not the immediate heirs or direct ancestors. See, for example, the monuments at Baginton: Dugdale, *Warwickshire*, p. 154.

28. Hamper, *Dugdale*, p. 99; SBT, DR422/165. Sir Simon Archer referred to both men as his cousins and was involved in the attempts to get them to pay in 1655: Hamper, *Dugdale*, pp. 287–8.

significance for individual gentlemen: Beeston and Halton castles for the catholic John Savage; Crewe Hall and Birkenhead Priory for John Crewe; his alleged ancestor Hugh Lupus for Sir Richard Grosvenor.[29] Such illustrations of family houses and ancestors also appeared in the *Antiquities of Warwickshire*, but they were less obvious among the crowd. Nevertheless, the *Vale-royall's* massed shields of arms across 11 pages of engravings did present a potent image of the continuity of Cheshire gentry society. The pages are divided into eight rows of six shields apiece, with the names of the associated families above.[30] No differentiation is made between the arms of modern and medieval families, which are displayed alongside the arms of the religious houses swept away in the sixteenth century in a roughly alphabetical order (Figure 2.2). This massed display of arms was an important expression of the status and continuity of the Cheshire gentry. As with the more extensive engravings of the *Antiquities of Warwickshire*, the effect was to present the gentry families of mid-seventeenth-century Cheshire as part of a larger community that had its roots in the medieval past. This suggested subliminally that, just as that community had survived civil wars and religious upheavals in the past, it would overcome the more immediate divisions.

The potentially most divisive subject for the Interregnum county historian wishing to preserve the illusion of a county community among the gentry was of course the recent conflict. One possible approach was simply to ignore it and to a large extent this is what they did. Such locally significant parliamentarian figures as Lord Brooke and William Purefoy are mentioned by Dugdale in the accounts of their families, but no details of their careers are given. Equally, the reference to Lord Leigh of Stoneleigh having been awarded his title in 1643 'in testimony of his stedfast loyalty' to Charles I is a rare example of an unequivocal reference to the royalist gentry.[31] The death of the Earl of Northampton at the battle of Hopton Heath is mentioned in his pedigree, but there is no description of his pivotal role in the early stages of the war.[32] Likewise, although the earlier service of William Feilding, the first Earl of Denbigh, as an admiral under his brother-in-law the Duke of

29. Smith, *Vale-royall*, in King, *The vale-royall of England*, p. 96; Webb, *Vale-royall*, in King, *The vale-royall of England*, pp. 75, 122, 130.

30. All but one includes some blank shields. The first page has the space for four shields in the top left corner taken up with the dedication to Venables and a further page has a blank space in the same place. The total number of arms is more than double the number of families that would record their pedigrees in Dugdale's visitation of Cheshire in 1663/4. Such massed displays of coats of arms became a staple of subsequent county histories. See, for example, those surrounding the maps of Robert Plot's *Natural history of Oxfordshire* (Oxford, 1677) and *Natural history of Staffordshire* (Oxford, 1686) and the plates of arms in Sir Robert Atkyns, *The present and ancient state of Glostershire* (London, 1712).

31. Dugdale, *Warwickshire*, pp. 61, 173, 789.

32. Ibid., p. 58. Dugdale was sent by the king to assist the Earl of Northampton with the Warwickshire commission of array in the summer of 1642: Broadway, *William Dugdale*, p. 424.

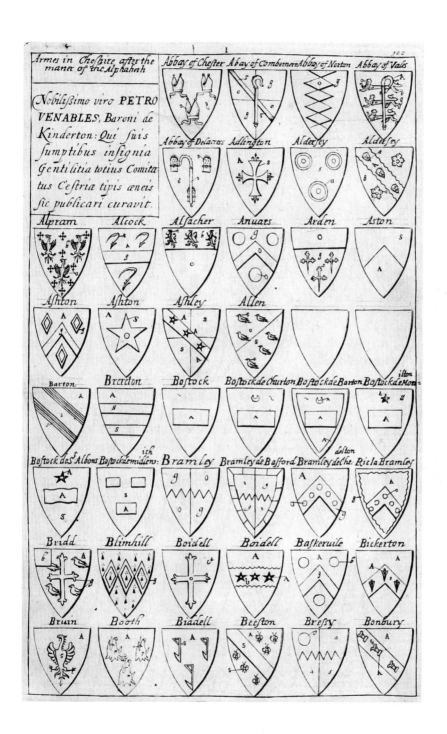

Figure 2.2 The first page of Cheshire coats of arms from Daniel King, *The vale-royall of England, or, the county palatine of Chester illustrated* (London, 1656).

Buckingham is mentioned, there is no reference to his later military service and subsequent death after the storming of Birmingham. The account of the Feilding family ends with the first Earl, no mention being made of his son, Basil Feilding, second Earl of Denbigh, who had briefly led the parliamentarian forces in Warwickshire, or of his daughter, the wife of the royalist James, Duke of Hamilton.[33] In the case of the Feildings, we know that the account of the family was shaped not simply by Dugdale's reticence about the recent conflict. Through the survival of his correspondence with the second Earl's agent, Henry Firebrace, we can trace the development of Dugdale's account of Newnham Paddox through 1654 and 1655.[34] This shows that the second Earl of Denbigh was far more concerned that his family's spurious Habsburg descent should be acknowledged by Dugdale than to have his own existence recorded. The desire to gloss over recent events was not limited to royalist antiquaries, but apparently extended to the parliamentarian gentry.

A reluctance to admit evidence of the breakdown of the gentry community did not mean that references to the recent conflict were completely absent from contemporary county histories. In dedicating the *Antiquities of Warwickshire* to Lord Hatton, Dugdale referred to 'our sad distractions', which had led his patron into exile in France.[35] Samuel Lee made a passing reference to the 'unhappy burning' of Foregate Street in 'the late uncivil Wars' in his account of Chester, but he did not identify which side was responsible or describe the other vicissitudes the city and county had suffered.[36] In his accounts of Edgbaston and Compton Wynyates, Dugdale described the destruction visited upon the churches while the neighbouring houses were parliamentarian garrisons.[37] His references emphasised the destruction of family monuments, which gentlemen of all but the most extreme political and religious views might be expected to find reprehensible. They echoed his observations on the damage that had been done during the religious upheavals of the sixteenth century to monuments and stained glass and, consequently, to the memory of those they recorded and the status of their descendents. In contrast, Dugdale's account of Kenilworth castle was written in 1640, and, while it gives a full description of the castle's role in Simon de Montfort's rebellion, it was not updated to give an account of its part in the more recent civil war. The views of Kenilworth engraved by Hollar show the castle as it was before it was slighted by parliament's order in July 1649 (Figure 2.3).[38]

33. Dugdale, *Warwickshire*, pp. 57–8.
34. WCRO, CR 2017/F101. See also R. Cust, 'William Dugdale and the honour politics of Stuart Warwickshire', in C. Dyer and C. Richardson (eds), *William Dugdale, historian, 1605–1686: his life, his writings and his county* (Woodbridge, 2009), pp. 104–6.
35. Dugdale, *Warwickshire*, sig. a4v.
36. Lee, *Chronicon Cestrensis*, in King, *The vale-royall of England*, p. 6.
37. Dugdale, *Warwickshire*, pp. 425, 655.
38. Ibid., pp. 159–67; L.F. Salzman (ed.), *The Victoria County History of Warwick*, vol. 6 (London, 1951), pp. 134–8.

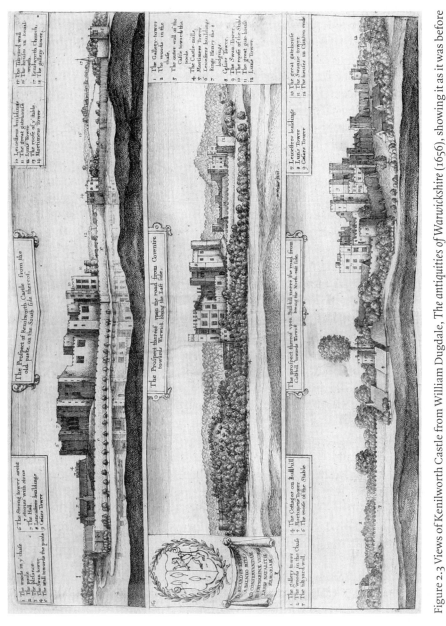

Figure 2.3 Views of Kenilworth Castle from William Dugdale, The antiquities of Warwickshire (1656), showing it as it was before its partial destruction in 1649.

In Thomas Phillipott's *Villare Cantianum* we find a reference to a family memorial being damaged in 'the late intestine war' that echoes Dugdale's observations on Edgbaston and Compton Wynyates. Phillipot blamed the destruction of the painted window on 'the tempestuous and ill managed, or rather over-heated zeal of these times, which like an over-heated brain still concludes in madness'.[39] As scholars working on nationhood have shown, negation – the identification of an other against which a community is contrasted – is an important element in the formation of communal identity.[40] This provides a definition of what a member of the county community of gentry was not: namely tempestuous, ill-managed or over-heated. With the fashionable neo-stoic emphasis on restraint, these were considered very ungentlemanly characteristics. If the excesses of the civil war and its aftermath could be blamed on the out-of-control urges of the lower classes and of religious extremists, then the gentry community could re-establish itself. There was an implicit continuity here between the iconoclastic rabble and greedy clerics who, according to the antiquaries, destroyed monuments in the sixteenth century and those responsible for more recent destruction.[41] This model also provided a means to acknowledge that some members of the gentry were guilty of excesses without undermining the idea of a county community. The recording of the visitation of God's judgement on those gentlemen who breached society's standards and their posterity was a staple of county histories and other antiquarian works.[42] In this interpretation the county community itself was identified with religious moderation and respect for the hierarchy of the church as of the state. Samuel Lee may have contributed little that was original to the *Vale-royall*, but his *Chronicon Cestrensis* did provide a concentrated catalogue of the temporal and spiritual hierarchy from the remote past 'to this day', when the exiled Charles II was Earl of Chester. His reference to the 'Vulgar' who denied John Bridgeman the title bishop in the last years of his life emphasised the idea of a division between the gentry community and the religious extremists, whose 'Sacrilege' was responsible for the 'sad Cathedral Ruines' in Chester.[43]

English history was of course full of civil wars and county historians were accustomed to incorporating accounts of these into a model of the gentry community based on continuity and respect for the established hierarchy. There was no denying that substantial numbers of the medieval gentry had rebelled

---

39. T. Phillipot, *Villare Cantianum* (London, 1659), p. 85.
40. See, for example, P. Sahlins, *Boundaries: the making of France and Spain in the Pyrenees* (Berkeley, 1989); L. Colley, *Britons: forging the nation 1707–1837* (New Haven, 1992).
41. J. Broadway, *'No historie so meete': gentry culture and the development of local history in Elizabethan and early Stuart England* (Manchester, 2006), pp. 197–8.
42. See, for example, J. Broadway, 'Aberrant accounts: William Dugdale's handling of two Tudor murders in *The antiquities of Warwickshire*', *Midland History*, 33 (2008), pp. 2–20.
43. Lee, *Chronicon Cestrensis*, in King, *The vale-royall of England*, pp. 34, 46.

against their kings on various occasions. Such conflicts had produced documents that could be extremely helpful in identifying the medieval gentry. Phillipot, for example, made use of a list of the Kentish gentlemen pardoned by the pacification of Kenilworth for their support of Simon de Montfort against Henry III.[44] Over the course of the succeeding generations many of the families that had taken part in medieval rebellions had naturally died out and in most cases any links to modern families were indirect. This was less true of what William Webb described as the 'horrible and bloody dissentions and civill warres between the Houses of York and Lancaster'. These were a recent memory when the first county histories were written and had affected many gentry families that were still extant.[45] The uncertainty of exactly who was the legitimate claimant to the throne at a particular junction assisted the integration of the Wars of the Roses into a model of the county community based on respect for hierarchy. If a gentleman was genuinely convinced he was supporting the legitimate claimant, then his actions were not necessarily rebellious. Hence, it was possible to describe rebellions against an individual king without necessarily impugning the community's respect for hierarchy. A providential explanation could also be employed. Of de Montfort's rebellion, Dugdale wrote that God 'sometimes permits rebellious Subjects to prevail in many wicked attempts against their Soveraigns, making use of them, only, for a while as his chastening rod'.[46] This mindset, that assumed rebels were the instruments of God's wrath, allowed royalists such as Dugdale both to believe that eventually the monarchy would be restored and to incorporate rebellions into their model of gentry society. Gentlemen could be provoked to such an extent that they would be led into rebellion, if God for his own mysterious purposes allowed it to happen. A variation on this idea was presented by Phillipot in his account of Rochester, when he wrote that Edward IV 'did not voluntarily fall into that sea of blood, which was let loose in the civil war, commenced between him and the partisans of the house of Lancaster, but was rather driven into it, by the tempest of his ill fortune'.[47] The parallels between past and more recent conflicts were implicit, but were no doubt understood by the readers of these works.

The promulgation of an illusion of county community during the 1650s was assisted by the unease felt by many former parliamentarian gentlemen about the execution of the king, the continuing influence of the New Model Army and the spread of religious radicalism. These concerns – which represented aspects of that 'other' against which the county community was defined – meant that they shared much common ground with their neighbours among the royalist gentry.

44. For example, Phillipot, *Villare Cantianum*, pp. 50, 80, 95.
45. Webb, *Vale-royall*, in King, *The vale-royall of England*, p. 148.
46. Dugdale, *Warwickshire*, p. 162.
47. Phillipot, *Villare Cantianum*, p. 284.

The appearance of Dugdale's and King's books and of the new edition of Lambarde during the rule of Cromwell's major-generals may not be entirely coincidental. Respect for hierarchy, continuity and property rights were ingrained in the psyche of the English gentry. The county community might be an illusion, but it provided a convenient fiction that could accommodate a wide spectrum of religious and political belief among the gentry while still providing a sense of group identity. It was a fiction that was more effectively manipulated by an initiate such as Dugdale than an outsider such as King. As a royalist gentleman living in Warwickshire it was also more personally important to Dugdale.

If the county community was a convenient fiction during the Interregnum, it might seem surprising that there were not more county histories published. There were certainly accounts of other counties similar to those published by King for Cheshire in circulation. By 1642 Thomas Habington had completed a draft of his account of Worcestershire for circulation among his friends and William Burton's revised *Description of Leicestershire* was with the printer. As we have seen, in 1656 Dugdale himself hoped to see Erdeswicke's *Staffordshire* in print, probably edited by himself. The non-appearance of these works was partly due to circumstances. Habington died in 1647. His manuscripts were preserved, but the death of his son William, the cavalier poet, in 1654 meant that there was no one to promote their publication. The second edition of the *Description of Leicestershire* foundered as the country descended into civil war. Burton's son Cassibelan preserved his father's manuscripts, but, as with his own translations, seems to have taken no steps to have it published. As for Dugdale's putative edition of Erdeswicke, this was overtaken by other projects, such as the *History of St Paul's* (1658) and a lucrative commission to write a history of fen drainage. Ultimately, though, to be successful such works needed the active involvement of the county gentry and that, it seems, could only be effectively orchestrated by a prominent member of that community. Even in Warwickshire Dugdale had lacked the status that would have ensured success without the active assistance of Sir Simon Archer. Dugdale was well aware of the vital role Archer had played in securing the support of the Warwickshire gentry for his work and knew he lacked an ally in the Staffordshire elite on whom he could rely for similar assistance. Hence the *Antiquities of Warwickshire* represented an expression of the county community that could not easily be replicated.

Charles Phythian-Adams has written of the development of county histories that culminated in the *Antiquities of Warwickshire* that they celebrated 'a newly invented cult of the gentle dead within its own traditionally bounded arena of local influence; a collective recitation of distinguished forefathers; a hymn to the descent of provincial property and office'.[48] This was the essence of the county

---

48. C. Phythian-Adams, 'Leicestershire and Rutland', in J. Simmons (ed.), *English county historians* (Wakefield, 1978), p. 230.

community as manifested in these works. The support that Dugdale secured to enable him to complete and publish his work is evidence that the county gentry continued to espouse this image of themselves in the aftermath of the civil war. It was the Warwickshire gentry as they wished to be seen, as perhaps they imagined themselves, but not in social, political or economic reality as they really were. As we have seen, King's work was far less embedded within the gentry community of Cheshire and consequently could not represent it so successfully. Yet both works demonstrate that the county community provided a convenient fiction which offered the gentry a sense of communal identity in the face of threats of political, religious and economic instability. The county community of the gentry might not exist, but an illusion of it could be created in the pages of a county history.

3

The cultural horizons of the seventeenth-century English gentry

IAN WARREN

Alan Everitt framed his county community thesis as an attempt to explain the origins and nature of the English civil wars of the 1640s and the period of political instability which followed.[1] The same agenda has dominated subsequent responses to Everitt's thesis, whether receptive or sceptical in tone.[2] Yet the historiography of the 1640s and 1650s is by no means the only potential framework for discussion of the county community. The political narrative supplied by Everitt was built on a wide-ranging and detailed account of the social and cultural experience of the English gentry, embracing deep-seated trends and structures relevant to a much longer period. This socio-cultural aspect of the county community thesis touches on themes far removed from debates surrounding the English civil wars, and commands considerable interest in its own right. By way of engaging with this aspect of the county community, the present essay will seek to revisit Everitt's intellectual legacy from the perspective of the cultural history of the gentry.

The fullest description of the county community occurred in Everitt's 1966 study, *The community of Kent and the Great Rebellion, 1640–60.* The society evoked in the second chapter of that work is well known. Everitt described a community of gentry whose social, political and cultural horizons were largely confined to their own shire, which provided both the main arena of their social life and the chief focus of their allegiance. These families had enjoyed long continuance in the

1. A.M. Everitt, *The county committee of Kent in the civil war*, Leicester University, Department of English Local History, occasional papers, 9 (1957); idem (ed.), *Suffolk and the Great Rebellion*, Suffolk Records Society, 3 (1960); idem, *The community of Kent and the Great Rebellion 1640–60* (Leicester, 1966); idem, *The local community and the Great Rebellion*, Historical Association, general series, 70 (London, 1969).

2. For example, A. Fletcher, *A county community in peace and war: Sussex 1600–1660* (London, 1975); C. Holmes, 'The county community in Stuart historiography', *Journal of British Studies*, 19 (1980), pp. 54–73; A. Hughes, 'Warwickshire on the eve of the civil war: a "county community"?', *Midland History*, 7 (1982), pp. 42–72.

possession of their local estates, and a proclivity towards intermarriage wove a dense web of kinship ties among them. Their conservative social and cultural values were reflected by their traditional and unpretentious dwellings, a sense of responsibility towards their inferiors and antiquarian interests in county history.[3] In subsequent writings Everitt acknowledged that the Kentish model was followed more closely in some English shires than others. Leicestershire thus contained a similar gentry community, while Northamptonshire and Suffolk did not.[4] Much of Everitt's rhetoric nonetheless suggested a fairly ambitious notion of the applicability of the county community thesis, not least his famous description of England in 1640 as 'a union of partially independent county-states or communities, each with its own distinctive ethos and loyalty'.[5]

These claims have been strongly challenged. Clive Holmes and Ann Hughes, Everitt's most searching critics, have expressed serious reservations about the applicability of the county community model, even in the case of Kent. They object that Everitt's association of gentry societies with county boundaries is assumed rather than demonstrated, and point to a range of administrative, geographical, economic and social factors which would have militated against shire cohesion. In opposition to Everitt's claims for the cultural insularity of the gentry, Holmes has also emphasised the role of education, travel and metropolitan contacts in broadening the horizons of the gentry. Hughes has pointed out, meanwhile, that antiquarian interests might just as well have suggested narrowly dynastic loyalties on the one hand or national intellectual horizons on the other as they did a specific fixation with a gentleman's home county. In their respective county studies of Lincolnshire and Warwickshire both historians also express scepticism about the ethos of conservatism and paternalism described by Everitt, pointing to the increasing prevalence among landed proprietors of a more commercial approach to estate management.[6]

These were probing criticisms, powerfully made, and they have gained widespread acceptance. Their contribution to our understanding of the social and cultural life of the gentry has nevertheless been in many respects a negative one, displacing Everitt's account without replacing it with any picture of comparable coherence. True, Holmes backs up his claim for the presence of a

3.   Everitt, *The community of Kent*, chapter 2.
4.   Everitt, *The local community*, pp. 15–22; idem, *Suffolk and Great Rebellion*, pp. 11–22.
5.   Everitt, *The community of Kent*, p. 13.
6.   Holmes, 'The county community'; idem, *Seventeenth-century Lincolnshire* (Lincoln, 1980), chapter 2; idem, 'Centre and locality in civil-war England', in J. Adamson (ed.), *The English civil war: conflict and contexts, 1640–1649* (London, 2009), pp. 152–73; Hughes, 'Warwickshire on the eve of the civil war'; idem, *Politics, society and civil war in Warwickshire, 1620–1660* (Cambridge, 1987), chapter 2; idem, 'Local history and the origins of the civil war', in R. Cust and A. Hughes (eds), *Conflict in early Stuart England: studies in religion and politics, 1603–1642* (London, 1989), pp. 224–53.

'national gentry culture' with a compelling account of the common intellectual framework, shaped by national legal institutions and principles, in which English gentlemen viewed political issues.[7] The wider nature and content of this national 'culture' nonetheless remains less clear. This may be asking too much of the opponents of the county community thesis, however. As already noted, the fundamental questions at issue related to the causes and course of the English civil wars, rather than the precise character of gentry culture. One criticism of Everitt's account was indeed that he placed too much emphasis on the role of the gentry, wrongly assuming the deference of their social inferiors to their leadership. Since Everitt, county studies of the civil wars have usually quite properly included a broader social canvass, thereby limiting the room for more intensive engagement with the elite.[8] So while the social and cultural life of the gentry loomed large, and perhaps too large, in the county community controversy, its treatment of the gentry was in some respects unsatisfactory.

If the county community debate tended to engage with gentry values on a relatively narrow front, however, this defect has been in some measure remedied by more recent works which, while largely unconnected to that discussion, have helped to illuminate the balance of local and national horizons within elite identity. Broadly, the more recent historiography of the gentry has served to reinforce the tide of opinion against Everitt's model. Further research on the education and formative experiences of the gentry has thus emphasised the exposure of the gentry to a wide range of national and international influences, rendering Everitt's claims regarding their narrow horizons increasingly implausible.[9] Other works, moreover, suggest an emerging consensus that the early modern period witnessed a major shift in which the cultural loyalties of the landed elite increasingly turned away from the life of the rural estate and its local surroundings towards a prestigious society closely associated with London and its provincial satellites.

This model is most explicitly stated in two books published in 1998: Anna Bryson's *From courtesy to civility: changing codes of conduct in early modern England*, and James Rosenheim's *The emergence of a ruling order: English landed society 1650–1750*. There are important differences between them. Bryson adopts a longer and earlier chronology than Rosenheim, roughly encompassing the sixteenth and seventeenth centuries. The two works also differ in methodology, with Bryson's intellectual emphasis and focus on conduct literature contrasting with the more

7.   Holmes, 'The county community', pp. 59–60, 61–73; idem, 'Centre and locality'.
8.   Holmes, 'The county community', pp. 72–3; D. Underdown, *Somerset in the civil war and interregnum* (Newton Abbot, 1973); idem, *Revel, riot, and rebellion: popular politics and culture in England 1603–1660* (Oxford, 1985); Hughes, *Politics, society*; M. Stoyle, *Loyalty and locality: popular allegiance in Devon during the English civil war* (Exeter, 1994).
9.   These findings are synthesised in V. Larminie, 'Gentry culture in the seventeenth century', in C. Dyer and C. Richardson (eds), *William Dugdale, historian, 1605–1686: his life, his writings and his county* (Woodbridge, 2009), pp. 109–25.

straightforwardly social-historical account provided by Rosenheim. The two nonetheless agree about the trajectory of elite cultural change in the early modern period. Bryson thus outlines a shift of elite identity away from what she defines as a social and cultural ideal of 'lordship' towards one of 'urbanity', arguing that this transition both underpinned and responded to the increasing resort of the English nobility and gentry to London and the court.[10] In similar vein, Rosenheim argues that his period witnessed a process of increasing cultural differentiation between the landed elite and society at large, as a nobility and gentry shaken by the political turmoil of the 1640s and 1650s reconstructed their prestige through the elaboration of an exclusive cultural sphere driven by metropolitan and urban forms of consumption and sociability.[11]

This basic model finds further support in other works treating more specific areas of elite life. Felicity Heal's *Hospitality in early modern England* documents a long-term shift whereby hospitality was transformed from a social obligation governing the relations of elite householders with their social inferiors into a more discretionary and socially exclusive activity.[12] Meanwhile, historians of the country house such as Mark Girouard, Nicholas Cooper and Paul Hunneyball have added an architectural dimension to this model of increasing physical and cultural differentiation. House plans, they suggest, point to the increasing segregation of the gentle nuclear family from their servants through the use of a self-contained network of service rooms, backstairs and corridors. The increasing stylistic conformity of country house architecture to a classicism imported from the continent and patronised by the Stuart court suggests a similar cultural tendency.[13] So, in various ways, these narratives suggest the increasing assimilation of the elite within a cosmopolitan culture whose tone was set by London society and the court, and beyond them by the wider aristocratic culture of western Europe.

The development of this broad consensus would seem to have largely completed the work begun by Everitt's original critics, suggesting that even those traits of the mid-seventeenth-century gentry that were genuinely traditionalist or localist were part of a vanishing world. Buried under this great edifice of interpretation, it is difficult to see how Everitt's model of gentry culture can be revived. It is telling that recent works by Anne Duffin and Mark Stoyle on the elite

10. A. Bryson, *From courtesy to civility: changing codes of conduct in early modern England* (Oxford, 1998), especially chapter 4.

11. J.M. Rosenheim, *The emergence of a ruling order: English landed society 1650–1750* (Harlow, 1998), especially chapters 4–7. For a local survey which chimes neatly with Rosenheim's account see P. Jenkins, *The making of a ruling class: the Glamorgan gentry 1640–1790* (Cambridge, 1983), especially chapters 7 and 9.

12. F. Heal, *Hospitality in early modern England* (Oxford, 1990), especially chapter 4.

13. M. Girouard, *Life in the English country house: a social and architectural history* (New Haven, CT, 1978), chapter 5; N. Cooper, *Houses of the gentry 1480–1680* (New Haven, CT, 1999), chapter 7; P.M. Hunneyball, *Architecture and image-building in seventeenth-century Hertfordshire* (Oxford, 2004).

of Cornwall, perhaps the most isolated and distinctive of all English shires, have held aloof from the county community model.[14] Viewed from the present-day historiographical landscape the concept now seems strangely remote, suggestive of a formative period of English local history in which the analytical categories of that discipline remained in ferment. Neither does it seem probable that the reintroduction of a reductive dichotomy of county and nation is now likely to aid further engagement with gentry culture. At the same time, if Everitt's specific conclusions now appear mistaken, his broader emphasis on the local and rural dimensions of gentry experience may still have something to contribute to our understanding of this period. Indeed, precisely because the historiographical pendulum has swung so decisively against the kind of localist and paternalistic picture which he evoked, a re-engagement with these facets of gentry life may help to restore a degree of balance to this field. This is not to accuse the scholars mentioned above of exaggerating the extent of change in elite culture in this period: indeed, they are for the most part careful to acknowledge the persistence of a strong element of provincialism. The danger is rather that, in the absence of a fuller elaboration of this facet of elite culture, a narrative of increasing cultural integration and cosmopolitanism may come to seem more emphatic and dominant than its individual proponents intend, leading to an overall view of elite experience in this period which is rhetorically, if not explicitly, unbalanced. The further development and enlargement of a sense of the place of local and rural loyalties in elite experience may thus serve not so much to contradict recent scholarly tendencies as to contextualise their findings more fully. With this aim in mind, let us remind ourselves of those facets of elite identity which were most attuned to Everitt's sympathies.

A key consideration is the extent to which the social status of individual gentry families was manifested and negotiated locally. This is especially apparent in the case of landownership, a criterion whose centrality to the identity of the gentry is easily taken for granted. It may of course be objected that over the course of this period notions of gentility came to embrace significant groups among the non-landed. The title of gentleman was, after all, used by an increasingly wide social constituency over the course of the seventeenth century, embracing in particular the prosperous professionals and urban rentiers who were to be found in many towns. This was associated with an increasing tendency to associate gentility with a certain kind of lifestyle rather than specifically with landed property.[15] As Henry French has argued, it also reflected the uprooting of

---

14. A. Duffin, *Faction and faith: politics and religion of the Cornish gentry before the civil war* (Exeter, 1996); M. Stoyle, *West Britons: Cornish identities and the early modern British state* (Exeter, 2002).

15. For a general discussion of the changing usage of the title see P. Corfield, 'The rivals: landed and other gentlemen', in N. Harte and R. Quinault (eds), *Land and society in Britain, 1700–1914: essays in honour of F.M.L. Thompson* (Manchester, 1996), pp. 1–33.

personal and moral definitions of gentility from their traditional socio-economic context, encapsulated in the assertion of the Tatler that 'the Appellation of Gentleman is never to be affixed to a Man's Circumstances, but to his behaviour in them'.[16] Whether we accept an assumed equation of gentility with rural landownership or not, however, it remains the case that Everitt's county community concept and the varied literature which has responded to it were concerned with a specifically landed social group. It was Everitt himself who coined the term 'pseudo-gentry' to distinguish town dwellers with gentle aspirations from the (presumably genuine) gentry who possessed country estates and seats.[17] Scholars emphasising the increasingly cosmopolitan orientation of the elite in our period echo this focus, with Rosenheim even referring repeatedly to the subjects of his study as 'the landed'.[18] Since it would be inappropriate to evaluate this historiography in relation to a social constituency which it does not claim to embrace, the present essay will retain this specific focus on the landed gentry. A relatively narrow definition of the gentry may in any case have more historical validity than the increasingly widespread adoption of the title of gentleman suggests. French thus argues that, notwithstanding the increasingly widespread use of that term, there remained an acknowledged distinction between those capable of vindicating such claims on the metropolitan and national stage and those only able to do so within their immediate local communities.[19] The suggestion of an exclusive kind of gentility to which not all 'gentlemen' had access recurs in James Boswell's observation, in relation to the status of Samuel Johnson's bookseller father, that 'the appellation of Gentleman ... was commonly taken by those who could not boast of gentility'.[20]

In acknowledging the centrality of landownership to the identity of the group with which we are concerned, we must furthermore accept that this was a cultural, and not merely an economic, fact. It might be tempting to suppose that the role of landownership within elite identity was merely that of an enduring economic framework within which a much more dynamic gentry culture operated. Some of the more ambitiously stated models of change in gentry culture in this period appear to adopt this template. To talk, as Rosenheim does, of 'the landed's uniquely metropolitan identity' seems to imply a distinction between the economic basis of elite power (land) and the cultural forms in which it was expressed (participation in fashionable metropolitan society).[21] A similar vision is

---

16. H.R. French, '"Ingenious & learned gentlemen": social perceptions and self-fashioning among parish elites in Essex, 1680–1740', *Social History*, 25 (2000), pp. 44–66. D.F. Bond (ed.), *The tatler*, 1 (Oxford, 1987), pp. 99–100 (no. 207, 5 Aug 1710).

17. A. Everitt, 'Social mobility in early modern England', *Past and Present*, 33 (1966), pp. 69–72.

18. Rosenheim, *Emergence of a ruling order*, pp. 1–12.

19. French, '"Ingenious & learned gentlemen"'.

20. J. Boswell, *The life of Samuel Johnson LL.D.*, 1 (2 vols, London, 1791), p. 8.

21. Rosenheim, *Emergence of a ruling order*, p. 215.

suggested by Bryson's mention of '"hard" factors of economic power and access to technologies of violence' being 'clothed in cultural legitimation'.[22] Yet if the possession of land was not the fundamental element of elite culture why discuss it at all, except to suggest that changing forms of gentry culture merely expressed a collective identity derived ultimately from the economic fact of landownership? The difficulty with the latter model is that it brings us close to a kind of Marxian distinction between economic base and cultural superstructure for which Mark Dawson has berated historians of early modern gentility.[23] This trap can only be escaped by recognising that the persistence of landowners' authority and coherence was due as much to the potency of the cultural associations conjured by their possessions as to the wealth and coercive power they conferred.

Such has been the tendency to take the landedness of the landed gentry for granted that the cultural associations of landownership remain relatively under-explored. Historians have never lost sight of this point entirely, however. Lawrence and Jeanne Stone's formidable An open elite? England 1540–1880 is thus founded on the assumption that possession of a large country house remained central to elite status over many centuries.[24] Some of the key facets of this relationship are, meanwhile, clear or well-established. A key function of the country estate was thus to anchor that sense of dynastic continuity and permanence which was a central facet of elite cultural authority. As Heal and Holmes have observed, the elite 'individual is seen as standing at the apex of a double helix intertwining land and blood'. The estate itself provided the focus of many forms of elite status assertion, including 'lavish heraldic display on their buildings and in the interior decoration of their mansions'. Other gestures included 'the heraldic and military motifs and the genealogical assertions graven on their marmoreal effigies', the memorials themselves usually being located in a church or mausoleum close to the family seat.[25] A further context for the prestige of the country estate and for the deployment of heraldic and military imagery lay in the feudal origin of English land law, with its suggestion of an active, personal and asymmetrical bond between lord and tenant.

To highlight the enduring and fundamental role of the landed estate within elite identity is not to deny that the cultural life of the gentry underwent change during the seventeenth century. It does, nonetheless, help us to keep certain aspects of that change in proportion. One point we are thus reminded of is the degree to which evidence of the gentry's engagement with metropolitan forms of culture, consumption and sociability continued to be focused on the country house. As

22. Bryson, From courtesy to civility, p. 23.
23. M.S. Dawson, Gentility and the comic theatre of late Stuart London (Cambridge, 2005), introduction, especially pp. 3–14.
24. L. Stone and J.F. Stone, An open elite? England 1540–1880 (Oxford, 1984), pp. 11–13.
25. F. Heal and C. Holmes, The gentry in England and Wales, 1500–1700 (Basingstoke, 1994), pp. 22, 46.

Rosenheim acknowledges, cultural change did not involve a diminution of the role of the rural mansion as a focus for display so much as a shift in the message it carried: 'The country house had always made an assertion about the character of its occupants, but this differed in the later seventeenth and early eighteenth centuries from what had been said in the past. Now the statement spoke more to the owner's taste than to his power.' The country house thus became a crucial advertisement of its owner's 'breeding and sensibility', where classical architectural forms, sumptuous furniture and decoration and collections of art, sculpture and books were increasingly 'displayed for the approving view of one's peers'.[26]

It would be easy to make the lazy assumption that the continuing cultural vitality and adaptability of the country house in this period was a simple result of inertia, largely inevitable and therefore insignificant. If we acknowledge that continuity in human affairs reflects its own kind of dynamism, however, a more interesting point emerges. The centrality of the country house to forms of fashionable display thus reminds us that increasing gentry cosmopolitanism was not simply about the substitution of a polite urban culture for a becalmed or moribund traditional one, but part of an ongoing process of negotiation between centripetal and centrifugal cultural forces. The provincial reception of metropolitan practices and objects involved a subtle change in their meaning, whereby the prestige of urban and continental influences was used to reinforce status within local society. This reflected a context in which, as Richard Cust has outlined, there remained an important local dimension to honour and reputation in which the demonstration of taste was an important factor.[27] This interface between metropolitan prestige and local reputation is exemplified particularly clearly by some of the grander London-manufactured funeral monuments deployed to the provinces in this period.[28] Much remains to be understood about these processes, however, and exploration of the local permutations and meanings of a seemingly uniform elite material culture offer a potentially rich avenue for further research into the balance of local and national considerations within elite identity.

The extent to which the country residence provided a focus for fashionable culture was also a reflection of another point which helps us to see cultural change in this period in proportion: namely the relatively limited extent to which elite families were prepared to invest in urban residences. It is clear that the

26. Rosenheim, *Emergence of a ruling order*, pp. 93–4.
27. R. Cust, 'William Dugdale and the honour politics of Stuart Warwickshire', in Dyer and Richardson (eds), *William Dugdale, historian*, pp. 89–108.
28. For a useful county study of this particular cultural form and the relative significance of regional and metropolitan influences see R. Richardson, 'The effigy tombs of the gentry of Worcestershire 1500–1700', in *Transactions of the Worcestershire Archaeological Society*, 3rd series, 19 (2004), pp. 149–75.

seventeenth century saw a significant widening of gentry engagement with town life, reflecting the increasing importance of urban areas as centres for professional services, administration, leisure and sociability. Nowhere was this truer than in the case of London, whose political, economic and cultural supremacy resulted in a cumulative increase in seasonal residence by the gentry which was stalled but not ultimately derailed by the civil wars and the political instability of the 1650s.[29] These advances nonetheless occurred within certain constraints. Permanent migration to urban centres by the heads of major families seems to have been rare, and where it did occur it may have had as much to do with a wish to save money on the cost of rural housekeeping as a desire to plunge into the delights of town life.[30] Most town-dwelling gentry continued to maintain and periodically inhabit their rural residences, thereby limiting the capacity for both financial and sentimental investment in an urban establishment. Thus constrained, they typically resorted to forms and habits of town accommodation which appear functional and short-term. In London, many chose to lodge in furnished rooms in a private house or commercial establishment for a weekly rent, or to take chambers in the Inns of Court.[31] Even where gentry families acquired townhouses these typically remained the poor relations of their rural counterparts. Most were leased or bought rather than built with gentry habitation in mind, ensuring that they rarely differed greatly from the residences of their middling-sort neighbours.[32] Across most of the country, furthermore, the available housing would have consisted of traditional-style vernacular properties

29. For provincial towns see P. Borsay, *The English urban renaissance: culture and society in the provincial town 1660–1770* (Oxford, 1989), especially chapters 8–9; idem 'The landed elite and provincial towns in Britain 1660–1800', *Georgian Group Journal*, 13 (2003), pp. 281–94. For London see F.J. Fisher, 'The development of London as a centre of conspicuous consumption in the sixteenth and seventeenth centuries', *Transactions of the Royal Historical Society*, 4th series, 30 (1948), pp. 37–50; L. Stone, 'The residential development of the West End in London in the seventeenth century', in B.C. Malament (ed.), *After the Reformation: essays in honour of J.H. Hexter* (Philadelphia, 1980), pp. 167–212; R.M. Smuts, 'The court and its neighbourhood: royal policy and urban growth in the early West End', *Journal of British Studies*, 30 (1991), pp. 117–49; I. Warren, 'The gentry, the nobility, and London residence c.1580–1680', DPhil thesis (Oxford University, 2007), chapter 1.

30. In 1642 Henry Peacham's *The art of living in London* addressed itself to those who travelled to the city 'to save the charge of Housekeeping in the Countrey'. For some actual examples see T. Habington, *A survey of Worcestershire*, ed. J. Amphlett, Worcestershire Historical Society (2 vols, Worcester, 1895), 1, p. 49, 2, pp. 28–9; Bodl., Bankes MS, 64/16: Sir Edward Peyton to the Duke of Lennox, 30 April 1635.

31. J. McEwan and P. Sharpe, '"It buys me freedom": genteel lodging in late seventeenth- and eighteenth-century London', *Parergon*, 24 (2007), pp. 139–61; L.C. Orlin, 'Temporary lives in London lodgings', *Huntington Library Quarterly*, 71 (2008), pp. 219–42; D. Lemmings, *Gentlemen and barristers: the Inns of Court and the English Bar 1680–1750* (Oxford, 1990), chapter 2.

32. For a hostile account of the London houses favoured by the gentry see H. Colvin and J. Newman (eds), *Of building: Roger North's writings on architecture* (Oxford, 1981), pp. 24–6.

with little claim to architectural distinction.[33] Even in London, where there was extensive building of more modern housing, the speculatively built properties inhabited by the gentry tended to be marked by a relatively uniform appearance, rapid turnover of owners and a marked absence of any strong sense of dynastic attachment.[34]

The continuing importance of the country house and estate, and the networks and forms of display associated with it, is not the only factor qualifying our sense of increasing gentry attachment to a national urban culture. Similar reflections arise if we consider the discursive construction of gentry identity in relation to real or imagined metropolitan and provincial entities. The county community concept itself was, of course, partly justified in relation to a number of intellectual and rhetorical tendencies which seemed, to Everitt and those he influenced, to articulate to a sense of shire unity. Everitt's citation of antiquarian activity as an index of county feeling and Hughes's rejoinder have already been noted.[35] Other apparent indications of county cohesion included the widespread use of the evocative term 'country' among the gentry to refer to the shire, and the numerous petitions and addresses which were organised at the level of the county during the troubled 1640s and 1650s.[36] Both inferences have been countered by Holmes, who in the first case draws attention to the widespread use of the term 'country' to express awareness of the wider political nation, and in the second emphasises the role played by national political figures and groupings during the English Revolution in orchestrating what might initially appear to be spontaneous expressions of local opinion.[37]

Persuasive as these objections may be, it remains difficult to deny that many gentry did at least acknowledge a strong loyalty to the unit of the shire. As Jan Broadway has observed, the rhetoric of the county historians and occasional effusions of shire patriotism from other quarters suggest that the county community existed as a powerful ideal and source of legitimation, even if it was never realised in reality.[38] Indeed, it has become increasingly clear that county loyalty had little to do with the kind of insular, clannish society with which both advocates and opponents of the county community thesis have associated it. Far from reflecting the narrow horizons of rustic backwoodsmen, these values seem to have been promoted by some of the more dynamic and cosmopolitan

---

33. The coming of regularly proportioned brick or stone-fronted housing to provincial towns was largely a product of the period after 1700. See Borsay, *Urban renaissance*, chapter 2.
34. Stone, 'Residential development', pp. 195–6.
35. See above, p. 74.
36. Everitt, *The community of Kent*, pp. 13, 95–107.
37. Holmes, 'The county community', pp. 61–2, 69–71; Holmes, 'Centre and locality', pp. 170–73.
38. J. Broadway, *William Dugdale and the significance of county history in early Stuart England*, Dugdale Society, occasional papers, 39 (1999), pp. 7–8; idem *'No historie so meete': gentry culture and the development of local history in Elizabethan and early Stuart England* (Manchester, 2006), p. 108.

intellectual currents of the period. County sentiment thus shows strong marks of humanist influence, including its association with a cult of public service, its nourishment from didactic history and its promotion through national and regional scholarly networks.[39] When in 1636 the Cheshire worthy Sir Richard Grosvenor, describing the duties of a JP, asserted that 'every man owes his countrey a tribute off action', his words closely echoed, perhaps consciously, Cicero's famous maxim *non nobis solum*, Englished by the grammarian John Brinsley in 1616 as: 'we are born not for our selves alone, but our Countrey doth chalenge a part of our birth'.[40] Seemingly, therefore, certain strands of humanist influence tended to foster rather than weaken the investment of the gentry in their localities.

This cult of local magistracy did not sit altogether easily with the prescriptions of the more courtly and urban-oriented strand of humanism, descended from Castiglione, with its emphasis on the role of manners, speech and cultural refinement in the projection of identity.[41] To this extent we can trace a tension within English humanism as a social programme which may have hindered the development of a homogeneous gentry culture in this period. It was certainly reflected to disruptive effect in the conflicted attitude of the early Stuart kings to the role of the elite, defined as it was on the one hand by attempts to harness them to the objective of transforming London into a Renaissance capital, and on the other by the insistence, repeatedly backed by royal proclamation, that the public duties of the gentry lay in the shires.[42] Some elements of the elite may have continued to experience this tension in the later seventeenth century. That a humanist ethos of localism retained some adherents following the Restoration is suggested by the production of further gentry-authored and -focused county histories, notably those by Robert Thoroton on Nottinghamshire in 1678, Sir Henry Chauncy on Hertfordshire in 1700 and Sir Robert Atkyns on Gloucestershire in 1712.[43] Even so, the ideological division, party conflict and

---

39. Broadway, 'No historie so meete', chapters 2, 3 and 6.

40. Grosvenor is quoted in R. Cust and P. Lake, 'Sir Richard Grosvenor and the rhetoric of magistracy', *Bulletin of the Institute of Historical Research*, 54 (1981), p. 37; J. Brinsley (tr.), *The first booke of Marcus Tullius Cicero, concerning duties* (London, 1616), p. 48.

41. Bryson, *From courtesy to civility*, chapters 3–4.

42. For evidence of the former tendency see K. Sharpe, *The personal rule of Charles I* (New Haven, CT, 1992), pp. 403–12; J.F. Larkin and P.L. Hughes (eds), *Stuart royal proclamations, I: royal proclamations of King James I 1603–1625* (Oxford, 1973), pp. 345–7, 485–8, 597–8; for the latter see F. Heal, 'The crown, the gentry and London: the enforcement of proclamation 1596–1640', in C. Cross, D.M. Loades and D.M. Scarisbrick (eds), *Law and government under the Tudors: essays presented to Sir Geoffrey Elton … on … his retirement* (Cambridge, 1988), pp. 211–26.

43. R. Thoroton, *The antiquities of Nottinghamshire* (London, 1677); H. Chauncey, *The historical antiquities of Hertfordshire* (London, 1700); R. Atkyns, *The ancient and present state of Glostershire* (London, 1712).

waning interest of the greater gentry in local government in these years all point to the retreat of the cult of the shire patriot.[44]

Other facets of gentry culture, less specific but more persistent than this humanist form of localism, also militated against the outright adoption of a cosmopolitan social identity. Elite culture was thus heavily marked by a diffuse range of associations which emphasised 'country' affiliations in the more general sense of the countryside and those things pertaining to it. These were not entirely dissociable from the localism outlined above. A prominent theme of 'country' values was thus an ideal of gentry hospitality, charity and paternalism that also featured in some of the more didactic passages of the county histories, notably Thomas Habington's unpublished collections for a history of Worcestershire, compiled over the early part of the century.[45] Yet these social virtues had a history and resonance which long pre-dated the heyday of the humanist-trained county patriot. The association of the gentry with bounteous household entertainment already enjoyed a long literary pedigree by the early seventeenth century, perhaps most famously exemplified by the Franklin in the general prologue to Chaucer's Canterbury Tales.[46] By the reign of James I it was so familiar a feature of social commentary as to enjoy its own literary conventions, such as the notion of decline from an imagined golden age.[47] These were to reach their apotheosis in the 'country house poems' of the period, of which Jonson's To Penshurst is the appropriately Kentish paradigm.[48]

Within the broad realm of 'country' ideals variously appropriated by and attributed to the seventeenth-century gentry, historically specific social virtues such as hospitality and charity were complemented by other notions. The increasing centrality of classical literature to the education and cultural formation of the gentry familiarised the elite with the terms in which authors such as Hesiod, Virgil and Horace discussed rural life. Here the countryside was represented as a place of natural bounty, honest labour and self-sufficiency, in contrast with the deceit, artifice, sterility and constraint of the city. The extent to

---

44. Heal and Holmes, *The gentry in England and Wales*, chapters 5–6; J.M. Rosenheim, 'County governance and elite withdrawal in Norfolk, 1660–1720', in A.C. Beier, D. Cannadine and J.M. Rosenheim (eds), *The first modern society: essays in English history in honour of Lawrence Stone* (Cambridge, 1989), pp. 95–125.

45. Habington, *Survey of Worcestershire*. The didactic thrust of Habington's county history is discussed in J. Broadway, '"To equall their virtues": Thomas Habington, recusancy and the gentry of early Stuart Worcestershire', *Midland History*, 29 (2004), pp. 1–24.

46. J. Winny (ed.), *The general prologue to the Canterbury Tales* (Cambridge, 1978), lines 333–62. The historical context of Chaucer's description is illuminated in G.H. Gerould, 'The social status of Chaucer's Franklin', *Publications of the Modern Language Association of America*, 41 (1926), pp. 262–79.

47. For the conventions of discussion of hospitality see Heal, *Hospitality*, pp. 108–12.

48. For an anthology based on a broad definition of the genre, resulting in some interesting comparisons, see A. Fowler (ed.), *The country house poem* (Edinburgh, 1994).

The Court and Country,
OR
A briefe Discourse Dialogue-wise set downe
betweene a Courtier and a Country-man:
Contayning the manner and condition of their liues, with many
Delectable and Pithy Sayings worthy obseruation.

Also, necessary Notes for a COVRTIER.

Written by N. B. Gent.

The Country-man.   The Courtier.

LONDON, Printed by G.E LD for Iohn Wright, and are to be sold at his shop
at the Signe of the Bible without Newgate. 1618.

Figure 3.1 Title page from Nicholas Breton, *The court and country* (London, 1618), illustrating a tendency to perceive that dichotomy in terms of distinct social and cultural types. By permission of the Folger Shakespeare Library.

which these notions infused elite discourse is evident in much gentry correspondence, as in July 1617, when Sir John Holles wrote from London to Lord Norris, observing: 'Your Lordship pleads well for the cuntry, and I say Amen: ther beeing less temptation to evill, and more diversion than heer, and yet sufficiency every way for naturall requisites.'[49] Rehearsing the same themes nearly a century later in a letter of July 1712, John, Lord Hervey was less shy about flaunting his erudition for the benefit of his son:

> It gave me a double satisfaction to read ye lively description you sent me of ye sweet delights a country life affords ... You'l find Cicero thought nothing more worthy the employment of a wise & honest man than husbandry; some have placed ye summum bonum in it; Virgill gives ye followers of it ye title of fortunate; & Horace ye epithet of blessed.[50]

Already by the end of Elizabeth's reign these rural associations seem to have crystallised in a sympathetic archetype of the 'country gentleman', and over the course of the seventeenth century we find this persona being appealed to by gentry and others, usually as a means of distancing them from the culture and values of the metropolis, court or other more exotic entities.[51] In the early 1620s Sir Arthur Capel of Little Hadham, Hertfordshire, pondering options for the education of his grandson and heir, drew up a memorandum entitled 'Reasons against the travellinge of my grandchild Arthur Capell into the parts beyond the seas'. First to occur to him was the objection that 'his caleinge is to be a cuntery gentillman, wherein is lyttell or no use of forrane experience'.[52] We might be inclined to associate such sentiments with the less affluent and more culturally isolated elements of the gentry. In fact, Capell was one of the wealthiest men in his county, which he had served as deputy lieutenant, and where he enjoyed seemingly cordial relations with the neighbouring Cecil Earls of Salisbury.[53] His example indicates that the assertion of a rural social identity was not simply the preserve of the more impoverished and untutored scions of the gentry, but something that was possible at the highest ranks of landed society (Figure 3.1).

Not all were quite so certain of the prestige and status which a country gentleman could assert in the face of a more courtly and cosmopolitan world. Thomas Knyvett of Ashwellthorpe in Norfolk thus applied the mantle to himself

---

49. P.R. Seddon, *Letters of John Holles, 1587–1637*, Thoroton Society, record series, 31, 35–6 (1975–86 for 1974–85), p. 175.
50. S.H.A. Hervey, *Letter-books of John Hervey, first earl of Bristol* (3 vols, Wells, 1894), I, pp. 331–2.
51. An early reference to the 'honest country gentleman' as a type occurs in G. Harvey, *Three proper, and wittie, familiar letters* (London, 1580).
52. HALS, Hertfordshire, 8,641.
53. A letter of November 1602 to Robert Cecil from Capel is dated from 'my poor lodging by the Savoy'; HMC, *Hatfield House*, 12 (London, 1910), p. 469. See also R. Hutton, 'Arthur Capel, first baron Capel of Hadham (1604–1649)', in ODNB.

in what seems a more diffident and self-deprecating tone. Writing to his wife from London in 1629, he wondered aloud whether his status as a 'countrye gentleman' permitted him to pass comment on the social behaviour of peers, while in February 1635 he revealed: 'I am this night for the Queens maske at court, And though a country Gentleman, yet am I graced with a Tickett of her majesty, but to tell thee true, if I doe not like my waye of going in, I doubt I shall let it alone.'[54] If Knyvett lacked Capel's confidence in the sufficiency of the life of a country gentleman, however, he apparently shared the same sense of the reality and familiarity of this social persona. The two cases therefore agree in indicating that a self-consciously rural social demeanour was both available and potentially useful to gentlemen of their status.

It is suggestive to turn from these examples to others suggesting the intrusion of a rural gentry identity into the national political arena. The frequent use of the term 'country' among Westminster politicians of the period is well attested, having been emphasised, among others, by Holmes in his efforts to wrest the term away from Everitt's county communitarians. For Holmes, as noted above, references to the 'country' at this level are to be understood as referring to the political nation at large, or what he calls the country/commonwealth: an entity with no necessary rural connotation.[55] This seems reasonable, and it may also apply in large measure to those recurrent periods throughout the seventeenth century which saw the mobilisation of a 'court' versus 'country' political rhetoric. Nonetheless, there was in practice some tendency in our period to view this dichotomy in cultural as well as political terms, conflating 'court' and 'country' with a metropolitan/rural divide. We see this in the assertion by Sir Robert Phelips, MP for Somerset, during a Parliamentary debate in 1625 that he was 'neither Courtier nor Lawyer but a plaine Countrey Gentleman'.[56] We see it also at the end of the century, when concerns arising from the cost of war with France and the burgeoning financial apparatus of the state seem to have given the figure of the country gentleman real political definition. One parliamentarian, writing to an acquaintance in the country in November 1696, observed that 'by the Votes you will see that there is a great majority who choose rather to be Courtiers than neglected country gentlemen'.[57] Another contemporary, recounting a debate in the House of Commons over the size of the army in January 1698, even identified three oppositionist 'country gentlemen' by name.[58] Literary responses to public affairs also provided a means of highlighting the wider cultural associations of

54. B. Schofield (ed.), *The Knyvett letters, 1620–1644* (London, 1949), pp. 75, 88.
55. Holmes, 'The county community', pp. 69–71.
56. P. Zagorin, *The court and the country: the beginning of the English revolution* (London, 1969), p. 35.
57. HMC, *Cowper MS*, 2 (London, 1889), p. 367.
58. E.M. Thompson (ed.), *Correspondence of the family of Hatton*, 2 vols, Camden Society, new series, 22–3 (1878), 2, p. 238: Charles Hatton to Christopher, Viscount Hatton, 19 January 1698.

the 'court'/'country' rivalry. Noting the association of the countryside with 'independence, innocence and integrity', John Spurr has highlighted the eagerness of political propagandists of the 1670s to couch their appeals in the form of 'Letters to "friends in the country" or Appeals to and from "the country"'. These pamphleteers were 'eager to associate their message with the sturdy political independence of the country gentry', who embodied 'a certain self-image, a set of convictions and attitudes, which were, for all their paternalism and tradition, a salutary political stance in the face of parliamentary "corruption" under Danby'.59

The apparent desire of politicians to appropriate rural associations of honesty and disinterestedness, while emphasising distance from the court, sheds some interesting light on the wider cultural connotations of rural and metropolitan affiliation. In associating opposition to the government with rusticity, political troublemakers were implicitly leaving the supposed cultural high ground of metropolitan civility to be appropriated by the court. This willingness to embrace a rural social identity, however tactical and insincere it might have been, thus reinforces the comments of Capel and Knyvett in pointing to the respectability of a gentry identity which defined itself not with but against the cultural claims of London and the court.

In making a case for the persistence and viability of the country gentleman persona, I do not mean to imply that its significance remained static over the course of the century. In fact, the continuity of language masks important shifts in its content and emphases. At one level there were certain anxieties linked to the figure of the country gentleman, whose prominence fluctuated over time. Among them were concerns about the role of gender in the gentry's relationship within the capital, which seem to have been especially prominent in the 1620s and 1630s, but which recurred throughout the century. One consequence of London's development as a focus for sociability and material display was to stir ancient perceptions of women as loquacious and luxurious. Assumptions gained ground that female gentry were especially fond of the capital, that it compounded their sinful tendencies and that, in particular, they used the conventions of fashionable society to resist and even challenge the authority of their husbands. From this perspective, the country and its advocates represented a masculine contrast to the effeminising capital.60 One figure to whom these notions seem to

59. J. Spurr, *England in the 1670s: 'this masquerading age'* (Oxford, 2000), p. 163.
60. For example, see James I's 1622 poem on London in J. Craigie (ed.), *The poems of James VI of Scotland*, 2 vols (Edinburgh, 1955–8), i, XIVa; D. Lupton, *London and the countrey carbonadoed and quartered into severall characters* (London, 1632), pp. 22–7; J. Shirley, *The lady of pleasure*, ed. R. Huebert (Manchester, 1986); HMC, *Salisbury*, 22 (London, 1971), p. 440: countess of Rutland to William, Earl of Salisbury, July 1661; Thompson (ed.), *Correspondence*, i, p. 227: Bishop John Fell to Lady Hatton, May 1680.

have appealed was John Verney, the merchant and landowner whose experience of the capital has been closely analysed by Susan Whyman. Following many years of subjection to a metropolitan visiting code policed by female relatives, Verney retired to the country upon inheriting his father's baronetcy and Buckinghamshire estate in 1696, readily throwing off the more constraining social conventions of the capital and asserting what Whyman describes as 'his Tory country ideology and a masculine resistance to excessive politeness'.[61]

Whyman's study of the Verneys also highlights another focus of 'country' hostility to London which waxed and waned over the course of the century, namely its perceived susceptibility to foreign influence. Both Sir Ralph Verney and his elder son Mun voiced conventional anxieties about the solvent influence of polite society on native English behaviour and expression, the former asking a correspondent to address him 'without compliment ... in plain English, which is the natural language of Buckinghamshire bumpkins'.[62] This defensiveness seems to have been a prevalent response to the power and cultural influence of France during the later seventeenth century, and was especially marked at moments when the scale of luxury imports became a political concern, as during the later 1660s and 1670s.[63] A noteworthy cultural artefact of this period is Sir Robert Howard's play *The country gentleman*, prepared for production in 1669 but suppressed before the premiere as a result of a politically sensitive scene inserted by George Villiers, Duke of Buckingham. The play's eponymous hero is Sir Richard Plainbred, a wealthy west country gentleman with a fierce dislike of London and its fashionable affectations, and whose taste for English cooking and beer is significantly contrasted with the Francophile tastes of his pretentious landlady and two town fops.[64] Howard was in fact himself a major figure in the 'country' opposition in Parliament in this period, so the play provides another link between the cultural and political connotations of that term.[65]

In other respects the period witnessed more decisive and permanent shifts in the connotations of 'country' values. One of these, already highlighted in Whyman's reference to John Verney's 'Tory country ideology', concerned political outlook. While country rhetoric remained a device of opposition throughout our

61. S.E. Whyman, *Sociability and power in late Stuart England* (Oxford, 1999), p. 106.

62. Ibid., pp. 106–7.

63. D. Ormrod, 'Cultural production and import substitution: the fine and decorative arts in London, 1660–1730', in P. O'Brien (ed.), *Urban achievement in early modern Europe* (Cambridge, 2001), pp. 210–30.

64. A.H. Scouten and R.D. Hume (eds), *The country gentleman*, by Sir Robert Howard and George Villiers, Duke of Buckingham (Letchworth, 1976), especially act 1. See also A. Patterson, 'The country gentleman: Howard, Marvell, and Dryden in the theatre of politics', *Studies of English Literature, 1500–1900*, 25 (1985), pp. 491–509.

65. J.P. Vander Motten, 'Sir Robert Howard (1626–1698)', in ODNB.

period, its ideological complexion shifted. During the reigns of Charles I and Charles II alike, the 'country' label was thus associated with a hostility to perceived court leanings towards popery and arbitrary government, and provided an important precursor to the emergence of a Whig position in the later 1670s.[66] The revolution of 1688–9 and its subsequent fallout disrupted these associations. The deposition of James II, the institution of a regime closely identified with the cause of international Protestantism and the passage of the Toleration Act transformed religious politics, notably by fostering a greater sense of insecurity among high churchmen and their lay allies. These anxieties steadily became identified with a renewed 'country' position, defined by reaction to the fiscal, administrative and military expansion of the period and the accompanying financial revolution.[67] The result was to give the political persona of the 'country gentleman' an increasingly Tory hue, as vividly realised in the figure of the foxhunting Tory squire Sir Roger de Coverley in the *Spectator*.[68]

The greatest shift within the galaxy of 'country' values to occur in our period, however, was probably associated with the decline of traditional gentry hospitality. As already noted, the valorisation of hospitality was a long-standing feature of gentry notions of rural identity. In linking the ideal of the country gentleman to particular norms of household management and social interaction it also gave substance to an otherwise rather nebulous cultural construct. This close relationship is emphasised by Felicity Heal, who credits 'country' values with a positive role in prolonging the life of traditions of elite beneficence into the middle decades of the century, and even into the 1680s in the case of the Yorkshire baronet Sir John Reresby.[69] For these reasons, the increasing curtailment of traditional forms of elite beneficence in the mid and later seventeenth century is likely to have diminished the resonance and scope of gentlemen's sense of their rural status. Significantly, however, it does not seem straightforwardly to have resulted in the triumph of metropolitan cultural ideals. Instead, a more undemanding and low-maintenance country gentleman persona seems to have persisted into the eighteenth century, underpinned by the continuing prestige of the country house and probably sustained in varying degrees by classical notions of rural retirement, an occasional desire to emphasise cultural distance from fashionable London society and, no doubt in many cases, a genuine enthusiasm for the life and pastimes of the countryside.[70]

66. Zagorin, *The court and the country*, pp. 33–9; Spurr, *England in the 1670s*, pp. 83, 226, 243–6.
67. G. Holmes, *Religion and party in late Stuart England*, Historical Association, pamphlet G86 (London, 1975); C. Rose, *England in the 1690s: revolution, religion, and war* (Oxford, 1999), chapters 3–6.
68. For example, D.F. Bond (ed.), *The spectator*, 2 (Oxford, 1965), p. 1–4 (no. 126, 25 July 1711).
69. Heal, *Hospitality*, p. 168 and the following.
70. For a later text which seems to engage with this archetype see Anon., *The tricks of the town laid open: or, a companion for country gentlemen. Being the substance of seventeen letters from a gentleman at London to his friend in the country, to disswade him from coming to town* (London, 1746).

In noting the various permutations of 'country' ideology we should remember that these rural loyalties could not be indulged too exclusively. If there were circumstances in which it was acceptable and even prestigious to assert a rural identity, and there was an accepted vocabulary through which this could be done, contemporary comments and literary representations testify that there was also a wrong kind of rusticity, evoking the boorishness, naivety and dullness that had been highlighted in hostile depictions of rusticity going at least as far back as the 'Boor' represented in the ancient Athenian *Characters of Theophrastus*.[71] The self-proclaimed independence, plainness and ingenuousness of the country gentleman could thus easily become an unattractive compound of eccentricity, boorishness and naivety, as the large number of satirical representations of country gentlemen makes clear. A particularly popular Jacobean collection of 'characters' included an account of a figure who could easily have just stepped out of Alan Everitt's Kent:

> His travell is seldome farther then the next market towne, and his inquisition is about the price of Corne ... Nothing under a Sub-poena can draw him to London: and when hee is there, he stickes fast upon every object, casts his eyes away upon gazing, and becomes the prey of every Cut-purse. When hee comes home, those wonders serve him for his Holy-day talke.[72]

It was presumably with such pitfalls in mind that the Gloucestershire knight Sir Richard Berkeley, no lover of metropolitan norms, recommended a middle course of manners and conduct in 1631: 'Covet not to win estimation by trimming up thy selfe in disguised habits & new fangled fashions ... Nor yet bee over-rusticall, as though thou didst condemne all things ... but be modest in attire, and temperate in dyet, and use a mean, observing decency'.[73] Berkeley's advice emphasises once again the fact that the forms of expression outlined here were not so much the unmediated product of instinct or predisposition as they were self-conscious acts of cultural positioning.

The sympathy which Alan Everitt brought to evidence of localism and rural paternalism in the life of the seventeenth-century English gentry has been little

71. J. Diggle (ed.), *Theophrastus: Characters. Edited with introduction, translation and commentary*, Cambridge Classical Texts and Commentaries, 43 (Cambridge, 2004), 3. This text also enjoyed wide contemporary exposure thanks to a 1592 edition and Latin translation by Isaac Casaubon.
72. Anon., *A wife now the widow of Sir Thomas Overbury ... Whereunto are added many witty characters ... by himselfe, and other learned gentlemen* (London, 1614), sig. D4–v.
73. R. Berkeley, *The felicity of man, or his summum bonum* (London, 1631), p. 621. For Berkeley see also J.S. McGee, 'The mental world of Sir Richard Berkeley', in M.C. McClendon, J.P. Ward and M. MacDonald (eds), *Protestant identities: religion, society, and self-fashioning in post-Reformation England* (Stanford, CA, 1999), pp. 85–9.

in evidence in the historiography of the elite since he wrote his seminal works on the local dimensions of the English civil wars and revolution. Among those scholars who engaged with his work as well as among others concerned with the focus of elite identity, the emphasis has tended to fall heavily on change and integration. This focus has produced some remarkable historical writing and greatly advanced our understanding of the gentry. In the end, however, change and continuity are mutually referential and illuminating, and the substantial imbalance between them in the discussion of this topic over the past generation has perhaps given us a lopsided perspective, tending to overlook the dynamic nature of those factors which resisted or countered the march towards a national, urbane, patrician culture. The intention of this chapter has therefore been to approach the evidence for a significant shift in gentry identity during the seventeenth century with a greater receptivity to factors that serve to limit, qualify and refine this narrative.

In many respects an integrationist model of gentry culture in this period emerges unscathed from such an analysis. Just as recent research into the formative experiences of the gentry has emphasised the breadth of their social and cultural horizons, so attention given here to the forms of expression practised by the elite, even where these initially appear conservative or insular, has tended to turn up evidence of national or metropolitan influence. If, in evoking a 'national gentry culture', Clive Holmes referred to the reach and penetration of that culture, his claim would seem to be substantially correct. If we turn to consider the content of the identity or identities concerned, however, an insistence on homogeneity becomes distorting. This was a highly integrated elite culture, yet one heavily grounded in symbols, values and foci of identity that were local in orientation, or otherwise linked to a more general 'country' ethos which defined itself against the polite life of the town. Looked at from this perspective, the dominance of an emphatically metropolitan culture is less evident than the extent to which local and national and urban and rural emphases implicated and fed off of one another. London's material culture was used to reinforce local status; rural independence was asserted in order to claim prestige in a metropolitan political forum; prejudice against city life was fomented within a highly London-centric literary culture; international currents of humanist thought and regional intellectual networks were used to celebrate an ideal of local magistracy and shire unity. These paradoxes hint at a closely woven elite culture in which the opposition of centre and locality was to a great extent smoothed and obscured by a dense web of more limited interconnections, and in which 'local' and 'national' occurred less as opposite poles than as differing shades. This does not invalidate the application of dichotomies of centre and locality, or metropolitan and rural, to the cultural life of the seventeenth-century English gentry. It does, however, give us some sense of the limits of what such analysis is likely to achieve. It is unlikely that this field of enquiry will offer much succour for models of polarisation between local and national loyalties, even without the exclusive concentration on the shire which marked the county community model. At the same time, sensitive analysis of the close interplay between, on the one hand, those forms of loyalties and forms of expression which were relatively localised and, on the other, those of a relatively national or cosmopolitan hue, offers the prospect of capturing contemporary experience with a rewarding degree of fullness and precision.

4

Fashioning communities: the county in early modern Wales

LLOYD BOWEN

Alan Everitt made a telling aside in his 1969 pamphlet, *The local community and the Great Rebellion*, the classic summary of his 'county community' thesis. In a passage discussing the conflicting loyalties of the local and the national in early modern communities he cited examples from Suffolk and Kent, with which he was most familiar, as well as work on 'Staffordshire, Nottinghamshire, Wales, and other districts'.[1] The taxonomic slippage is telling, with 'Wales' being treated as a unit of analysis comparable to an English county. Although some uneasiness with the frame of reference may be seen in the complicating addition of 'other districts' (which, confusingly, seems to make the English shire one such 'district'), the statement is suggestive of a more general historiographical tendency to treat Wales as a separate and distinctive historical category in 'local' history. The brevity of the reference is also illustrative of another trend in the literature: to leave Wales well alone. Wales is often seen as best left to the Welsh. As a result, Wales has been a rather spectral presence in the county community debate, while, conversely, Everitt's methodology and insights have made only a limited impact on the historiography of early modern Wales.

The county in early modern Wales was comparatively new, as the Welsh shires were settled in their final forms only in the 1530s and 1540s. This chapter investigates the social, cultural and political purchase that these new shires obtained among the Welsh gentry community in the century between the Henrician Acts of Union and the civil wars. It discusses how sixteenth- and seventeenth-century Welsh gentlemen paralleled their English counterparts by producing county histories and antiquarian treatises and serving in county government. It also considers the ways in which they represented and discussed their counties in transactions with the central state. However, it will be argued that the idea of the county was only one of several 'local' allegiances available to the early modern Welsh gentleman at this time. The comparatively novel county jostled

---

1. A. Everitt, *The local community and the Great Rebellion*, Historical Association, general series, 70 (London, 1969), p. 10.

in the contemporary mind with alternative social, political, historical, spatial, linguistic and cultural constructions of place which were both more circumscribed and more capacious than the county. The gentry of this period were aware of, and could invoke, ancient Welsh administrative and cultural domains which long pre-dated the imposition of the English shire. These could range from sub-county divisions such as the *cantref* (which approximated the English hundred) and *cwmwd* (or '*commote*' – generally two or three of these comprised a *cantref*) to the kingdoms of medieval Wales, such as Gwynedd, which comprehended several post-union counties.[2] Moreover, there was another sub-regnal identity which could be conjured – that of Wales itself, which continued to have cultural, social and political ramifications long after incorporation with England. Beyond this, the Welsh were also particularly committed to the historical and geographical community of Britain, and enthusiastically proclaimed themselves heirs of an ancient British tradition. It is argued that, while the county had a place in all of this, it is best understood as one discursive community among many, some of which were unique to early modern Wales.

The 'hard' Everittian county community thesis has had only a limited impact in Welsh historiography, but there is a long tradition of Welsh county studies. An influential early example of this genre is Henry Rowland's *Mona antiqua restaurata* (1723), which surveyed Anglesey's material remains to argue that it had been the chief seat of the druids.[3] Later Welsh antiquaries produced a rich vein of local studies which took the county as their subject. Several were multi-volume works that brought together a wealth of primary evidence along with some synthetic analysis. Among these were the works of Theophilus Jones (Breconshire), Richard Fenton (Pembrokeshire), Jonathan Williams (Radnorshire), Sir Samuel Meyrick (Cardiganshire), G.T. Clark (Glamorgan) and Sir J.A. Bradney (Monmouthshire).[4] Welsh county history journals were founded with a particular flourish in the early twentieth century and again during the 1950s with the encouragement of the Standing Conference on Local History and its Welsh president, Sir Frederick Rees.[5] The 1950s also saw plans revived for a multi-volume history of Glamorgan, which began to appear in the 1970s.

2. R.R. Davies, *The age of conquest: Wales, 1063–1415* (Oxford, 1987), pp. 3–23 offers a masterful treatment of the complex administrative, territorial and cultural divisions in medieval Wales.
3. H. Rowlands, *Mona antiqua restaurata* (Dublin, 1723).
4. T. Jones, *History of the county of Brecknock*, 2 vols (Brecon, 1805–9); J. Williams, *History of Radnorshire* (Brecon, 1905); S.R. Meyrick, *History and antiquities of the county of Cardigan* (1810); R. Fenton, *A historical tour through Pembrokeshire* (London, 1811); G.T. Clark, *Limbus patrum Morganiæ et Glamorganiæ* (London, 1886); J.A. Bradney, *A history of Monmouthshire*, 4 vols (London, 1904–33).
5. See London Metropolitan Archives, 4230/A/07/020, 032–038; R.F. Treharne, 'The National Council of Social Service: the Standing Conference on Local History and the work of local antiquarian societies', *Ceredigion*, 1 (1950–51), pp. 73–6.

By the time that Everitt's pioneering work appeared, then, the county was established as an important framework for Welsh history and, although the work produced was often antiquarian in character, there were signs of a critical awareness of the subject and the development of closer ties between amateur enthusiasts and professional historians, particularly those working in the University of Wales.[6] Despite this, the impact of the county community thesis on the smaller, less contentious and less volatile world of Welsh historiography was more limited, subtle and understated than in England. It generated no thoroughgoing localist county community studies of any Welsh shires and none of the controversy and historiographical debate which was to be found in England. As Stephen Roberts observed recently, there was a 'by-passing of most of Wales by the "county" historians of the 1960s and 1970s'.[7] This is not to say that there was no impact in the principality at all, however, and something of a Welsh response to Everitt can be found in the influential work of Professor John Gwynfor Jones.

Jones has produced a number of studies of the sixteenth- and seventeenth-century Welsh gentry which discuss their role in county government and society. Unlike many of his contemporaries, his work has adopted (albeit in a piecemeal and unsystematic fashion) elements of the county community thesis, particularly in relation to his postgraduate research area of Caernarfonshire.[8] In an early article he maintained that the gentry of the county had 'an intense sense of belonging to a particular locality', and that 'national policies in an age of rapid change were interpreted in their essentially local context'.[9] Elsewhere he asserted that the Caernarfonshire gentry were 'intensely provincial in their loyalties and in their interpretation of the many obligations thrust upon them', that 'British politics ... were normally defined on a county basis', and that there was an 'overriding sense of attachment to a region or locality [which] governed the attitude of the squires to the wider implications of increasingly burdensome duties'.[10] These statements were supported by reference to Everitt's recent work and, although their implications were not fully pursued, an emphasis on a rather indeterminate and amorphous 'corporate unity' on the part of the 'shire community' can be found throughout Jones's voluminous and influential writings.

6. See, for example, the reflections on the possibilities and problems of a county-based approach in A.H. Williams, 'The teaching of local history', *Morgannwg*, 1 (1957), p. 46.
7. S.K. Roberts, 'How the west was won: parliamentary politics, religion and the military in south Wales, 1642–9', *Welsh History Review*, 21 (2002–3), p. 648.
8. J.G. Jones, 'The Caernarfonshire justices of the peace and their duties during the seventeenth century', MA thesis (Bangor, 1967).
9. J.G. Jones, 'Caernarfonshire administration activities of the justices of the peace, 1603–1660', *Welsh History Review*, 5 (1970–71), pp. 162–3.
10. J.G. Jones, 'Aspects of local government in pre-Restoration Caernarfonshire', *Transactions of the Caernarfonshire Historical Society*, 33 (1972), p. 7.

Jones developed elements of this at greater length in a 1996 monograph on Caernarfonshire administration between 1558 and 1640. This came close to asserting that there was a corporate gentry identity centred on the shire which was dynamic, parochial and exclusivist. He described a conservative gentry society which had a 'symbolic' and geographical unity and was possessed of 'close family and social relations, economic superiority and marriage ties'. This, he went on, 'created an integrated and organic community', and he also maintained that the gentry, the local 'political nation', sought to 'steer clear' of direct involvement with central government and its contentious politics, preferring instead to safeguard the interests of county society. Moreover, he argued that the county's quarter sessions were 'an integrating force which helped to preserve the regional [sic] identity of Caernarfonshire people'.[11] This seems redolent of a county community along the lines suggested by Everitt, but the factor operating against political and social insularity was the creeping influence of Anglicisation in culture and language among the gentry, which led Jones ultimately to conclude that 'the exclusivity of county society should not be exaggerated'.[12]

Whereas in Everitt the county was ranged conceptually against the intrusions of the state, in the work of Gwynfor Jones and other historians of early modern Welsh counties the apparatus of the English state is seen to have been assimilated fairly easily. It was the attendant and insidious 'corruption' of the 'native' gentry order, principally by English language and culture, which militated against any thoroughgoing adoption of the localist model. Such a position draws upon an established theme in nineteenth- and twentieth-century Welsh public discourse which saw the Welsh gentry as destined to 'betray' their county, their country and their culture.[13] The Welsh gentleman was stereotyped in this discourse as a Tory, Anglophone, Anglican, absentee landowner and contrasted explicitly with the radical, nonconformist, Cambrophone, plebeian *gwerin* (folk) who were the true bearers of the national spirit. It is perhaps for reasons such as these that the wave of gentry-focused English county community studies which appeared in the wake of Everitt's work was not replicated in Wales.

It seems unlikely that any thoroughgoing county community study of a Welsh shire will now emerge after the penetrating critiques of 'hard' county community localism offered by scholars such as Ann Hughes and Clive Holmes.[14] Despite this, there is a growing recognition that the shire formed *one* important context

11. J.G. Jones, *Law, order and government in Caernarfonshire, 1558–1640* (Cardiff, 1996), pp. 19, 148, 218–19. He also wrote of a 'co-operative spirit' among the Caernarfonshire gentry which was 'inextricably linked to a sense of corporate unity within the shire and an underlying awareness that gentility had a fundamental role in the creation and sustaining of that unity': *ibid.*, p. 111.
12. *Ibid.*, p. 19.
13. H.M. Vaughan, *The south Wales squires* (London, 1926); M. Cragoe, *An Anglican aristocracy: the moral economy of the landed estate in Carmarthenshire, 1832–1895* (Oxford, 1996).
14. A. Hopper, 'Introduction', above, pp. 1–12.

for early modern gentry society and politics, albeit not Everitt's *dominant* context. Indeed, the essays presented in the current volume suggest stimulating avenues for pursuing the early modern county, and there is a new opportunity to integrate Wales into this developing picture.

The shires of Wales were not the indigenous early medieval entities found in England. They were instead symbols of defeat and subjugation, structures for civilising and pacifying rebellious subjects.[15] Most of the first counties were carved out of the lands of the last native prince of Wales, Llywelyn ap Gruffydd, after his defeat by Edward I in 1282.[16] The Statute of Wales of 1284 created the counties of Anglesey, Caernarfonshire, Cardiganshire, Carmarthenshire, Flintshire and Merioneth, and introduced the apparatus of English law and governance which, in theory, if less and less in practice as time went on, were to be exercised by English governors and officials. The remaining 'modern' Welsh counties of Breconshire, Denbighshire, Glamorgan, Monmouthshire, Montgomeryshire, Pembrokeshire and Radnorshire were products of Henry VIII's Acts of Union (1536–1543), and generally were formed from the marcher lordships in the east and south of the country.[17] These acts annexed Wales to England and provided for the universal jurisdiction of English statute and common law under the Westminster courts and the Council in the Marches. They also introduced into Wales the office of justice of the peace, and allowed Welsh constituencies to return members to the national parliament. In addition, this legislation altered the boundaries of the Edwardian shires and effectively gave Wales territorial and administrative integrity for the first time.

The most salient features of the counties of Wales in the sixteenth century, then, were that they were English and of comparatively recent origin. Even their borders seemed provisional, and several were changed between the passing of the first act in 1536 and the second in 1543. The shire was considered by English officials as an essential adjunct of civility and order, but there were some, such as the Lord President of the Council in the Marches, Rowland Lee, who felt that the Welsh were not ready for the responsibilities of local self-governance.[18] Given such opinions,

---

15. M.C. Noonkester, 'The third British empire: transplanting the English shire to Wales, Scotland, Ireland, and America', *Journal of British Studies*, 36 (1997), pp. 251–84.

16. Cardiganshire and Carmarthenshire were already inchoate counties under royal control in the 1240s: J.G. Edwards, 'The early history of the counties of Carmarthenshire and Cardiganshire', *English Historical Review*, 31 (1916), pp. 90–98.

17. By this time Pembroke and Glamorgan were royal lordships administered like counties, and were referred to as such. Monmouthshire is something of an anomaly as it was excluded from the Welsh legal system of great sessions courts and annexed to the Oxford circuit, its financial accounts were rendered separately from Wales and, unlike other Welsh counties, it was given two MPs after the English model. However, culturally it was thoroughly Welsh, it was created out of Welsh lands, was subject to the jurisdiction of the Council in the Marches of Wales, and was treated as a Welsh county by contemporaries.

18. TNA, SP1/102, fo. 149; SP1/101, fos 198–200.

one could understand a reluctance on the part of the Welsh gentry to adopt the English county and its attendant legal and administrative apparatus. Yet, on the contrary, Welsh squires rushed to fill the new shire offices, some as early as 1536 reportedly being prepared to 'giff ... large money to be made iustices of the peace'.[19] A year later the English bishop of Bangor claimed that it was 'the nature of a Welsheman ... to bear office & to be in authoritie. He will not let to runne thorow the fyer of hell & sell & geve all he can make of his owen & of his frends for the same.'[20] The Welsh had been filling posts in local administration for many years, but the proliferation of county offices after the union opened up new opportunities for honour, prestige and wealth which were simply not available beforehand.[21]

In terms of willing participation in county government and administration, then, the county represented important new opportunities for the Welsh gentry which they seized enthusiastically and moulded to their own cultural predilections. The legal and administrative structures of the union provided a framework for constructing a sense of corporate belonging which consolidated with usage over time.[22] There is, however, little evidence of any kind of concerted attempt by the London authorities to publicise the benefits of union or to promote a sense of allegiance to the counties. Despite this, the Welsh gentry became active in constructing a sense of shire community. According to one of the leading historians of early modern Wales, by the reign of Elizabeth the Welsh counties 'had become fully absorbed into the popular consciousness as the natural units for government, administration, justice, and politics'.[23] It should be noted, however, that the articulation of a shire identity in some areas was not wholly new but built on older practices. In Merioneth, for example, some settlements with the Crown in the fifteenth century were made '*pro tota communitate comitatus Meryon*' ('for the whole community of the county of Merioneth'), with leading Welsh figures assuming a role in representing their county compatriots.[24] The county had a presence in the political lives of important Welsh *uchelwyr* (gentlemen) before the union, then, but it was in the sixteenth century that it became a key reference point for them.

One important index of the development of county-centred identities among

19. TNA, SP1/106, fo. 245.
20. BL, Harleian MS 283, fo. 153.
21. W.R.B. Robinson, 'The Tudor revolution in Welsh government, 1536–1543: its effects on gentry participation', *English Historical Review*, 103 (1988), pp. 1–20.
22. J. Gwynn Williams, 'Rhai agweddau ar y gymdeithas Gymreig yn yr ail ganrif ar bymtheg', *Efrydiau athronyddol*, 31 (1968), p. 43.
23. G. Williams, *Renewal and reformation: Wales, c.1415–1642* (Oxford, 1987), p. 340. J. Gwynn Williams maintained that 'an awareness of belonging to a county' ['ymwybyddiaeth o berthyn i sir'] was well established by the seventeenth century: 'Rhai agweddau ar y gymdeithas Gymreig', p. 42.
24. D.H. Owen and J. Beverley Smith, 'Government and society, 1283–1536', in J. Beverly Smith and Ll. Beverly Smith (eds), *History of Merioneth. II. The Middle Ages* (Llandysul, 2001), p. 105.

Welsh elites was their production of histories (or sometimes 'chorographies') for several Welsh shires.[25] These were part of the burgeoning interest in local histories which was a feature of later Elizabethan and early Stuart society. Rhys Meyrick's work on Glamorgan, Morganiæ archaiographia, was explicitly modelled on Lambarde's *Perambulation of Kent*, and was one of the first responses to Lambarde's call for the production of county histories to form a corpus of national geographical and historical works. It is noticeable that most of these antiquarian studies were concerned with counties which were outside the historic principality which had possessed a form of shire government since 1284. This might suggest that in these post-union shires antiquarian study was a way of constructing and asserting such a corporate identity in a comparatively new cultural space, and that such an identity was more developed in the old Edwardian counties.

These works often evinced a genuine pride in the county, even where these institutions were ('officially' at least) only decades old, as in the case of Glamorgan and Pembrokeshire. On the latter, for example, George Owen declared that if he was fervent in his praise of Pembrokeshire, 'yett I should therefore partelye deserve pardon (the love and affection of my countrey eggeinge me thereunto)'. He described Pembrokeshire as 'famouse for … love, loyalltie and service to the kinges of this realme', adding 'let not therefore the same be buryed in oblivion'. He concluded emphatically that God had 'bestowed particular blessings … more upon this country than upon the rest of Wales'.[26] In his work on Glamorgan, meanwhile, Meyrick asserted that one reason for his writing the tract was that 'the present estate [of Glamorgan] should be as well unto posterity known as unto us that live at this present'.[27] Humphrey Lhuyd's tract on Anglesey related how the island had continuously rebuffed attempts at invasion, and he accounted it 'the principalest of the four regions' of the ancient kingdom of Gwynedd. He also insisted on using the island's ancient name, 'Mona' ('Môn' in Welsh), as its original designation before the English named it 'Anglesey' ('The English ile'). He was also clearly gratified to refer twice in his short tract to the common appellation of the county as 'Môn mam Cymru', 'Anglesey, Mother of Wales', on account of its fertility.[28]

In works such as those of Meyrick and Rice Lewis on Glamorgan, enumerating the county's chief landowners and judicial officers invoked a gentry

25. See D. Powel, *The history of Wales*, ed. W. Wynne (Merthyr Tydfil, 1812), pp. xxv–xlvi; H. Lhuyd, 'De Mona druium insula', in Sir J. Price, *Historiae Brytannicae defensio* (London, 1573), sigs. Aa–Ccii; A. Ortelius, *Theatrum orbis terrarium* (Antwerp, 1608), sigs. I3, XLVi–XLViv; R. Merrick, *Morganiæ archaiographia. A book of the antiquities of Glamorganshire*, ed. B. Ll. James, South Wales Record Society, second series, 1 (1983); G. Owen, *The description of Pembrokeshire*, ed. D. Miles (Llandysul, 1994); R. Lewis, *A breviat of Glamorgan*, ed. W. Rees, South Wales Record Society, first series, 3 (1954), pp. 92–150; BL, Harleian MS 6,108, fos 1–33v.
26. G. Owen, *The description of Penbrokshire*, ed. H. Owen, 4 vols (London, 1892–1936), 1, p. 256.
27. Merrick, *Morganiæ archaiographia*, p. 1.
28. Ortelius, *Theatrum*, sigs. XLVi–XLViv.

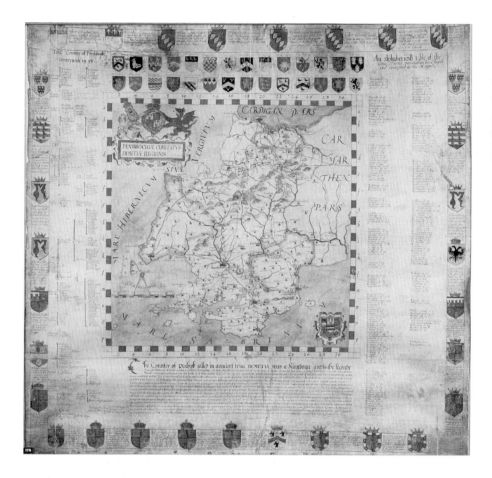

Figure 4.1 George Owen, *Penbrochiae comitatus olim Demetiae regionis descriptio* (1602). By permission of Llyfrgell Genedlaethol Cymru/The National Library of Wales, MAP1001, PZ3681.

community held together by the bonds of the shire. This was echoed in the activities of genealogists during this period who anchored the elite in their locality by tracing their long tenure and ancient familial ties to the area. Several of these county historians were also deeply concerned with genealogy, and the sense of the legal and topographical identity of the shire that they described was often intimately related to the family histories of the shire gentry.[29]

There was also a visual element to the inculturation of the shire in sixteenth- and seventeenth-century Wales through a new interest in the representation of the county in maps. Christopher Saxton's were the first set of county maps available for Wales. These visually arresting and detailed productions were prepared with local knowledge in the summer of 1576 when the Privy Council ordered that two or three

29. B.G. Charles, *George Owen of Henllys: a Welsh Elizabethan* (Aberystwyth, 1973), pp. 107–26.

'honest men such as do best know the cuntrey' assist Saxton, and that a horseman who could 'speke both Welsh and Englishe' accompany him on his journey.[30] Individual Welsh county maps based on those produced by Saxton were incorporated into William Camden's *Britannia* in 1607 and John Speed's *Theatre* in 1610. Jan Broadway's observation that 'seeing a county represented by a map gave visual form to what had previously been an abstract idea' is particularly relevant to Wales, where the county boundaries were settled only decades before these works were produced.[31] The vogue for cartography was taken up by George Owen, who produced a splendid colour map of Pembrokeshire in 1602 which Camden later incorporated into his *Britannia*.[32] Owen's manuscript map included a border displaying the coats of arms of the Earls of Pembroke, while another frame was occupied by 28 coats belonging to leading Pembrokeshire gentry. Owen thus contributed to the developing awareness of the post-union shire in Wales, but also tied it to the gentle and noble communities which controlled its government and administration (Figure 4.1).

The rhetorical ideal of the shire community was articulated in several discrete spheres of gentry culture in the century after the Acts of Union, and the 'new' shire of Glamorgan offers some interesting examples of these. The literary trope of the county as Elysian retreat was expressed in a poem of c.1620 ascribed to Sir John Stradling of St Donats, 'A song in praise of Glamorganshire'.[33] He maintained 'This countrie justlie may be named / The arcadie of Wales; / So faire and fruitful are the plaines / Soe riche the grassie vales', and went on to detail its fecundity and plenty. The kind of sentiments behind this panegyric presumably moved Rice Lewis in the dedication of his 1596 'Breviat of Glamorgan' to remind Thomas Morgan of Rhiwperra that 'it hath pleased God by his providence to make you a Glamorganshire man'.[34] The community of county gentry was a potentially powerful rhetorical device in the public sphere, and came to be seen as capable of collective action. The chaplain to the second Earl of Pembroke, Gervase Babington, drew on this idea in a pamphlet of 1583. He dedicated it 'To the gentlemen of Glamorganshire', but reproved them for failing adequately to support and sponsor able ministers in the county and entreated them to discharge their public duties in this respect.[35]

30. J.R. Dasent (ed.), *Acts of the Privy Council, 1575–1577* (London, 1894), p. 159.
31. J. Broadway, '*No historie so meete*': *gentry culture and the development of local history in Elizabethan and early Stuart England* (Manchester, 2006), p. 207.
32. Charles, *George Owen*, pp. 151–9; W. Camden, *Britannia* (London, 1607), pp. 508–9.
33. Only known from later copies: NLW, MSS 21,327A, 6,513B.
34. Lewis, *Breviat of Glamorgan*, p. 94.
35. G. Babington, *A very fruitfull exposition of the comaundements by way of questions and answeres* … (London, 1583), sigs. ¶¶1–¶¶¶4. See also his letter to Sir Edward Stradling presenting him a copy of this text and addressing him as 'a pyller of this country', and thus, presumably, one who could galvanise the local gentry community to act on these matters: J.M. Traherne (ed.), *The Stradling correspondence* (London, 1840), p. 277.

The image of a gentry county community was a pervasive presence in the protracted dispute between 1577 and 1581 over the provision of money to repair the collapsed bridge at Cardiff.[36] County and town disputed the levels of payment which should be borne by each, and this ultimately led to the introduction of a bill in parliament which placed four-fifths of the costs on the county. This was vigorously resisted by many county gentlemen, who feared that this apportionment, in addition to being inequitable, would also make them liable for the upkeep of other bridges in the county. The matter was complicated by the fact that it was the knight of the shire, William Mathew of Radyr, who had introduced the bill in parliament, not the member for Cardiff boroughs. Led by Sir Edward Stradling, the squire of St Donats, the county lobby attempted vigorously to influence interested parties in the Commons and the Lords, and even the Queen herself. The surviving correspondence reveals the perceived potency of mobilising in the name of the county community. The gentry described themselves as suitors 'in the behalf of the whole countrye', and reduced the dispute to the townsmen on one side 'and the gentlemen and the inhabitants of the contry' on the other.[37] In a remarkable mobilisation of aggressive local sentiment, 100 county gentlemen 'of no yll sorte' petitioned Henry Herbert, second Earl of Pembroke, a powerful Glamorgan magnate, over the matter. After receiving the Earl's reply, they subsequently assembled a kind of county parliament to which 'certaine of the discretest of ev[e]ry parish' were invited to discuss the Earl's answer, and 'by this means to publish the letter to the whole of the county'. At this meeting they resolved to oppose the prospective bill.[38]

Ultimately their efforts failed and the bill found its way into law, but there was some revealing discussion of the social and political constituency which Mathew was seen to have betrayed in promoting the bill on behalf of Cardiff rather than the county freeholders who elected him. He was described as 'working againste the inhabitants of this countie' and 'forgeatinge by whom he was chosen and by whom he is feaed [fee'd], p[er]secuitinge whom he should protecte'.[39] This was an 'unaturall attempte' by a man 'chosen for us and waged by us yet [he] furthereth the cause of oure adversaryes'.[40] The magnitude of the betrayal and the sense of accountability to the county electorate was conveyed graphically by Sir Edward Mansell, who maintained that 'if my deere father had beene living &

36. L. Bowen, 'Wales at Westminster: parliament, principality and pressure groups, 1542–1601', *Parliamentary History*, 22 (2003), pp. 117–20; P. Williams, 'Controversy in Elizabethan Glamorgan: the rebuilding of Cardiff Bridge', *Morgannwg*, 2 (1958), pp. 38–46.
37. NLW, Penrice and Margam MSS 1,822, 2,770.
38. NLW, Penrice and Margam MSS 3,585, 2,770, L.44; A. Collins (ed.), *Letters and memorials of state* (2 vols, London, 1746), i. 274–5.
39. Alnwick Castle, Northumberland papers, III, fo. 101r–v. I am most grateful to the Duke of Northumberland for allowing me to cite from his family papers.
40. NLW, Penrice and Margam MS L.28; Alnwick Castle, Northumberland papers, III, fo. 78.

partye against my contrey, tho[u]ghe hee had been of estate as highe as princce [sic] of Praga, I would & ought to have opposed my self against him whatt I mought'.⁴¹ In this case, the 'contrey' was very clearly the constituency of Glamorgan gentry who had supported Mathew's election and who, ultimately, would be picking up the bill for repairing the bridge in Cardiff. There was, then, clearly a gentry county community which could be summoned into being over such an issue, and the indignation of Stradling and his associates testify to the strength of the communal bonds which could tie such a constituency together. Clearly the post-union shire had a potency in the public discourse of south Wales which could help structure the language of local politics and alignments within county elites.

The sense of the shire as a community in which honour was constructed, and to which gentlemen were accountable, can be seen in early modern Wales as in England. The sense of serving one's 'country' as a parliamentary representative was evident in the Cardiff bridge dispute, and was articulated elsewhere too. In the disputed Caernarfonshire election of 1620, for example, John Gryffudd of Llŷn lobbied Sir William Maurice to support his candidacy, observing 'you knowe best the experience yt is obtained by beeinge of a parliament & that every true lover of his countrie shold endeavoure to do service ther'.⁴² When he attacked the bishop of Bangor in the 1626 parliament, he claimed that he was acting 'in further dischardge of his duety to that county for which hee did serve'.⁴³ There was obviously a sense of duty and obligation to the 'country' here, but there is little indication that such language implied the kinds of godly public accountability to the 'commonwealth' which has been seen as important in understanding such claims elsewhere.⁴⁴ Rather, this was a rhetoric of service to the community which was of a piece with other kinds of local office. Poets presented MPs as the incarnation of their communities, and their principal role was to defend its interests.⁴⁵ As in the case of the justiceship of the peace and the shrievalty, the county was a context for service and honour which helped fabricate and fortify county identities. Thus we find local gentlemen praised in Welsh poetry as sturdy defenders of the shire and its institutions. They were 'blaenor Môn' ('the leader of Anglesey'), or 'llywiawdwr Môn' ('the governor of Anglesey'), 'ustus heddwch gwastad' ('an equitable justice of the peace'), 'ymgeleddu gwlad' ('cherisher of the

41. NLW, Penrice and Margam MS L.44. Mathew was moved to defend himself against such accusations of partiality: TNA, SP12/148, fo. 35r–v.
42. NLW, Clennenau MS 398.
43. TNA, SP16/30/8.
44. The work of Richard Cust is crucial to this interpretation: see his '"Patriots" and "popular spirits": narratives of conflict in early Stuart politics', in N. Tyacke (ed.), *The English revolution, c.1590–1720* (Manchester, 2007), pp. 43–61, and sources cited.
45. J.G. Jones, *Concepts of order and gentility in Wales, 1540–1640* (Llandysul, 1992), pp. 177–9.

community'), '*Salmon i'r sir*' ('Solomon of the county').[46] Thomas Mansell, who represented Glamorgan three times in parliament and served thrice as sheriff and as a prominent justice, was described by one bard as '*enaid Morgannwg uniawn*' ('virtuous soul of Glamorgan').[47] The county was thus a key site for the construction of gentility through public service, although the Ciceronian model in Wales was largely shorn of its oppositional Calvinist edge.

In addition to such positive images of the shire as have been discussed hitherto, Tudor and Stuart gentlemen also mobilised a very different idea of the Welsh county in the public sphere – that of a distant and impoverished space. This was particularly the case in discussions over the provision of men and money for the state. Taking advantage of the hazy and imperfect knowledge of early modern governors concerning Wales, county justices not infrequently presented their communities as barely able to bear the burdens of the state.[48] Particularly prominent in this respect was Anglesey. The island was perceived as a weak spot in the nation's defences and a potential landing site for Catholic invasion. As a result, for much of the period its militia was exempted from mobilising beyond the county, a privilege which its JPs defended forcefully for decades thereafter.[49] The island's governors were also keen to play up the county's impecuniosity and thus alleviate the weight of taxation. When the Privy Council demanded a greater subsidy yield from Anglesey in 1626, the bench responded that they had always paid as much as their estate could support, 'and as great as eny countie in England proportionablie did'. Arguing that they had 'strayned our selves' to meet the king's demands, they reminded the Council that the authors of the Henrician union legislation, 'knowing the povertie of Wales … whereof this countie is the least & poorest', had waived the £20 property qualification for JPs in Wales so 'that men of meaner meanes might bee justices of peace'.[50] It was vanishingly unlikely that London would send anyone to ascertain the real economic capacities of the island's gentry, so the image of an impoverished county community established at the union provided the Anglesey justices with a useful precedent for alleviating the demands of the Caroline state. And in this it was not alone. The 'ould generall plea … [of] the extreame povertie of those remote partes' mentioned by one Welshman in a private letter was deployed by a number of other counties in this period.[51] Under Charles I,

46. Ibid., pp. 169–71; idem, 'Anglesey after the union', *Transactions of the Anglesey Antiquarian Society* (1990), p. 41.
47. A.D. Thrush and J.P. Ferris (eds), *The history of parliament: the House of Commons, 1604–29* (6 vols, Cambridge, 2011), 5, p. 254.
48. L. Bowen, *The politics of the principality: Wales, c.1603–42* (Cardiff, 2007), pp. 85–206, 265–73.
49. E.G. Jones, 'Anglesey and invasion', *Transactions of the Anglesey Antiquarian Society* (1947), pp. 30–36.
50. TNA, SP16/25/37. See also TNA, SP14/130/100.
51. NLW, MS 9061E/1424.

Flintshire, Breconshire and Pembrokeshire all claimed at different times that they were poorest in the kingdom.[52]

The Welsh county had become a source of pride and a focus for poetic eulogy and antiquarian study, but it was also a malleable resource in the currency of the public sphere. Different images of the county could be summoned for different audiences by the gentry who populated it – that of the verdant shire overflowing with riches or of an impoverished and remote backwater toiling to meet even the minimum demands of early modern governors. Anglesey was simultaneously the fertile mother of Wales and the vulnerable and impoverished island of limited means.

In all of the domains discussed to this point – local government, antiquarian study, politics and local culture – the post-union shire became an important framework for gentry life – important but not, however, exclusive. The most telling criticism of the 'hard' county community has been its restrictive concentration on the shire as the determining variable in gentry culture and politics. A more fruitful enterprise has been to see the county as only one of several discursive fields in which the early modern gentleman operated. The remainder of this chapter explores how the county in early modern Wales was a rather unstable and pliable category which jostled with older territorial and conceptual loyalties. Some of these loyalties were more localised and restricted than the county, but there were also larger domains to be considered, which included ancient medieval kingdoms such as Gwynedd, the country of 'Wales' itself, and a particularly Welsh take on the significance of Britain.

Although the shires were important arenas of public service for the Welsh gentry, there remained a persistent and pervasive awareness of the continued significance of their antecedents. Given the nature of the union settlement this is hardly surprising. The shape of the post-union counties was often determined as much by immediate political considerations as by ancient territorial affiliations. For example, the county of Glamorgan was centred on the old Welsh kingdom of Morgannwg (which incorporated the medieval lordship of Glamorgan), but the union legislation annexed this to the western lordships of Gower and Kilvey, which historically, linguistically, administratively and ecclesiastically had closer ties with the territory to the west in Carmarthenshire. The final shape of Glamorgan was determined by aristocratic politics, as Gower and Kilvey were owned by Henry, Earl of Worcester, who had administered Glamorgan lordship for the Crown, while Worcester's rivals the Devereux family were influential in Carmarthenshire. Thus the early modern shire reflected dynastic and political interests as much as topography or established administrative arrangements, and this seems to have been institutionalised in the post-union dispensation, with the county bench dividing into eastern and western divisions to discharge its

52.   TNA, SP16/24/58; SP16/30/85; SP16/32/66; E178/7154, pt. 2, fo. 135.

business.[53] Local politics was also important in determining the boundaries of Pembrokeshire and Carmarthenshire. George Owen related how the original shape of Pembrokeshire under the 1536 act was changed drastically in 1542 by Sir Thomas Jones, who was Pembrokeshire's MP but a Carmarthenshire man. Intending to 'work his native country ... some good', Jones had several of Pembrokeshire's eastern lordships transferred to Carmarthenshire, much enlarging it, but the lands 'were lost before any Pembrokeshire man knew thereof'.[54] Flintshire, Denbighshire and Merioneth also had their original boundaries changed by statute, and an act was passed shortly after the first tranche of union legislation allowing the king to apportion lordships to the shires for three years because the territories allocated to the counties in 1536 had not been 'indifferently allotted'.[55] Although many counties had important medieval precursors, the union settlement could seem arbitrary and sometimes even capricious. The historians of the union in Monmouthshire have asserted that the 1536 shire 'had all the marks of a county designed by committee'.[56] This probably served to temper enthusiasm for these new administrative units and may have helped sustain the ongoing association with pre-union units of governance and loyalty in Welsh gentry culture.

Although there is no question that the gentlemen of sixteenth- and seventeenth-century Wales increasingly saw the county as the stage for public service, their horizons were often much more restricted than this – although this does not necessarily translate into their being simply localist backwoodsmen. The building blocks of the shires were much older territorial forms, the *commote* and the *cantref*, and a good deal of gentry life was lived and constructed within such sub-county units. George Owen recalled that these divisions of Wales were made 'in the tymes of the Brittaines', but that they were still very much a presence in Elizabethan society as 'manye ... names as yet remaine and the places well knowne by the same'.[57]

When antiquarians discussed the histories of their counties they were often thrown back on reflecting how these were relatively recent additions grafted onto established and well-known congeries of medieval lordships, *commotes* and *cantrefs*. The first part of Meyrick's *Morganiæ archaiographia* was concerned with delineating the difference between the county of Glamorgan and the lordship of Morgannwg, and described the errors made in this respect by some

53. W.R.B. Robinson, 'Henry, earl of Worcester and Henry VIII's legislation for Wales', *Bulletin of the Board of Celtic Studies*, 21 (1966), pp. 344–5; TNA, SP16/31/44.
54. G. Owen, *The dialogue of the government of Wales* (1594), ed. J.G. Jones (Cardiff, 2010), pp. 133–5, 138–42.
55. *Statutes of the realm*, 10 vols (London, 1810–28), 3, p. 653.
56. W.R.B. Robinson and M. Gray, 'The making of Monmouthshire', in M. Gray and P. Morgan (eds), *The Gwent county history, vol. 3: the making of Monmouthshire* (Cardiff, 2009), p. 1.
57. Owen, *Penbrokshire*, 1, p. 45.

commentators. This history of 'Glamorgan' was enumerated hundred by hundred, recalling the old *cantrefs* 'whereof is derived the division now used whereunto our shires be now severed'.[58] George Owen's *Pembrokeshire* was written alongside his attempts to press his claims as lord of Cemais in the north of the county, a franchise which, he claimed, had not been removed by the acts of union. Sir John Wynn of Gwydir's most influential antiquarian endeavour was a history of his own family. Asserting his descent from the princes of Gwynedd, it was little concerned with the present-day realities of Wynn's county of Caernarfonshire, but was rather a study of upward mobility by one family in the *commote* of Eifionydd.[59]

The appearance of older ideas of place and local loyalty can be seen in many areas of gentry life, and they serve to complicate and sometimes undercut the role of the shire in the gentry's administrative and cultural worlds. In north Wales, for example, the medieval kingdom of Gwynedd continued to stalk the governors of the region. Indeed, to a degree Gwynedd was institutionalised in the union settlement by the creation of the north Wales circuit for the court of great sessions, which encompassed the three counties of Gwynedd: Anglesey, Caernarfonshire and Merioneth.[60] Discussing Anglesey, John Gwynfor Jones has observed that Welsh language poets of the sixteenth century not infrequently represented their gentry patrons as governors of a 'distinct political region ... with a specific obligation to maintain its independence as a coherent entity ... The power exerted by officials in Anglesey was often fitted within the context of a broader provincial entity or gwlad of Gwynedd'.[61] For example, the mid-sixteenth-century Anglesey gentleman Rowland Bulkeley was praised by one poet as '*Ymherodr holl Wynedd*' ['The Emperor of all Gwynedd'], while Sir William Glynne, a Jacobean justice in Anglesey and Caernarfonshire, was described as '*plaid gweiniaid Gwynedd*' ['a party working for Gwynedd'].[62] Although the shire becomes more prominent in such material as the period progresses, Gwynedd never fully disappears. The careers of the Caernarfonshire gentlemen Sir John Wynn of Gwydir and Sir William Maurice of Clenennau can provide some further illustration of Gwynedd's continued presence in post-union Wales.

As with those of several other gentlemen of north Wales in this period, Wynn and Maurice's careers of public service were not restricted to a single shire. Wynn was appointed sheriff for Caernarfonshire, Merioneth and Denbighshire, and

58. Meyrick, *Morganiæ archaiographia*, p. 9.
59. J. Wynn, *The history of the Gwydir family and memoirs*, ed. J.G. Jones (Llandysul, 1990).
60. The south-western circuit similarly reproduced the broad boundaries of the medieval kingdom of Deheubarth.
61. Jones, 'Anglesey after the union', pp. 32–3.
62. *Ibid.*, p. 40; idem, 'Awdurdod cyfreithiol a gweinyddol lleol yng nogledd Cymru yn y cyfnod 1540–1640 yn ôn tystiolaeth y beirdd', *Llên Cymru*, 12 (1972–3), p. 182.

served as a JP in all three counties for much of his public career.[63] In addition to representing Caernarfonshire and Beaumaris in parliament, Maurice was a justice in Anglesey, Caernarfonshire and Merioneth, and also served as sheriff for the latter two counties.[64] These men seem to have had a regional rather than county-based view of government and administration in north-west Wales, and this region had significant echoes of the medieval Principality of North Wales, itself based on the native kingdom of Gwynedd. An ode written to Maurice by Thomas Prys of Plas Iolyn (Denbighshire) is illuminating in this respect. Prys recounted the major offices Maurice had held and portrayed him as the guardian of a distinct province. Specific reference was made to his prominence in Gwynedd, while mention was also made to his offices in Caernarfon and Merioneth, and Maurice was described as 'ruwliwr i'n tir' ['ruler of our region'].[65] Here, then, the shire sat alongside the medieval kingdom – the two were not in tension but could be accommodated simultaneously in the construction of Maurice's gentility and public service. Indeed, the two arenas were mutually reinforcing, the shire helping constitute the rhetorical space of the older kingdom, while prominence in the wider region reflected back on Maurice's status in the county.

Issues of security in this part of Wales also recalled medieval bonds of affiliation structured on the kingdom of Gwynedd. Defending the strategic weak point of Anglesey animated these older ties, with the other Gwynedd counties of Caernarfonshire and Merioneth being expected to assist the island as a discrete administrative bloc when invasion threatened.[66] The arrangement was still in place during the Elizabethan wars with Spain, and in the 1580s these counties were organised together under a single muster master.[67] None of this was explicitly modelled on the old kingdom of the north-west, but the connections between the three shires in this and other contexts indicates how the ghosts of native Welsh territories were not fully exorcised by the Henrician settlement.

This regional aspect of gentry life and culture sat alongside other local loyalties. Significant in this regard was the division of Wales into northern and southern administrative provinces. This partition was partly a product of the topographical barrier of the central upland massif, but it also reflected

---

63. P.W. Hasler (ed.), *The history of parliament: the House of Commons, 1558–1603*, 3 vols (London, 1981), 3, p. 671. In this he was following a family precedent – his father Morus and his uncle John (Gwynne) had also been JPs in three counties, while a poem had hailed his grandfather as an equitable justice who held three regions ('tair gwlad') in his grasp: S.T. Bindoff (ed.), *The history of parliament: the House of Commons, 1509–58*, 3 vols (London, 1982), 3, p. 676; Jones, *Concepts of order*, p. 12.
64. Thrush and Ferris, *House of Commons, 1604–29*, 5, p. 288.
65. J. Fisher (ed.), *The Cefn Coch mss* (Liverpool, 1899), pp. 152–3.
66. NLW, MS 9051E/9; TNA, SP1/150, fo. 108.
67. TNA, SP12/170, fo. 125r–v; SP12/195, fo. 162.

differences in dialect as well as long-standing administrative practices and historical and cultural affiliations.[68] One could be identified, and identify oneself, as belonging to either north or south Wales. An unfortunate collector of Crown rents in Jacobean Cardiganshire was opposed by the local community in part because he was 'a north Wales man'.[69] The early 1600s saw a good-natured historical debate between Welsh antiquaries as to whether the medieval kings of south Wales or the north had the greater dominion in the country – something that evidently reflected contemporary senses of pride and precedence.[70]

The north–south divide echoed the separation of the old principality into northern and southern constituencies, but it also had institutional ramifications in early modern Wales. For example, regional offices, such as the Chamberlainship of north and south Wales, occupied by prominent local gentlemen such as John Puleston of Caernarfonshire (north Wales, 1547–51) and Sir Thomas Mansell of Glamorgan (south Wales, 1585–1631), continued after the union.[71] The vice-admiralty was also split into northern and southern divisions with leading gentry serving as deputies.[72] North and south Wales had separate receivers and auditors of Crown revenues, and central government routinely viewed the country as split into six counties in the north and six in the south (Monmouthshire was generally accounted as part of England). This could be seen, for example, when the Privy Council levied troops in Wales and when the country was assessed for payments such as ship money or the semi-feudal levy known as the 'mize'. The powerful Commission for the Propagation of the Gospel (1650–53) divided itself between commissioners in the north and south, an arrangement repeated in successor commissions for ejecting scandalous ministers in Wales.[73] The business of sequestrating the estates of royalists was similarly partitioned, and when the constituency of 'Wales' sent members to the Nominated Assembly in 1653 its allocation of six was divided equally between north and south.[74] The division of Wales into two halves was to be found primarily in the sphere of policy and politics.[75] It was generally London and Ludlow which dealt with Wales on these terms, and although the north–south divide did have some important administrative

68. G.H. Jenkins (ed.), *The Welsh language before the industrial revolution* (Cardiff, 1997), pp. 98–106.
69. Williams, 'Rhai agweddau ar y gymdeithas Gymreig', p. 42.
70. R. Vaughan, *British antiquities revived* (Oxford, 1662); College of Arms, London, Box 36/XX; Charles, *George Owen*, pp. 140–45.
71. *Calendar of patent rolls, 1547–8* (London, 1924), p. 163; TNA, E315/310, fo.12; E214/371.
72. Commissions for piracy and coastal defence were similarly arranged.
73. C.H. Firth and R.S. Rait (eds), *Acts and ordinances of the interregnum*, 3 vols (London, 1911), 2, pp. 976–7.
74. M.A.E. Green (ed.), *Calendar of the committee for compounding with delinquents*, 5 vols (London, 1882–92), 1, p. 172.
75. Although the inhabitants of these areas could deploy such labels polemically, as in the lobbying activities of the 'clothiers of north Wales' against the activities of the Shrewsbury Drapers' Company in the early 1620s: TNA, SP14/121/58; 14/131/21, 23; 14/134/23.

implications, much more significant in this period was the notion of a unified country of 'Wales' and, developing out of this, a wider sense of Britishness.

The notion of Welshness long pre-dated the settlements of 1284 and 1536, and continued to shape concepts of identity and loyalty throughout the early modern period. In part the idea of 'Wales' was a linguistic one, with the unifying preponderance of the Welsh language being far more significant than the dialect differences that divided it. The most common term approximating 'nationhood' in this period was iaith, which literally translates as 'language' – this was a community of language much more than one constituted by the administrative boundaries or social ties of the county.[76] Individuals could be said to personify and protect this linguistic, historical and geographical space. Thus the second Earl of Pembroke could be lauded as '*llygad holl Cymru*' ('the eye of all Wales'), and the third Earl of Worcester was presented as '*Cymro o ierll Cymru wyd ... Cymro iawn, Cymru enaid*' ('A Welshman sprung from Welsh earls ... A right Welshman, the soul of Wales').[77] Patriotism of the country trumped that of the county, and I have argued elsewhere that the cultural significance of Welshness could translate into the political arena, and may, for example, help explain the strength of civil-war royalism there.[78]

The cultural freight of early modern Welshness can be seen in the field of historical study, where a central event was the publication in 1584 of David Powel's *The historie of Cambria, now called Wales*. This was based on earlier work by Humphrey Lhuyd and provided a translation of medieval chronicles which charted the history of Wales from the time of King Cadwaladr in AD 680 down to the death of the last native prince in 1282. Powel claimed his work was intended to place the history of Wales impartially before the reader, in contrast to the 'slanderous report of such writers as in their bookes do inforce everie thing that is done by the Welshmen to their discredit'.[79] An exercise in patriotic revisionism, this work was keen to present Wales as a locus of loyalty and pride, and it enjoyed an enduring popularity as the ur-text of Welsh historiography.

In addition to providing the translation at the core of Powel's Welsh history, Humphrey Lhuyd also produced two works which are emblematic of the national Welsh allegiance articulated by many gentlemen in this period. The first of these works was a striking exercise in historical cartography – a map of Wales entitled

76. P. Schwyzer, *Literature, nationalism and memory in early modern England and Wales* (Cambridge, 2004), p. 19.

77. G.H. Hughes (ed.), *Rhagymadroddion, 1547–1659* (Cardiff, 1976), p. 114; J.G. Jones, 'Language, literature and education', in M. Gray and P. Morgan (eds), *The Gwent county history, vol. 3: the making of Monmouthshire* (Cardiff, 2009), p. 287.

78. Bowen, *Politics of the principality*, pp. 70–80, 235–78; idem, 'Representations of Wales and the Welsh during the civil wars and interregnum', *Historical Research*, 77 (2004), pp. 358–76.

79. D. Powel, *The historie of Cambria, now called Wales* (London, 1584), sig. ¶v^{r}.

'Cambriae Typus' which Lhuyd sent, along with his discussion of Anglesey, to Abraham Ortelius in 1568. The map was incorporated into an edition of Ortelius's *Theatrum* five years later.[80] This showed a distended Wales whose eastern border was the River Severn – which is to say that 'Wales' incorporated large areas of western English counties as delineated by the Acts of Union. Furthermore, Wales was divided into its three medieval regions of Gwynedd, Deheubarth and Powys, which themselves were composed of traditional divisions such as Morgannwg, Gwent and Arfon; the counties were nowhere to be seen. The reasons for what may seem like his idiosyncratic disregard of the union settlement were laid out in the second of Lhyud's works under discussion, *Commentarioli Britannicae descriptionis fragmentum*. This was published in Cologne in 1572, but was translated into English a year later by Thomas Twyne as *The breviary of Britayne*. In this work Lhuyd maintained that those who claimed the boundaries of Wales were those established at the union were describing the new region of 'Wales', not the ancient 'Cambria', which was his subject of study.[81] 'Wales', he explained, was a word imposed by the Saxons which derived from 'Welsh' or 'stranger'. The Welsh referred to themselves as 'Cymry', the inhabitants of 'Cymru'. His was thus a historical map of Cambria based on the writings of Geoffrey of Monmouth and the story of the founding of Britain by the Trojan Brutus who divided the land between his three sons, with Camber's province defined by the rivers Severn and Dee.[82] Further gradations were based on the tripartite division of Wales into three kingdoms in the ninth century, and Lhuyd's virtual tour of the country took the old *cantrefs* and *commotes* as the basic building blocks of this territory.[83] Cambria was a historical and linguistic community tied together by blood, language and common memory, a place where one found 'the very true Britaynes by birth' who 'use the Brytish tongue'. Lhuyd maintained that he was motivated in his endeavours by 'love of my country', and there is no question that in this context he was referring to Wales (or 'Cambria'). His commentary did not wholly ignore the shires, but made it clear that these were comparatively recent intrusions into a much older Welsh landscape: 'This is nowe calle[d] Caernarvon shire', 'hit … nowe of late is joyned with other and made a shire', 'Mawddwy … is nowe in Merionydh shire', 'two of these partes which are both

80. P. Schwyzer, 'A map of greater Cambria', in A. Gordon and B. Klein (eds), *Literature, mapping and the politics of space in early modern Britain* (Cambridge, 2001), pp. 35–44; F.J. North, *Humphrey Lhuyd's maps of England and Wales* (Cardiff, 1937).

81. H. Lhuyd, *The breviary of Britayne*, trans. T. Twyne (London, 1573), fo. 50. Similar sentiments were expressed by Rice Meyrick: *Morganiæ archaiographia*, p. 11.

82. On this, see P.R. Roberts, 'Tudor Wales, national identity and the British inheritance', in P.R. Roberts and B. Bradshaw (eds), *British consciousness and identity: the making of Britain, 1533–1707* (Cambridge, 1998), pp. 8–42.

83. H. Lhuyd, *Chronica Walliae*, ed. I.M. Williams (Cardiff, 2002), pp. 13–15.

Figure 4.2 Humphrey Lhuyd, Cambriae Typus (1573). By permission of Llyfrgell Genedlaethol Cymru/The National Library of Wales, MAP 1002, PB01129.

Powis and Gwenedh [Gwynedd] are at this daye callyd Northwales and devided into 6 shires' (Figure 4.2).

The discourse of Britishness which framed Lhuyd's studies was also extremely important to most Welshmen and women. This was despite the attacks on Geoffrey of Monmouth's works by Polydore Vergil in the early sixteenth century which rendered the Welsh attachment to Brutus, Troy and their version of British history decidedly suspect and even comical in England.[84] This corpus of historical lore remained a potent and practical referent of Welsh identity and was ubiquitous in early modern gentry culture. As we have seen, bardic poetry addressed to the gentry frequently discussed their status in the county, but it was often equally concerned with the patron's ancient British lineage. Individuals were variously described as 'a baron of the pure stock of Brutus ... [a] generous Briton', 'the pride of the Brythonic inheritance', and 'the mirror of Britain'.[85] Pedigrees often reached back to the lines of the ancient 'British' kings to legitimate their ancestry, gentility and status; sometimes they went back as far as Brutus himself. For example, the impressive roll produced for William Blethyn, bishop of Llandaf, in the late sixteenth century by the herald-bard Dafydd Benwyn traced his line back to Brutus (with a helpful panel going back from thence to Adam), but also contextualised him very much in a Welsh, and indeed Glamorgan-centred, milieu, with descents from kings of Morgannwg who just happened to be the founders and benefactors of Llandaf Cathedral.[86] Some, like Humphrey Lhuyd, presented themselves to the public as 'Cambro-Britons', individuals who enjoyed a dual allegiance to Wales and its broader (and more ancient) political incarnation under a British monarch. In practically all historical endeavours undertaken by Welsh scholars at this time, be they based on county, family or country, the concept of Britain was a significant presence and an important framing device.

Wales as Britain became particularly prominent in public discourse during the reign of James I. The Welsh rushed to greet him in 1603–4 as the heir of Brutus who was restoring the island to its ancient political unity. The Radnorshire lawyer John Lewis wrote a spirited defence of the Galfridian tradition and praised the king as 'the absolutest King of Britain since Brute's time', describing how he had 'conjoined and united' the historic lands of Britain.[87] The Pembrokeshire

84. T.D. Kendrick, *British antiquity* (London, 1950); W.A. Bradley (ed.), *The correspondence of Philip Sidney and Hubert Languet* (London, 1912), pp. 36–9.
85. J.G. Jones, 'The Welsh poets and their patrons, *c.*1550–1640', *Welsh History Review*, 9 (1979), p. 245.
86. Glamorgan Archives, Cardiff, CL/Ped/1. Benwyn also composed several odes of praise to Blethyn and his wife: D.H. Evans, 'The life and work of Dafydd Benwyn', DPhil thesis (Oxford University, 1982), pp. 503–11.
87. BL, Royal MS 18 A. xxxvii, fo. 6v. Cf. BL, Harleian MS 4,872; NLW, Peniarth MS 252, fos 265–374; J. Lewis, *The history of Great Britain, from the first inhabitants thereof, till the death of Cadwalader, last king of the Britains*, ed. H. Thomas (London, 1729).

clergyman George Owen Harry published a genealogy of James 'King of Great Brittayne' which traced his ancestry back to the ancient ruling houses of Britain, while his associate Robert Holland translated the king's Basilikon Doron into Welsh, observing that he was 'Brutus right heire ... one lineally descended of him'.[88] It is notable that one of the very few enthusiasts for James's British project in his first parliament was Sir William Maurice, a man who repeatedly supported proposals for full union with Scotland bestowing the title of 'King of Great Britain' on the new monarch. One bard even described him as 'the chief of the British party' ('*penn plaid Brytaniaid*').[89]

The project was an abject failure, but the concept of Britain was deployed much more fruitfully in the context of the Reformation in Wales. Here the change in religion was presented by churchmen and scholars such as William Salesbury and Bishop Richard Davies as the recovery of an ancient and pristine British faith – a national faith of the Welsh. It was thus no English innovation but rather the rediscovery of an unpolluted strain of elemental Welsh piety.[90] This seems to have elicited a genuinely enthusiastic response from the Welsh, and such appeals to the discourse of Britishness helped smooth the path of religious change there.[91] Such success seems to have derived in no small measure from the historical framing of the new faith in line with prevailing currents in Welsh popular culture.

The idea of Britain and Britishness in early modern Wales resonated with a pluralist and inclusivist patriotism. The early modern Welsh gentry did not see the tension between being Welsh and British, men of the *commote* and leaders of the county. Sir William Maurice, for example, could present himself simultaneously and without contradiction as a magnanimous freeholder of Eifionydd, an influential Caernarfonshire justice, a stout defender of Gwynedd and a proud Briton. We have come rather a long way, then, from the original framework of the county community, and yet we have not fully abandoned it. In discussing the various arenas in which identity, politics, culture and history were conceived and practised we find that the county could ramify or play a supporting role in early modern Wales. All of these arenas were concerned with the relationships between the local, the regional and the national, but the relative weight given each within a particular context varied, and further study needs to be given to this contextualisation of localism rather than Everitt's privileging of it. The occasions when such localist discourses became more strident need to be better historicised and understood, and not necessarily folded into a continuum

---

88. G.O. Harry, *The genealogy of the high and mighty monarch James ... king of Great Brittayne* (London, 1604); NLW, MS 9,853E; R. Holland, *Basilikon Doron ... fragment of a Welsh translation*, ed. J.G. Ballinger (Cardiff, 1931), sig. A4.
89. J.E. Lloyd, *et al.* (eds), *Dictionary of Welsh biography* (London, 1959), p. 624.
90. L. Bowen, 'The battle of Britain: history and Reformation in early modern Wales' (forthcoming).
91. Hughes, *Rhagymadroddion*, p. 92.

of provincial ignorance and localism. Rather, such occasions should be seen as strategic choices within a complex field of discourse.[92] The more thoroughgoing county community localism of Everitt and his followers is not convincing unless we are considering the deployment of county loyalty in local histories, rhetorical constructions of kin or its polemical deployment to safeguard the shire from taxation, military involvement or other burdens. In place of this localist–neutralist construction we should enhance our understanding of the social, political and cultural horizons of the gentry as being both more limited and more expansive depending on context.

The legitimation of gentry power was rooted in historical constructions of personality and place, and the shire had an important role to play in this process in post-union Wales. Despite being imposed by an English parliament, the shires structured Welsh social and political realities in significant ways. Although not the only domains in which the complex processes of identity formation and political practice occurred, they became increasingly significant as the institutional and conceptual structures of the Henrician union incorporated themselves into the lives of the Welsh elites. At all times, however, the shire was only one of several interconnected and often interdependent physical and imagined spaces in which Welsh gentry culture was fabricated.

---

92. Jan Broadway's chapter in the present volume is an important contribution in this respect.

5

The Restoration county community: a post-conflict culture

DAVID J. APPLEBY

In 1969 Alan Everitt joked that the rewriting of the past undertaken by families seeking to conceal embarrassing associations during the civil wars had rendered the Restoration period 'no more conducive to scholarship in the field of local history than to common sense in the field of politics'.[1] The complex historiographical debates of the English Revolution had so dominated early modern British history that few academics cared for an aftermath whose historical problems seemed trivial by comparison. Despite this, the appearance of edited collections in the 1970s demonstrated that the Restoration did have its enthusiasts, and publications began to appear on various topics.[2] By the end of the twentieth century, having attracted a critical mass of new scholars, Restoration historiography had begun to change dramatically.

The chronological boundaries of Restoration scholarship have always been elastic. Many have chosen to focus on the years from 1658 to 1667, because the period from the death of Cromwell to the fall of Clarendon was one during which the monarchy very obviously underwent a process of restoration. Others have

*   I am grateful to the British Academy for financing research visits during 2010–11, during which several sources used here were collected. Thanks are also due to Stephen Roberts, the editors, and colleagues at the Universities of Leicester and Nottingham for their comments on earlier drafts.

1.   A. Everitt, *The local community and the Great Rebellion* (London, 1969), p. 3.
2.   W. Sachse (ed.), *Restoration England 1660–1689* (Cambridge, 1971); J. Thirsk (ed.), *The Restoration* (London, 1976); J. Jones (ed.), *The restored monarchy, 1660–88* (Basingstoke, 1979); J. Miller, *Popery and politics in England, 1660–88* (Cambridge, 1973); C. Sommerville, *Popular religion in Restoration England* (Gainsville, 1977); I. Green, *The re-establishment of the Church of England* (Oxford, 1978); J. Jones, *Country and court: England 1658–1714* (London, 1978); M. Mullett, 'The politics of Liverpool, 1660–88', *Transactions of the Historic Society of Lancashire and Cheshire*, 124 (1973), pp. 31–56; J. Hurwich, 'Dissent and Catholicism in English society: a study of Warwickshire, 1660–61720', *Journal of British Studies*, 16 (1976), pp. 24–58; J. Pruett, *The parish clergy under the later Stuarts: the Leicestershire experience* (Urbana, IL, 1978); L. Glassey, *Politics and the appointment of justices of the peace, 1675–1720* (Oxford, 1979).

commenced their study in 1659 or 1660, or ended with the Declaration of Indulgence (1672), the resolution of the Exclusion Crisis (1681), the death of Charles II (1685) or the Glorious Revolution (1688–9). The Restoration has also been placed within timeframes harking back to the Interregnum or forward to the long eighteenth century. These choices and the agendas which lie behind them all carry implications for local as well as national studies.

Several trends have emerged in this new history, not least a re-evaluation of the centrality of religion in local and national political culture after 1660.[3] Restoration scholars working in political and economic history have followed the lead of civil-war historians in situating domestic issues in a British rather than an Anglo-centric context.[4] The emergence of Atlantic studies has broadened horizons further, although Clive Holmes had already noted that many ancient county families were involved in enterprises overseas.[5] An even more recent development has been the increasing collaboration between historians and scholars working in the field of post-conflict culture. Social scientists have learned that truth and reconciliation committees existed in seventeenth-century England, while historians have begun to gain new insights into the interplay of conflict and culture, not least, given the themes in this present chapter, ways in which 'conflicts challenge and rearrange pre-existing systems of cultural control', particularly 'when they encounter modes of historicisation linked closely to unifying discourses of (gendered) national identity'.[6] This in turn has fed into an even more obvious trend in the new Restoration history: a renewed emphasis on the localities.

3. For example, D. Lacey, *Dissent and parliamentary politics in England, 1660–89* (New Brunswick, NJ, 1969); T. Harris, P. Seaward and M. Goldie (eds), *The politics of religion in Restoration England* (Oxford, 1990), pp. 1–2, 4, 5. For surveys of the historiography up to 1997 from different standpoints, see V. Stater, 'Reconstructing the Restoration', *Journal of British Studies*, 29 (1990), pp. 393–401; T. Harris, 'What's new about the Restoration?', *Albion*, 29 (1997), pp. 187–222; J. Miller, *The Restoration and the England of Charles II*, 2nd edn (London, 1997).
4. Harris, 'What's new about the Restoration?', p. 189; T. Harris, *Restoration: Charles II and his kingdoms 1660–1685* (London, 2005), pp. xvii–xviii; R. Hutton, *The Restoration: a political and religious history of England and Wales 1658–1667* (Oxford, 1985), p. 5, passim; R.L. Greaves, *Deliver us from evil: the radical underground in Britain 1660–1663* (Oxford, 1986); idem, *Enemies under his feet: radicals and nonconformists in Britain, 1664–1677* (Stanford, CA, 1990); J. Morrill, 'The Britishness of the English Revolution', in R. Asch (ed.), *Three nations: a common history?* (Bochum, 1990), pp. 83–115; idem, 'Three kingdoms and one Commonwealth? The enigma of seventeenth-century Britain and Ireland', in A. Grant and K. Stringer (eds), *Uniting the kingdom? The making of British history* (London, 1995), pp. 170–90; B. Bradshaw and J. Morrill (eds), *The British problem c.1534–1707: state formation in the Atlantic archipelago* (Basingstoke, 1996).
5. C. Holmes, 'The county community in Stuart historiography', *Journal of British Studies*, 19 (1980), p. 56; C. Pestana, *The English Atlantic in an age of revolution 1640–1661* (London, 2007).
6. C. Demaria and C. Wright, 'What is a post-conflict culture?', in C. Demaria and C. Wright (eds), *Post-conflict cultures: rituals of repression* (London, 2006), p. 6.

The new history has seen the traditional preoccupation with high politics counterbalanced by a movement towards what Tim Harris has termed a 'social history of politics' – uncovering experiences of, and participation in, political processes at the level of the local community.[7] The political culture of provincial communities and their relationship with the centre has therefore come under increasing scrutiny. Whilst Harris, along with Paul Seaward and Mark Goldie, has again been a prominent supporter of this approach, this was a development anticipated by Ronald Hutton. Hutton declared his central theme in Restoration (1985) to be 'the formation and implementation of national policy, and the interplay of central and local interests in this process'.[8] His narrative of events between 1658 and 1667 was therefore presented largely through the prism of provincial sources. Pondering on the political machinations at the end of the reign in his subsequent biography of Charles II, Hutton wondered whether 'the role of central government seems so mysterious because we are looking at it from the wrong angle. The proper perspective', he suggested, 'could be from below, from the localities.'[9]

By an accident of history, the rise of Restoration studies and its concomitant emphasis on provincial political culture coincided with the demise of the county community model. Everitt and his fellow travellers had produced a body of work on the provinces that even critics acknowledged to be consistent and coherent.[10] Although criticisms of the so-called county community school have lapsed into caricature at times, it can be argued that in the 1960s the perception of English shires as semi-autonomous states governed by inward-looking, paternalistic county elites became the default starting position from which students approached issues such as allegiance, neutralism and the efficacy of royalist and parliamentarian war efforts.[11] This consensus was shattered by Clive Holmes (1980) and Ann Hughes (1985), who insisted that the county gentry of the mid-seventeenth century were inextricably integrated into a national political culture.[12] From the outset, therefore, much as the disciples of the new Restoration history

7.   Harris, 'What's new about the Restoration?', p. 189; T. Harris, 'Introduction: revising the Restoration', in T. Harris, P. Seaward and M. Goldie (eds), *The politics of religion in Restoration England* (Oxford, 1990), p. 1.
8.   Hutton, *Restoration*, p. 2.
9.   R. Hutton, *Charles II: king of England, Scotland and Ireland* (Oxford, 1989), p. 434.
10. A. Hughes, 'The king, the parliament, and the localities during the English civil war', *Journal of British Studies*, 24 (1985), p. 236; A. Everitt, *The community of Kent and the Great Rebellion 1640–60* (Leicester, 1966); J.S. Morrill, *Cheshire, 1630–1660: county government and society during the English revolution* (Oxford, 1974); A. Fletcher, *A county community in peace and war: Sussex 1600–1660* (London, 1975); J.S. Morrill, *Revolt of the provinces: conservative and radicals in the English civil war, 1630–1650* (London, 1976).
11. For example, A.M. Johnson, 'Buckinghamshire 1640 to 1660: a study in county politics', MA dissertation (University of Wales, 1963), pp. 7–8, 25–6.
12. Holmes, 'The county community', pp. 54–73; Hughes, 'The king, the parliament', pp. 236–65.

urged their colleagues to study the political culture of the English provinces, they were also encouraged to distance themselves from the now unfashionable county community school.[13] The most strident voice belonged to Tim Harris, who in a review of Restoration historiography in 1997 went so far as to declare that 'the ultimate sterility of the county community debate for the early seventeenth century did much to dampen the enthusiasm of publishers (or commissioning editors) for local studies'.[14] Such works had indeed become rare by this time, but a number of local studies had already appeared. Everitt had even included a chapter on the Restoration in his work on the community of Kent.

Everitt's interpretation of the course of the Restoration was consistent with his wider thesis: he perceived a gradual rapprochement of the divided Kentish gentry, with diehard cavaliers, moderate royalists, neuters and conservative parliamentarians inexorably drawn together by a mutual abhorrence of the regicide and fears of social revolution. The republicans on the Kent committee (such as there were) were gradually recruited as a result of their revulsion for the Protectorate. Finally, alarmed by the chaos that followed the abdication of Richard Cromwell in May 1659, moderate Cromwellians returned to the bosom of the county community, drawn by a mutual desire for stable government. Anthony Fletcher presented a similar picture in Sussex.[15] Everitt even had a plausible explanation as to why this reunification had failed to produce regime change at a national level: Booth's rising in Cheshire and plots in various other localities had failed to bring back the monarchy in 1659 because the county elites had lacked the vision to extend the process of unification beyond the boundaries of their shires. However, he believed that this shortcoming was irrelevant because a centralised Commonwealth was bound to fail. He argued that the Protectorate and the headless republican regime that succeeded it could never hope to control the provinces without the support of the traditional county gentry.[16] This was proof that the Great Rebellion (to use Everitt's chosen term) had been an internecine dispute among the gentry, temporarily hijacked by ideological hoi-polloi in the shape of the New Model Army. As the political experiments of the Interregnum became ever more desperate, gravitational forces were drawing the county gentry back together and allowing the natural order to re-emerge. The return of Charles II confirmed that equilibrium had been successfully restored; a remote and sacerdotal monarchy had returned to govern *de juro* in order that the county elites could again govern *de facto*. Fletcher wrote of Sussex that 'the county gentry flooded back into power'.[17] In Kent, after the Rump had failed to preserve

13.   Harris *et al.*, *The politics of religion*, p. 2.
14.   Harris, 'What's new about the Restoration?', pp. 198–9.
15.   Everitt, *The community of Kent*, p. 302; Fletcher, *A county community*, pp. 311–20.
16.   Everitt, *The community of Kent*, pp. 302–4.
17.   Fletcher, *A county community*, p. 321.

its authority by governing through elements of the minor gentry (because those gentlemen were themselves fatally divided along national political and ideological lines), the major county families regained their traditional hegemony by default.[18]

Having explained how the monarchy could have been restored without serious bloodshed, Everitt briefly previewed the subsequent decades. He perceived a gulf quickly opening up between those he defined loosely as 'cavaliers' and 'moderates': the former concentrating on national political affairs in parliament and court whilst the latter dedicated themselves to the good government of Kent.[19] His model predicted that tension between the centre and the Kentish gentry would thus quickly re-emerge:

> They had supported the Restoration because they wanted stable government; but they had little sympathy with the Cavalier Court. They were appointed to office because they alone had the power to govern the community. Ultimately they proved as recalcitrant to the government of Charles II as to that of Cromwell and Charles I.[20]

Everitt's Restoration epilogue reinforced his hypothesis regarding Kent in earlier decades. He conceded that the civil wars and Interregnum had changed the fabric of county society in several ways – particularly the nature of royalism. Apart from the traditionally minded squires whose paternalistic instincts still embodied the ideal of the county community, a new species of cavalier had now emerged: men more intent on furthering their personal interests by soliciting favours at Whitehall or Westminster than shouldering the mundane responsibilities of the shire. Nevertheless, Everitt contended that the main effect of the Interregnum had been to create an intense longing for traditional, local, government. Kent once again aspired to 'live a life of its own apart from the mainstream of national developments'.[21] Far from eroding the power of the traditional county gentry, Everitt believed that the Great Rebellion had confirmed it.

The view that the county gentry had emerged from the republican experiment stronger than ever would continue to be widely accepted, even by those who chose to distance themselves from the county community hypothesis per se. In his 1983 survey of the government of provincial England under the later Stuarts, G.C.F. Forster pointed out that local rulers had always received orders from the centre, but had invariably put the interests of their locality before those of the state. He argued that the expansion of the tax system initiated during the Interregnum had increased the power of the justices of the peace, an advantage which continued after the Restoration, allowing county magistrates to mitigate

---

18. Everitt, *The community of Kent*, pp. 310, 312.
19. *Ibid.*, p. 319.
20. *Ibid.*, p. 322.
21. *Ibid.*, p. 326.

or ignore government directives, even in matters of finance, security and religion. Privy councillors, hampered by the absence of traditional institutions such as Star Chamber, quickly lost interest in micromanagement and turned their attentions to international diplomacy and high politics. The county elites would be left to their own devices until the Exclusion Crisis, when Charles II found it necessary to reassert royal authority in the provinces in order to safeguard the succession.[22] Believing that the apparatus of local government had survived the Interregnum substantially intact, Forster argued that the restored monarchy had not engaged in wholesale reform but had simply weeded the magistrates' benches and council chambers, replacing dubious individuals with nominees from the leading county families.[23] He conceded that variations in the availability of politically reliable replacements had required wholesale changes of personnel in some counties and compromise in others. In Everitt's hypothesis the revival of traditional county government after the Restoration had relied on a level of consensus, mutual interest and shared identity sufficient to smooth out the ideological divisions between the gentry that had developed during the previous decades. For Everitt the unity of the leading gentry families in Kent had been demonstrated by the declaration of a broad alliance headed by Sir Edward Hales in April 1660, which had stated that in the greater interest 'all revengeful thoughts against any party or persons whatsoever' were to be repudiated and utterly abhorred.[24] But even if this was the authentic voice of Restoration Kent such magnanimity was often lacking elsewhere. In Stafford, for example, recriminations were still being exchanged by aging aldermen almost three decades after the Restoration.[25] For many cavaliers the continued presence of former rebels in county government was insufferable. As late as April 1675 Lord Aston of Tixall in Staffordshire, having been traduced for the umpteenth time as a result of his Catholicism, reflected the grievances still held by many old royalists when he confided to Sir Joseph Williamson:

> I have that pride not to bear with patience, abiding in a country where my family has been eminent twenty descents and bore always places of trust under their kings, now to be trampled on and falsely accused by such as, till their fighting against the king and buying the estates of his loyal subjects, were not in the least known.[26]

22. G.C.F. Forster, 'Government in provincial England under the later Stuarts', *Transactions of the Royal Historical Society*, 5th series, 33 (1983), pp. 32, 42–3.

23. Ibid., pp. 29–30.

24. *The declaration of the gentry of the county of Kent* (London, 1660), quoted in Everitt, *The community of Kent*, p. 312.

25. William Salt Library, S.MS 402, fos 338v–339, quoted in D.A. Johnson and D.G. Vaisey (eds), *Staffordshire and the Great Rebellion* (Stafford, 1964), p. 85.

26. Walter, Lord Aston to Sir Joseph Williamson, 3 April 1675, F.H. Blackburne Daniell (ed.), *Calendar of state papers domestic, 1675–6* (London, 1907), p. 52.

Clearly, the process of reconciliation was more easily advanced in some shires than others. It was hampered not so much by the exclusion and harassment of Catholics such as Aston as by antagonism between the various shades of English Protestantism. The provincial cavalier gentry's reverence for tradition and precedent, coupled with a keen sense of their families' sufferings and diminished social exclusivity, often defined their relations with their neighbours and by implication their identification with the interests of the 'country' round about. Naturally, attitudes varied depending on personal circumstances. Family ties, personal friendship and mutual vested interests often overcame past differences; but hostility towards former enemies was made manifest not only in private correspondence but also in more public and permanent forms. Soon after the Restoration the Lucas family in Essex and the Capels in Hertfordshire both erected memorials which were intended to declare to posterity that their relatives had been murdered by parliamentarians.[27] Many of Lord John Lucas's neighbours had been active participants in the events which had led to the executions of his brother Sir Charles Lucas, Sir George Lisle and Lord Capel.

The bitter experience of the Lucas family highlights a further obstacle to the reification of the county community: the Lucases were far from unique among royalist gentry in failing to recover the wealth and influence that they had lost during the civil wars. Many found themselves at the Restoration with insufficient resources to secure county offices which their forefathers had occupied as a matter of course. Those who managed to do so often found that their reduced circumstances prevented them from performing their duties efficiently.[28] Others were in a worse position: over 5,000 impoverished royalist officers can be seen in the 1663 List of indigent loyal officers. Hundreds more petitioned the authorities for relief.[29] Even relatives of the county elite were not immune from a plight that critics condemned as a national scandal.[30] Everitt may well have been correct in identifying a new breed of self-serving metropolitan cavalier after the Restoration, but it should not be assumed that they were motivated by ambition and greed.[31] A

27. The tombstone of Sir Charles Lucas and Sir George Lisle is still in St Giles's, Colchester. That of Lord and Lady Capel is sited beside the altar of St Cecilia's, Little Hadham, Hertfordshire.

28. For example, Sir Henry Coker, JP, in Wiltshire; P.J. Norrey, 'The Restoration regime in action: the relationship between central and local government in Dorset, Somerset and Wiltshire, 1660–1678', *Historical Journal*, 31 (1988), p. 798.

29. *A list of officers claiming to the sixty thousand pounds, etc.* (London, 1663). A sample of the petitions addressed to the Crown can be seen in Gervase Holles's Register Book of Petitions, 1660–1670, BL, Additional MS 5,759.

30. Witness the troubles of Henry Kingsmill, son of a leading Hampshire JP at the Restoration: petition of Hester Kingsmill, to the King, July 1661, HRO, 5M48/78; further petition of Hester Kingsmill to the King, 1661–2, HRO, 5M48/79; C. Hammond, *Truth's discovery; or the cavalier's case clearly stated* (London, 1664), p. 5.

31. Everitt, *The community of Kent*, pp. 320–21.

disproportionate number of indigent officers of provincial origin were recorded in the 1663 List as residing in London and Westminster, which suggests that destitution, rather than avarice, drove many provincial cavaliers into the capital. For these economic migrants as much as for those remaining in the localities, the bitter experience of financial loss and diminished local status presaged not reunification but prolonged and acrimonious division. P.J. Challinor (1982), whilst supporting the view that the leading provincial gentry had closed ranks to bring back the monarchy, observed that divisions quickly re-emerged in counties such as Cheshire.[32] That matters did not then degenerate into renewed conflict can be ascribed to the chastening memories of civil war and the unifying influence of the Crown embodied in the Act of Indemnity and Oblivion (1660).[33]

The extent to which conflict or consensus existed within the ranks of the county gentry continued to exercise the minds of those historians who ventured into the Restoration localities during the 1980s. As it was manifestly still the 'principal administrative unit' with which the central Restoration regime engaged it was inevitable that these scholars remained predicated on the structure and process of county administration.[34] Nevertheless, the county community model was no longer considered an adequate explanation of the political culture of early modern England. Stephen Roberts described the county community hypothesis as a 'suspect artefact', whilst Andrew Coleby opined that it had 'obscured more than it clarified about English politics in the 1640s and beyond'.[35] This new historiography sought to explain the government of provincial England by focusing on centre–local relations. The localities were now viewed, as Holmes had always urged, in the context of an integrated national political culture. Many of the county community historians had also moved on. Anthony Fletcher conceded that Holmes had provided a 'useful corrective against too exclusive a concentration on the county', and structured Reform in the provinces (1986) accordingly.[36]

The main arena for investigating the nature of centre–local relations remained the Commission of the Peace, which Fletcher declared to be at 'the heart of the struggles for power in the localities'.[37] The demographics of each county bench

32. P. Challinor, 'Restoration and exclusion in the county of Cheshire', Bulletin of the John Rylands University Library of Manchester, 64 (1982), p. 360.
33. R. Rudge, 'The Acts of Indemnity and Oblivion: the legal process of reconciliation', MA dissertation (Nottingham University, 2011).
34. S.K. Roberts, Recovery and Restoration in an English county: Devon 1646–1670 (Exeter, 1985), p. xi. See also P. Jenkins, The making of a ruling class: Glamorgan gentry, 1640–1790 (Cambridge, 1983); A. Coleby, Central government and the localities: Hampshire 1649–89 (Cambridge, 1987); Norrey, 'Restoration regime', pp. 789–812.
35. Roberts, Recovery and Restoration, p. 214; Coleby, Central government and the localities, p. 2.
36. A. Fletcher, Reform in the provinces: the government of Stuart England (New Haven, CT, 1986), p. 308.
37. Ibid., pp. 12, 18.

varied, but even in Sussex and Devon (where large numbers of magistrates had been removed soon after Charles II's return) the national authorities made an effort to accommodate many former enemies in the interests of continuity.[38] Fletcher concluded that in the decade that followed there were 'few omissions from the commissions, no purges and no full-scale factional struggles'.[39] There was, as Norrey observed, an 'uneasy balance between cavaliers and those with a less presentable record of service in the 1640s'.[40] In many shires former enemies were willing to coordinate their efforts against those they jointly perceived to pose a threat to law and order. Such expediency allowed the royalist Sir Courtney Pole and the conformist Presbyterian Coplestone Bampfield to patrol Devon with their respective vigilante squads.[41] In other counties divisions were more evident: the Wiltshire ex-royalist colonel and JP Sir Henry Coker was continually frustrated by 'many mongrel justices that were for Oliver, who proceed coldly and neglect duty'.[42] But Everitt's model had never required the rulers of the shire to love one another. Insofar as the studies published in the 1980s showed that those in positions of local power after the Restoration were able to put aside their differences and work together to bring peace and order (if not uniformity) to their localities, relations only needed to be sufficiently cordial to facilitate coherent government. Unlike the solidarity Everitt had perceived in Kent, however, these rulers were more often motivated by their mutual distaste for radicalism than by a spirit of forgiveness.

The conclusions reached in the county studies of the 1980s were reasonably consistent and endorsed some of Everitt's claims. Fletcher argued that the influence of the provincial gentry had proved remarkably resilient during the Interregnum, and that as a result they had been able to reassert their traditional hegemony after 1658.[43] Roberts contrasted the declining influence of the Assizes with the 'self-confidence and power' of the county justices, concluding that, unlike Interregnum regimes, Charles II's government had tamely ceded control of the localities to the county gentry.[44] In no way, however, were these 'natural rulers' uninterested in national events: they interacted fully with the national political culture, principally because (at least in the early 1660s) they saw their desire for stability as being best served by working with central government.[45] Rather than those in the provinces being dependent on the centre, Charles II's regime relied on 'the active co-operation', or at least the 'tacit support, of large

38. Ibid., pp. 18–19; Roberts, *Recovery and Restoration*, pp. 148–9; Coleby, *Central government and the localities*, pp. 90–91.

39. Fletcher, *Reform in the provinces*, pp. 19, 20.

40. Norrey, 'Restoration regime', p. 791.

41. Roberts, *Recovery and Restoration*, p. 140.

42. Quoted in Norrey, 'Restoration regime', p. 805.

43. Fletcher, *Reform in the provinces*, p. 18; see also Roberts, *Recovery and Restoration*, p. 214.

44. Roberts, *Recovery and Restoration*, pp. 141, 143, 146, 184, 186.

45. Coleby, *Central government and the localities*, p. 233.

elements of the landed classes'.[46] As Everitt had argued nearly two decades earlier, the fear of social upheaval which had unnerved increasing numbers of moderate Puritan gentry during the late 1640s had returned after the fall of the Protectorate. For Presbyterians and Anglicans alike the monarchy came to be seen as the best chance of political stability and social order. The restored monarchy subsequently profited from its perceived fragility, because the gentry were thereby all the more motivated to protect it and less inclined to challenge it. The unpalatable alternatives to monarchy prompted many to identify 'their fortunes with those of the central government in a way they had not done before the 1650s'.[47] However, both Roberts and Coleby argued that by the mid-1660s the county elite saw their interests begin to diverge from those of central government, and were ready to demonstrate (as Everitt had always claimed) that it was only possible to govern the provinces through them.[48]

There was, of course, more to governing the country than law and politics: before the civil wars provincial life had also been shaped by the legal, administrative and moral authority of the state Church. In July 1660 the link between the parishes and the centre was made abundantly clear, with each and every church required to take down the arms of the Commonwealth and replace them with those of the king.[49] Despite such symbolism, during the period in which the county community debate was in full flow historians habitually underestimated the cultural and political significance of religion. Everitt did not mention religion whilst exploring the question of allegiance in *The local community and the Great Rebellion*; neither did Clive Holmes when mounting his challenge over a decade later. Most historians had long assumed that after 1660 there had been a reaction against the excessive religiosity of the previous decades which had resulted in the secularisation of politics.[50] John Morrill would later complain that seventeenth-century attitudes to popery (and, by implication, to religion in general) had been treated by his colleagues as 'a form of "white noise", a constant fuzzy background in the rhetoric and argument of the time against which significant changes in secular thought were taking place'.[51] In *The community of Kent* Everitt presented the county community's response to the religious controversies of Charles I's reign largely through the dilemmas of Sir Edward Dering, caught between the centralising tendencies demonstrated by Laud in his desire to micromanage the Church of England and those evident in Presbyterian

---

46. Ibid., p. 88.
47. Ibid., pp. 109–10.
48. Roberts, *Recovery and Restoration*, p. 146; Coleby, *Central government and the localities*, p. 233.
49. As recorded in West Ham churchwardens' accounts, ERO, D/P265/5, fo. 103.
50. For example, Jones, *Restored monarchy*, p. 7. Douglas Lacey was an early dissenter from this view.
51. J.S. Morrill, 'The religious context of the English civil war', *Transactions of the Royal Historical Society*, 5th series, 34 (1984), p. 173.

aspirations to turn the Church into an English Kirk.[52] Everitt's dismissive attitude towards the topic of religion dovetailed with the historical metanarrative current at the time he was writing: as part of the process of restoring 'natural' order to the shires, the Restoration religious settlement had replaced the centralising doctrines of the Commonwealth not with Laudianism but with an unassuming Anglicanism which minded its own business and only required lip service on Sundays. The vast majority of nonconformists were assumed to be politically quietist, which caused nonconformity to be marginalised in the historiography and outbreaks of repression to be blamed on narrow cliques of neurotic provincial cavaliers.

The county studies of the 1980s could have challenged these assumptions, and in doing so strengthened the case for viewing English political culture in terms of centre–local relations. However, with religious history then only just beginning to re-enter the mainstream, the treatment of such issues was uneven.[53] Stephen Roberts suspected that the parochial clergy and church courts had exerted a 'highly significant influence' on Devonian society as it recovered from the civil wars, but chose not to pursue the matter.[54] Other historians alluded to religious aspects of centre–local relations but underestimated the implications of their comments. Coleby, for example, suggested that the reinstitution of episcopacy after 1660 had given the central authorities a useful lever in Hampshire, and that bishops' visitations had yielded valuable intelligence concerning religious observance and nonconformist networks.[55] Patterns of religious toleration were repeatedly utilised in these studies as a gauge of centre–local relations, leading the 1980s generation to question assumptions that the persecution of nonconformity was driven from below.[56] Although there were certainly cavalier–Anglican gentry in the provinces eager to harass nonconformists, nowhere did they have sufficient resources to eradicate nonconformity itself. Nonconformist networks survived and went on to represent a constituency that would exist independently of any gentrified county community. Similarly, the inability of the central authorities in the early years of the Restoration to curb corporations who persisted in electing persons of suspect religious leanings indicates that there were limits to their ability to impose religious uniformity

---

52. Everitt, *The community of Kent*, pp. 85–95.
53. See M. Todd (ed.), *Reformation to revolution: politics and religion in early modern England* (London, 1995), pp. 1–10.
54. Roberts, *Recovery and Restoration*, p. xiv.
55. Coleby, *Central government and the localities*, p. 131.
56. Roberts, *Recovery and Restoration*, pp. 140, 151, 184; Norrey, 'Restoration regime', pp. 803–5; A.M. Coleby, 'Hampshire and the Isle of Wight, 1649–1689', DPhil thesis (Oxford University, 1985), pp. 222–4. For orthodox views at this time, see: R. Bosher, *The making of the Restoration settlement* (London, 1957), pp. 201–4; G. Cragg, *Puritanism in the period of the great persecution, 1660–1688* (Cambridge, 1957), p. 13.

from above.[57] This was, of course, also a reflection of the fact that those at the centre – king, privy councillors, Lords and Commons – were hardly a model of religious uniformity themselves.

Preaching frequently brought parsons and congregations into close contact (and conflict) with local and national authorities. From the outset Charles II's ministers and bishops were well aware of the relationship between preaching and local opinion, and attempted to control the output of the pulpits. They sponsored parliamentary legislation, periodically ordered state homilies on obedience to authority to be read in place of normal sermons and instituted a compulsory programme of annual services and preaching to commemorate the restoration of Charles II and the 'martyrdom' of his royal father.[58] The Act of Uniformity and the subsequent mass ejection of dissenting ministers in August 1662 was a blatant example of intervention in the localities: Gilbert Sheldon, then bishop of London, set up a nationwide clearing system and a pool of candidates ready to fill the livings vacated by nonconformist ministers, whilst those facing ejection used their pulpits to posit highly critical comments on the national situation.[59] Many provincial farewell sermons were published alongside those of London ministers; indeed, provincial congregations themselves were sometimes responsible for bringing their minister's words to a national audience, demonstrating not only a readiness to participate in a national political culture but also the ability to do so.[60]

In 1987 support for the idea of a Restoration county community came from an unlikely quarter, when Ann Hughes suggested that a desire for political and societal stability had caused the gentry of Warwickshire to close ranks and coordinate their activities. This new community spirit, which she argued had revealed itself in electioneering for the Convention Parliament and efforts to secure the militia, seemed 'less qualified [than previously] by the complexity of the county's economy or the variety of relationships the gentry had with their social inferiors'.[61] In one of the few county studies to appear in the 1990s, A.R. Warmington followed a similar line, suggesting that a county community had emerged in Gloucestershire between 1660 and 1672, with justices, deputy lieutenants and tax commissioners working in unison.[62] This resonated with

57. Coleby, *Central government and the localities*, pp. 91–2; Norrey, 'Restoration regime', p. 809.
58. Starting with the Treason Act 1661 (13 Charles II. St. I. Cap. I). See J. Sawday, 'Re-writing a revolution: history, symbol and text in the Restoration', *The Seventeenth Century*, 7 (1992), pp. 171–99; A. Lacey, *The cult of King Charles the martyr* (Woodbridge, 2003).
59. D. Appleby, *Black Bartholomew's day: preaching, polemic and Restoration nonconformity* (Manchester, 2007), pp. 79, 80; Bodl., Tanner MS 48, fo. 49.
60. For example, R. Fairclough, *A pastor's legacy* (London, 1663), frontispiece; P. Lamb, *The royal presence* (London, 1662), sig. A2.
61. A. Hughes, *Politics, society and civil war in Warwickshire, 1620–1660* (Cambridge, 1987), p. 336.
62. A.R. Warmington, *Civil war, Interregnum and Restoration in Gloucestershire 1640–1672* (Woodbridge, 1997), p. 208.

earlier studies which had argued that the justices had put aside their past differences in order to provide leadership in their localities. Viewed through the prism of the Commissions of the Peace, the emergence of a semi-autonomous county community seems a plausible deduction. However, the Restoration also saw the return of the county lieutenancy, a development which would have profound implications for the localities.

In the only paragraph to mention the Restoration lieutenancy in *The community of Kent* – a tussle in 1668 between the county's lord lieutenant and one of his deputies over the financing and equipping of the militia – Everitt chose to see not a demonstration of the hegemony of central authority (in that the deputy lieutenant, Sir Roger Twysden, was forced to resign) but a victory for localism in that the argument had occurred in the first place. Surely, however, it is significant that the long-serving and conscientious Twysden, who had suffered sequestration and imprisonment during the Interregnum, could be described by the Duke of Richmond as 'troublesome, unreliable and disaffected to the royal service' because he had insisted on due process of law and respect for local custom (Figure 5.1).[63]

County historians continued to underestimate the significance of the Restoration lieutenancy until well into the 1990s. Norrey believed the system to have consisted of absentee lord lieutenants who left the supervision of county militias to lacklustre deputies, 'many of whom would rather solicit rewards for past loyalties at court than spend endless mornings in draughty provincial taverns'.[64] This was unduly harsh on provincial gentry whose fortunes had been degraded by the civil wars and who were obliged to seek additional income in order to maintain the social standing on which their effectiveness as deputy lieutenants depended. Other historians portrayed the lieutenancy as a useful point of contact between the centre and the localities, although invariably a creature of the provincial elite rather than the Crown. They saw no incongruity in noting at the same time that Charles and his Privy Council selected each lord lieutenant with care and vetted their local nominees.[65]

Victor Stater's *Noble government* (1994) demonstrated that the Restoration lieutenancy was very different in scope and character from that which had existed before the civil wars. Charles II had made the re-establishment of the lieutenancy

---

63. Everitt, *The community of Kent*, pp. 322–3. Richmond had replaced the Earl of Winchelsea in May 1668.

64. Norrey, 'Restoration regime', p. 790; see also Forster, 'Government in provincial England', pp. 41–2.

65. Roberts, *Recovery and Restoration*, pp. 140, 151–2; Coleby, *Central government and the localities*, pp. 89, 90–91; Fletcher, *Reform in the provinces*, p. 20; Warmington, *Civil war, Interregnum and Restoration*, p. 176. See also V. Stater, *Noble government: Stuart lord lieutenancy and the transformation of English politics* (London, 1994), pp. 78–9; R. Dunn (ed.), *Norfolk lieutenancy journal 1660–1676*, Norfolk Record Society, 45 (1977), p. 8. See also Challinor, 'Restoration and exclusion', p. 365.

Duke of Richmond.

Figure 5.1 Charles Stuart, Duke of Richmond (1639–1672). Special Collections of the University of Leicester, Fairclough Collection, EP42B/3/R.

a priority in 1660, appointing each lord lieutenant primarily on the basis of their commitment to Church and state.[66] Unambiguous, proactive loyalty to the Crown, rather than social cachet, was now the primary requirement of the office. Horatio Townshend, appointed in Norfolk in 1661, was one of a number of Restoration lord lieutenants who entered the office as commoners; but his impeccable cavalier–Anglican credentials were the vital qualification, and it was a simple matter to ennoble him (Figure 5.2).[67]

Letters from the Privy Council to the county lieutenancies were not merely aspirational. County officials regularly received precise orders which they were expected to carry out promptly. A communication received by the Earl of Oxford, lord lieutenant of Essex, in March 1661 included specific directions regarding the release of Quakers who had been imprisoned in response to earlier instructions.[68] Unsurprisingly, as they were now carefully vetted and closely supervised, deputy lieutenants could be extremely zealous, assessing their neighbours' ability to contribute to the financing of the militia and punishing slow payers. Such activities, as Stater points out, would have been anathema to their predecessors, and emphasised their commitment to central government (Figure 5.3).[69]

The deputy lieutenants were particularly punctilious in following directions from the centre in times of political tension. Energised by letters sent out by the Privy Council immediately after Venner's Rising in London in January 1661, Essex deputies conducted detailed interrogations of very ordinary people such as a group of former troopers whom witnesses had observed drinking together in a Braintree pub.[70] Before the civil wars such examinations would have been beneath their dignity, and would have been left to local justices. Deputy lieutenants and militia were kept extremely busy for some time after Venner's Rising, confiscating weapons and ammunition from ex-parliamentarians, administering the oaths of allegiance and supremacy and reporting their activities to the Privy Council.[71] In October 1661 Hampshire deputies received reinforcements in the shape of a troop of the King's Lifeguard, and soon after began to apprehend persons passing through their county who were wanted by colleagues in counties as far away as Monmouthshire and Herefordshire. During the Uniformity crisis of 1662 they again participated in a nationwide operation, being instructed by the Privy Council to apprehend one John Woodman and convey him to London for

---

66.   Stater, *Noble government*, pp. 6, 71, 73–4, 84–5.
67.   Dunn, *Norfolk lieutenancy journal*, p. 9; Stater, *Noble government*, p. 67.
68.   ERO, D/DEb/95, fo. 127.
69.   Stater, *Noble government*, pp. 67–8.
70.   ERO, D/DEb/95, fos 113, 115–26.
71.   For example, for Essex, ERO, D/DEb/95, fos 123–26; for Hampshire, BL, Additional MS 21,922, fos 240, 240v, 241; for Norfolk, BL, Additional MS 11,601, fo. 2 (transcribed in Dunn, *Norfolk lieutenancy journal*, p. 24); also NRO, HMN 7/223; for Huntingdonshire, Bodl. MS Carte 74, fo. 204.

Etched by W.C.Edwards.   from a Portrait at Rainham.

THE RIGHT HON, HORATIO VISCOUNT TOWNSHEND.

LORD LIEUTENANT OF NORFOLK 1660.

Figure 5.2 Horatio, Viscount Townshend (1630–1687). Special Collections of the University of Leicester, Fairclough Collection, EP36/3/332.

S. Harding Del.   London Pub. April 13. 1792. by E. Harding Fleet Street   Schencker Sculp.

AUBERY DE VERE, XX & LAST EARL of OXFORD

From an Original Picture in the Possession of the Late Geo Drummond Esq.r at Stanmore.

Figure 5.3 Aubrey De Vere, Earl of Oxford (1627–1703). Special Collections of the University of Leicester, Fairclough Collection, EP36/3/357.

questioning.[72] In Shropshire the lord lieutenant, the Earl of Newport, received similar orders for the extradition of Richard Salwey, a notable ex-parliamentarian. Newport, in acknowledging the warrant, gave the Privy Council details of Salwey's personal network and suggested further arrests.[73] At the same time as these extraditions were taking place, local authorities in areas such as Staffordshire and Chepstow were compiling lists of ex-parliamentarian soldiers and their places of abode, and forwarding details to Whitehall.[74] These and myriad other documents show that deputy lieutenants were fully cognisant of affairs outside their shire and were ready both to act instantly on orders from central authority and to coordinate their efforts with colleagues in other counties.

The lieutenancy's increasing tendency to encroach on the preserve of other county institutions was effectively legitimised by the Militia Acts of 1662 and 1663, by which justices were often required to act under the direction of the deputy lieutenants. The Militia Acts settled the rivalry between the justices and the lieutenancy by placing the militia unambiguously under the command of the latter.[75] As the king's personal representative in each county, lord lieutenants had always played an informal part in the appointment of justices and parliamentary candidates, and their influence in this regard became more marked after the Restoration.[76] If the Militia Acts indicated that the counties were increasingly coming under the thumb of the lieutenancy, the rare incidences of obduracy in the provinces serve to demonstrate the extent to which the lieutenancy was (at least initially) under the thumb of royal authority: in 1666 and again in 1667 Norfolk deputies resisted demands for money from the county – but Charles rode roughshod over their scruples.[77] Small wonder that 'by the 1670s and 1680s the time when a lord lieutenant could be counted on to defend the interests of his county neighbours against an intrusive central government was long past'.[78] Charles II had been able to establish this new, centralised lieutenancy because his regime had enjoyed a honeymoon period with the provincial landed classes. In 1660 most Presbyterian gentry agreed with their cavalier–Anglican neighbours that a restored monarchy was the surest guarantor of property. Both constituencies were fearful that revolutionary fervour still lurked among the population, particularly among demobilised soldiers, and it was this that drove

72. BL, Additional MS 21,922, fos 249, 250, 253v.
73. TNA, SP29/57, fo. 235.
74. TNA, SP29/58, fos 139–46; SP29/56, fo. 216.
75. 13/14 Car. II, c. 2; 15 Car. II, c. 4; P. Hyde and D. Harrington (eds), *Faversham Tudor and Stuart muster rolls*, Faversham Hundred Records, 3 (Lyminge, 2000), p. xxx (a reference I owe to the kindness of Duncan Harrington); M.A. Faraday (ed.), *Herefordshire militia assessments of 1663*, Camden Society, fourth series, 10 (1972), p. 7.
76. Stater, *Noble government*, p. 22; Fletcher, *Reform in the provinces*, p. 25.
77. Quoted in Dunn, *Norfolk lieutenancy journal*, p. 18.
78. Stater, *Noble government*, p. 4.

Charles' early parliaments to emphasise the authority of the Crown rather than their own. In the localities, therefore, to support the work of the lieutenancy was to demonstrate one's loyalty to the monarchy – an important consideration for a Presbyterian seeking to hang on to local office and for a cavalier–Anglican hoping to gain it. In any case, both were eager to support an institution which had the capacity to protect them from political and religious extremists.

The Exclusion Crisis, which followed the 'Popish Plot' of 1678, revived an older fear: popery. Charles had by this time lost much of his early popularity due to his repeated attempts to introduce religious indulgence. Over the same period, with the vast majority of its officers staunchly committed to the traditional Church and state, the lieutenancy had gradually come under the influence of a hardening Tory–Anglican interest. When he turned to the lieutenancy to help him secure the royal succession (which it did by organising loyalist demonstrations, intimidating the opposition and influencing the outcome of parliamentary elections) Charles became a client of the Tory party. Inheriting the obligation, James II attempted to undermine the party – not least by inserting Catholics and Dissenters into the lieutenancy – and lost his throne. If the waning of the radical threat had ever allowed the centre to leave the provincial elite to their own devices during the 1670s, the emergence of party politics and the centralised lieutenancy system pulled them back into a national political culture.

An older and stronger tie to the centre was taxation, which Fletcher rightly considered to be 'central to the relationship between the centre and the localities'.[79] Michael Braddick's fine study of parliamentary taxation (1994) endorsed the impression evident in county histories that the later seventeenth century witnessed a growth in fiscal management by the centre. Localism, he argued, 'was not in fact opposition to the state but (at its worst) an evasion of the local realities of its obligations'.[80] There were, of course, variations in the pattern in and speed with which the counties of England and Wales were persuaded to acknowledge these obligations. In contrast to the fiscal triumph discerned by Coleby in Hampshire during the 1660s and 1670s, Norrey argued that tax-gathering in south-western counties was 'characterized by inefficiency, corruption and even opposition'.[81] However, even in these localities the state was frequently able to intimidate obstructive justices, and responded to erratic performance by transferring tax-gathering responsibilities successively from local officials (torn between the locality and their duty to the Crown) to county receivers, to tax farmers (very often London merchants and financiers) and finally to centralised tax offices and customs houses. C.D. Chandaman, noting the 'increase in

---

79. Fletcher, *Reform in the provinces*, p. 360.
80. M. Braddick, *Parliamentary taxation in seventeenth-century England: local administration and response* (Woodbridge, 1994), p. 296.
81. Norrey, 'Restoration regime', p. 796; Coleby, 'Hampshire and the Isle of Wight', pp. 210–14.

efficiency in all the main branches of revenue administration' during the course of Charles' reign, has concluded that the king's problems with finance were less to do with raising tax (particularly after 1670) than with inherited economic problems and imprudent spending.[82] The county receivers, sub-commissioners and sub-farmers were invariably local men, but their introduction perhaps represented an earlier, more decisive shift to centralisation than has sometimes been appreciated. Many tax officials, such as Captain Henry Lester in Somerset and Colonel Edmund Chamberlain and Colonel Thomas Veel in Gloucestershire, were deserving ex-royalist officers. It would be useful to establish how many of their former comrades were similarly employed, not least because the frequently acrimonious exchanges between Lester, Veel and Chamberlain and their respective localities indicate that all three men identified with the centre rather than the county.[83] County elites were informed that it was their patriotic duty to acquiesce to such developments in order to avoid the kind of divisions that had previously led to civil war.[84]

The impetus for fiscal centralisation came as a direct consequence of the previous 20 years of conflict. From the outset the newly restored regime needed almost £1 million to pay off the old Cromwellian army and reduce the navy. Apart from posing an obvious military threat, the armed forces represented a huge tax burden. It was in the interests of the new regime to alleviate this burden, particularly as it was widely assumed that the restoration of monarchical government would mean a return to pre-civil-war levels of taxation – an expectation which had caused many to welcome Charles' return. This would turn to widespread resentment when the hated excise was retained and schemes such as the hearth tax were instituted to ensure the financial survival of the monarchy. The poll tax of 1660–61 was a harbinger of things to come, being conceived and coordinated by the centre to fund a national objective. The initial arrangements to finance demobilisation were rushed, the revenue required was grossly underestimated and even after the main Act for disbanding the army had been passed in August 1660 many of those appointed as local commissioners were mystified as to their duties.[85] Furthermore, although most taxpayers wanted to see the back of Cromwell's army many were reluctant to pay for it. These faltering beginnings have led some historians to believe that local commissioners and taxpayers, although recognising the necessity of the government initiative, were relatively free from coercion.[86] That Hampshire had made no contributions by the

82. C. Chandaman, *The English public revenue 1660–1688* (Oxford, 1975), pp. 273–7.

83. Norrey, 'Restoration regime', pp. 797, 799; Warmington, *Civil war, Interregnum and Restoration*, pp. 203–5.

84. Norrey, 'Restoration regime', pp. 799, 802, citing Wiltshire Record Office, A1/150/11, Michaelmas 1667; Somerset Record Office, Q/SR/127/44; 131/31; TNA, T54/6/117–18.

85. For example, Lancashire Record Office, DDKE/acc 7848.

86. Coleby, *Central government and the localities*, p. 118.

end of October Coleby ascribes largely to the reluctance of the new regime to deploy soldiers to enforce collection and a certain amount of complacency as regards the unpaid army.[87] However, Hampshire did ultimately pay up, and more coercion may have been used there than surviving archives suggest. The central authorities were brusque enough when dealing with other counties: Kentish commissioners had already been advised that it was in their interests to expedite matters quickly in order to avoid having soldiers billeted in the county at free quarter.[88] In November, a parliamentary committee allotted the cost of disbanding O'Neil's and Ingoldsby's regiments to specific towns and counties in the West Country, the East Midlands and East Anglia. That the regiments in question had already been quartered in these same localities proves that free quarter was not an empty threat.[89]

Some £8 million was collected in taxes during the 1660s alone.[90] Given that this was extracted from an economy which had suffered grievously during the upheavals of the previous 20 years, this was indeed a fiscal triumph – but not for the provinces. The depleted finances of so many of the provincial gentry, the degradation of infrastructure and the desperate financial needs of thousands of incapacitated soldiers, war widows, orphans and others whose lives had been ruined by the wars posed intense economic challenges in many localities. In times past the paternalistic instincts of the county elite would have impelled them to protect their 'country' from heavy centralised taxes. After the Restoration, although the county elite were uncomfortable with increasingly centralised tax regimes, the trauma of civil war had reduced their will – and their ability – to resist. The detailed records of the poll tax of 1660–61, and the government's success in raising the huge amounts of money needed, do not suggest the emergence of a confident, independent provincial gentry so much as the reification of a determined and often ruthless centre.[91]

Governmental interest in the plebeian population was not confined to picking their pockets. In this respect, the Compton census of 1676 should be seen in the context of earlier surveys of parliamentarian veterans and the activities of the lieutenancy. Although Henry Compton, bishop of London, was appointed to oversee the project, it had been conceived by the Lord Treasurer. The Earl of Danby's purpose in surveying the nationwide distribution of papists and

87. Ibid., pp. 118, 125.
88. CKS, U1107/C30.
89. BL, Additional MS 36,832, fos 74v–75v.
90. Coleby, *Central government and the localities*, p. 117.
91. For example, TNA, E179/311/57 (Buckinghamshire poll tax returns for the disbanding of the army); E179/272/2 (Hertfordshire returns); E179/323/11 (Caernafonshire and Cheshire returns); E179/176/555 (Hampshire, Andover division returns); E179/321/29 (Anglesey returns). See also, for example, corresponding documents in Buckinghamshire Record Office, D/LE/17/3–6 (army poll tax assessments for various divisions and hundreds of Buckinghamshire, 1660–64).

nonconformists was to confirm that sufficient military resources existed to suppress any resistance should the penal laws be enforced more aggressively.[92] Ironically, Danby's plans to do this were derailed by subsequent events, not least because he overreached himself and lost his grip on the lieutenancy. The inconsistent quality of the census and the government's failure to act on its findings does not detract from its significance as a barometer of centre–local relations. Stephen Roberts has argued with reference to the Interregnum that '"centralization", if it means anything in this period, means the acquisition by government of a more finely tuned awareness of the behaviour of citizens.'[93] The Compton census and the veterans' lists demonstrate that the Restoration regime was extremely ambitious in this respect.

Events during the previous 20 years had left the authorities in no doubt that the plebeian population was capable of thought and agency. Indeed, politicians such as Arlington and Danby habitually exploited the gentry's anxieties in this regard to bolster support for their national policies. However, with notable exceptions such as David Underdown and Richard Greaves, historians have not always taken these anxieties as seriously as they might.[94] One of Holmes' criticisms of Everitt was that the latter had underestimated the extent to which the middling and poorer sorts were 'perfectly capable of forming political opinions and of expressing them forcibly in action, independent of the gentry'.[95] In fairness, no historian of Everitt's generation ever denied the fact that the general population might have political opinions. J.R. Jones, indeed, drew attention to the comments of foreign visitors during the early modern period, who 'were astonished by the interest shown in state affairs by ordinary people, including many who had no votes in parliamentary elections'.[96] News was greedily consumed at every social level, whether delivered from the parish pulpit, in travellers' gossip at the local inn or in printed pamphlets read out in the market place or alehouse. Such inquisitiveness had been encouraged during the civil wars, as royalists and parliamentarians competed for hearts and minds in order to sustain their respective war efforts. Large numbers of soldiers and civilians had travelled widely during the conflict, with a resulting impact on their

92. See A. Whiteman, 'The Compton census of 1676', in K. Schurer and T. Arkell (eds), *Surveying the people: the interpretation and use of document sources for the study of population in the later seventeenth century* (Oxford, 1992), pp. 78–96.

93. S.K. Roberts, 'Local government reform in England and Wales during the Interregnum: a survey', in I. Roots (ed.), *'Into another mould': aspects of the Interregnum*, 2nd edn (Exeter, 1998), p. 63.

94. D. Underdown, *Revel, riot and rebellion: popular politics and culture in England* (Oxford, 1985); idem, *A freeborn people: politics and the nation in seventeenth-century England* (Oxford, 1996); Greaves, *Deliver us from evil*; idem, *Enemies under his feet*. See also B. Manning, *Aristocrats, plebeians and revolution in England 1640–1660* (London, 1996).

95. Holmes, 'The county community', p. 72.

96. Jones, *Restored monarchy*, p. 4.

mental horizons.[97] The interrogations conducted by deputy lieutenants and justices suggest that the middling and poorer sorts were more minded than ever to involve themselves in matters beyond their immediate locality and to embrace abstract ideologies. For many such people, 'county' and 'country' were no longer necessarily synonymous terms.

Newton Key went some way towards uncovering an alternative provincial mentality in articles published in 1994 and 1995. These focused on county feasts held regularly in London during the later seventeenth century by exiles from western and midland counties living and working in the capital, and events held in the counties themselves. The merchants and displaced middling sort who attended the London events articulated a shared cultural identity, which incorporated an intense inter-county rivalry with an unmistakable sense of county community. In the process of doing this, Key argued, the feasters laced their political rhetoric with an embryonic Tory partisanship.[98] Published accounts of these county feasts propagated the view that stable national government was grounded in well-defined, consensual county communities. Perceived threats to this 'natural' order, from Presbyterians to Quakers, were regularly excoriated in the feast sermons.[99] Members of the county elite frequently attended as guests of honour and as late as 1680 Worcestershire and Herefordshire exiles were still being urged by feast organisers to donate money for the relief of 'loyal ex-Cavalier sufferers' in their native counties.[100] However, Key argued that although the feasters thereby appeared to be promoting the hegemony of the county gentry, the very act of organising county feasts and charitable donations served to bring 'the politics of association to social groups at the margins of the governing elite'.[101] The fact that the virtues of localism could be propagated by groups so closely connected with the commercial life of the capital is particularly poignant. If the notion of the county community has thus enjoyed an extended lease of life through Key's work, it has taken a very different path from that which Everitt and his colleagues envisaged.

A recent survey has indicated that some 540,000 people died in the British civil wars. In England and Wales (whose populations suffered proportionately less than those of Scotland or Ireland), Ian Gentles estimates the per capita loss to have been almost twice that of the First World War.[102] If the trauma of that

---

97. Witness the contributions of 'Bedfordshire man', 'Buffcoate' and 'Agitator', to the Army debates of 1647; C.H. Firth (ed.), *The Clarke papers*, 1 (London, 1992), pp. 235, 236, 251, 273, 276, 349.

98. N. Key, 'The political culture and political rhetoric of county feasts and feast sermons, 1654–1714', *Journal of British Studies*, 33 (1994), p. 224; idem, 'The localism of the county feast in late Stuart political culture', *Huntington Library Quarterly*, 58 (1995), p. 217.

99. Key, 'Political culture', p. 231.

100. Ibid., pp. 245–6.

101. Ibid., p. 225.

102. I. Gentles, *The English revolution and the wars of the three kingdoms, 1638–1652* (Harlow, 2007), pp. 436–7.

conflict is still etched in the modern psyche, Restoration communities were far more deeply affected and immeasurably more divided by the civil wars of the mid-seventeenth century.[103] Given these factors, not least the divisions caused by the cultural shock of the regicide, the idea that the Restoration somehow represented a return to 'normality' is bizarre. The maimed, the bereaved, the traumatised and the indigent were everywhere to be seen, visible reminders of the troubled past in communities burdened by heavy taxation, damaged local economies and degraded infrastructure.

If, as has been claimed, the Restoration saw elite county families recover their former wealth and position in the provinces, they were still hamstrung in many counties by tensions between ex-parliamentarians and embittered cavalier–Anglicans. Fears of radicalism and dissent encouraged the provincial gentry to cooperate with central government in order to ensure stability in their localities. Their feelings of insecurity were understandable: the common people had been exposed to unfamiliar stimuli and new ideas; plebeians had not only seen and participated in attacks on and humiliation of members of the gentry, but had been actively encouraged to do so. Such experiences had not transformed the middling and poorer sorts into a revolutionary proletariat; nevertheless, many had never lived under a functioning monarchy in their adult lives. Certainly, enough were known to be disaffected for Charles II and his ministers to desire a new model lieutenancy and a reorganised militia in order to police the localities. In the pursuance of this objective, the lesser gentry and yeomanry had a vital role to play in the parishes and hundreds. Further research is required on these so-called 'local elites', not least because the state of their personal finances and the extent of their willingness to act as agents for the centre might yet prove key to understanding changes in centre–local relations between 1660 and 1689.

It is a mark of the residual influence of the county community model that so many studies since the 1960s have continued to underplay the extent to which Charles II's ministers were able to intervene in the provinces. Having said this, they did not have the capacity to micromanage every aspect of provincial life, nor was it necessary to do so, provided each county remained secure, stable and willing to pay its taxes. The civil wars and Interregnum had affected local communities in different ways, and as a consequence each faced the Restoration with a different (sometimes very different) cultural legacy. Towns such as Taunton and Lyme actually continued to celebrate the anniversary of their deliverance from royalist sieges.[104] Such popular historicism, though it provoked alarm in the cavalier–Anglican press, was invariably designed to provide those communities with comfort and certainty, both instinctive priorities in a world where conflict had

---

103. See, for example, R. Gough, *The history of Myddle*, ed. D. Hey (Harmondsworth, 1981), pp. 71–5.
104. R. L'Estrange, *Toleration discuss'd* (London, 1663), p. 70.

inevitably obliterated both.[105] On the other side of the hill, the county feasts were one way in which provincial cavalier–Anglicans could provide themselves with equal comfort and certainty. A more neutral solution, as Everitt observed in Kent, was for a community to retreat into its shell. But the tranquil rhythm of life discernible in local administrative records is often misleading: at the same time as reassuringly mundane alehouse licences and recognizances were being issued by the authorities in New Romney and Folkestone, justices attending county quarter sessions were required to grapple with problems arising directly from the civil wars and national regime change.[106] The post-conflict culture of the Restoration developed along lines which would be instantly recognisable to those studying the aftermath of more recent conflicts: the restored monarchy was reproduced and consolidated by inscribing the memory of the civil wars and regicide into both local and national culture. This meant, among other things, that after 1660 the harder local communities tried to pretend that life had returned to 'normal', the more apparent it became that much had changed.

105. See modern parallels in Demaria and Wright, *Post-conflict cultures*, p. 7.
106. East Kent Archives, NR/J/Q/1; Fo/JQ1/1; CKS/Q/SO/E1, fos 66v, 68v; CKS/Q/SO/W1, fo. 71.

Conclusion
County counsels: some concluding remarks

STEPHEN K. ROBERTS

The essays in this volume demonstrate that whatever the limitations of Everitt's original thesis may have been, historians studying early modern society and its relationship to the concepts and practice of governance must still reckon with the county. Ian Warren reminds us that 'many gentry did at least acknowledge a strong loyalty to the unit of the shire', Jan Broadway argues for the symbolic importance of the county community in the minds of the gentry, and Jacqueline Eales's discussion of the petitioning that went on in Kent between 1640 and 1649 shows how political activity was orchestrated on a county basis. Lloyd Bowen challenges Everitt's 'privileging' of the county among the 'interconnected and often interdependent physical and imagined spaces of Welsh gentry culture', and it is the monarchy, rather than the county, which seems the dominant entity in David Appleby's account of the Restoration, but even so, both argue for the continuing relevance of the county as a factor to be reckoned with.

There was an irreducible core of political activity common to every county in England and Wales, before, during and after the trauma of civil war. Annually a high sheriff was chosen from a shortlist of usually three in each county by the king or his advisers. The sheriff was responsible for collecting dues to the crown and played an important part in meetings of the assizes when the judges visited the county. He was the returning officer at parliamentary elections for the shire and was in charge of ensuring that writs and returns were made in elections for the boroughs. The commission of the peace was compiled on a county-by-county basis, and was an index of status for the gentry in each shire.

The militia, the most important military entity capable of a rapid turn-out, was under the overall direction of the lord lieutenant of each county, with under him a body of deputy lieutenants. By the 1640s it was common practice for each county to employ a muster master, whose task it was to drill the militia. This was not really an equivalent of the marginal territorial army, still less was it a faintly absurd Home Guard in which military-minded civilian men turned out to run around in woods at weekends. As a recent study of the early seventeenth-century militia in Monmouthshire by Tony Hopkins has shown, the militia made demands of everybody, including women.[1] The gentry had to provide men, horses and arms and were often commissioned in it as officers; the middling sort had to pay towards items of arms and armour, and the labouring sort contributed brawny manpower. Wives and widows could find themselves burdened with providing, or at least funding, muskets and calivers for the menfolk's muster drilling. David Appleby's essay shows how historians have tended to underestimate the significance of the militia, and demonstrates how after 1660 its potential as a reliable agency of the monarchy came to be realised. Its officer cadre was finely tuned according to its demonstrated political loyalties, but its pre-1640 collectivist antecedents and the militarising process of the 1640s and 1650s all contributed towards making it the perfect vehicle for harmonising social relations in the interests of the restored monarchy.

When we consider the ineluctable demands of the state on propertied individuals in early modern society, in terms of taxation and labour demands such as mustering for the militia or repairing roads and bridges by the direction of county quarter sessions courts, the primacy of the county in thinking about one's place in society is undeniable, at least as far as secular obligations went. Even the unpropertied were affected. As is well known, the unit of poor law administration was the parish, but the provision of such housing for the poor as existed, houses of correction or workhouses, was a county responsibility, and every kind of appeal on poor law matters went from the parish to the county and usually no higher.

In this world of county administration, in which office as well as an impressive and ancient coat of arms was a mark of prestige, status was defined by appropriate public conduct. Thomas Gerard, a contemporary commentator on Somerset in the 1630s, picked up on the way Sir John Wyndham of Orchard Wyndham did not seem to be taking his social obligations seriously. Wyndham, a justice of the peace, made Orchard Wyndham 'the chief place of his abode, in which he strives rather to please his affection than to suit himself according to his rank'.[2] A twentieth-century historian picked up on this example of a gentry figure not conforming to social expectations in a study that preceded Everitt on Kent: that by T.G. Barnes, an American historian, on Somerset 1625–40. We might here incidentally remind ourselves that Everitt was not the first academic historian of early modern England in the twentieth century to focus on a county. There was a strong modern tradition of studying counties BE: Before Everitt. This was a product partly of university expansion and a rise in the numbers of trained

1.   T. Hopkins (ed.), *Men at arms: musters in Monmouthshire, 1539 and 1601–2*, Publications of the South Wales Record Society, 21 (2009).
2.   T. Gerard, *The particular description of the county of Somerset, 1633*, ed. E.H. Bates, Somerset Record Society, 15 (1900), p. 27, quoted by T.G. Barnes, *Somerset 1625–1640: a county's government during the 'personal rule'* (Cambridge, MA, 1961), p. 24.

historians, but also of the emergence of county councils in 1889, which took their county records seriously.

We should remember that county councils themselves published records: the Warwickshire series of edited quarter sessions records, for example, appeared between the wars. From the same time, just before the Second World War and then strongly just after it, dated the creation by county and city councils of record offices. A third influence in the 1950s and 1960s was a strong and visible county tradition itself. Before the successive waves of local government reorganisation from 1974, before the building of edge-of-town council offices which followed, and before the scepticism that recent governments of both main parties have shown towards local government, county towns were in many if not all counties very visibly the material expression of an unbroken county culture, only weakening in our own time in the early decades of the twenty-first century. Lloyd Bowen's essay brings out strongly the concept of loyalty to the Welsh shires, artefacts that are (in historical terms) relatively recent. He shows how the county was one of a number of 'discursive fields' in which the Welsh gentry lived their cultural, social and political lives. It is interesting to note that Monmouthshire, arguably the most problematic and most argued-over of Welsh counties because of its structural Janus face, looking towards both England and Wales for its institutional models, was in fact the one to produce the most thorough and substantial history on a grand scale: the monumental History of Monmouthshire, by Sir Joseph Alfred Bradney (1859–1933).

Most counties in England established county record societies in the late nineteenth century or the first quarter of the twentieth. Wales was slower, and as late as the 1950s only two of the pre-1974 counties could claim their own single-county societies. The editing and study of records for Wales as a whole, either generally, as in the publications of the University of Wales Board of Celtic Studies, or in specific-interest bodies, such as the Historical Society of the Church in Wales, was much stronger. Perhaps this alternative model of the county as one of a number of entities competing for cultural loyalty helps explain why Welsh historians did not rush to emulate or challenge Everitt's county orientation. Nevertheless, there was a great deal of material for academic historians of counties to build upon when they started work, and Everitt's predecessors as county historians of the early modern period who assumed a degree of primacy in the county as a meaningful community included, as well as Barnes, A.L. Rowse, Mary Coate and A.C. Wood.[3] The rationale for studying counties as units of government and of representative politics, especially parliamentary politics, cannot be attributed to Everitt, major although his contribution turned out to be.

3.   A.L. Rowse, Tudor Cornwall, 2nd edn (London, 1969); M. Coate, Cornwall in the great civil war and Interregnum: a social and political study, 2nd edn (Truro, 1963), A.C. Wood, Nottinghamshire in the civil war (Oxford, 1937).

Jan Broadway argues in this volume that the county gentry 'belonged to an imagined community ... which grew out of a perceived affinity based on shared values', a view which Lloyd Bowen's essay broadly endorses. Most notions of community do depend on perceived affinity to be meaningful, whether we are discussing the early modern gentry or the miners during the strike of 1984–5. Some of the efforts of the county historians who wrote in the sixteenth and seventeenth centuries to position themselves in the county community were somewhat laboured. Thomas Habington's list of dedicatees for his work on Worcestershire, which Jan Broadway mentions, illustrates this. Baron Coventry was the son of a lawyer who had bought his estate only in 1592; the tenth Earl of Shrewsbury was a Catholic who acquired the title only because another branch of the family had died out; Baron Windsor had been forced by Henry VIII to surrender his demesne in return for abbey lands; Sir William Devereux was the illegitimate half-brother of the third Earl of Essex and spent all his life in the Essex household. Sir Richard Berkeley, the ship money judge who notoriously brought in a verdict in favour of Charles I, was the son of a clothier who bought, rather than inherited, Spetchley Park, near Worcester. Not one of the five conformed to the definition of gentry, with deep and ancient roots in landed property in their county, which would have satisfied the Devon historian Thomas Westcote. Westcote, writing in the 1630s, denounced these newly arrived type of people as

> upstart golden asses, whose niggardly covetous fathers have infatuated with an insolent arrogancy, by leaving them a mass of ill-gotten wealth ... their gentility hangs as ill on them as if they had borrowed it of some near-like name, or bought it with their pennies; and then fret if they be not saluted with 'your worship'; vouchsafing faint salute to their honest poor kindred; casting a squinting eye on their equals; yea vaunting themselves above their betters ... if some able pen were at leisure to undertake against such mushrooms, dipped in strong satirical ink, it would soon embowel these windpuff bladders ... and restore worship to his right seat and habitation ...[4]

Here we have two historians writing at much the same time who have quite different perspectives on the county societies they wrote about. For Westcote, Devon was a county much invaded by lawyers and merchants, whose new wealth threatened to destabilise older values of gentility. His book is a prose equivalent of Ben Jonson's poem, 'To Penshurst', which in similar terms denounced the upstarts and their new houses, 'proud, ambitious heaps', in contrast to the values of community and neighbourliness upheld at Penshurst Place by the Sidneys. For Habington, writing in a county where he, as a Roman Catholic, was at least partly an outsider, the arriviste and somewhat contorted gentility of his

4.   T. Westcote, *A view of Devonshire in 1630*, eds G. Oliver and P. Jones (Exeter, 1845), pp. 451–2.

dedicatees was invisible. As E.H. Carr said: 'Study the historian before you begin to study the facts.'[5]

Jan Broadway points out that only one county history was published between 1620 and 1640. The work of others, including that of Thomas Westcote, was circulated in manuscript, in a tradition of scribal publication that ran in parallel to work in print. Given the number of manuscript county histories written at this time that had to wait until the eighteenth century to find their way into print, we need to explore the motives of those who took the minority route to London to find a bookseller and someone willing to take the financial risk involved in publishing anything. If you judged your readership to be the tightly defined county community you were writing about, the safer option would be to circulate copies within your county among the readership about whose mores, houses and ancestors you were writing. The best-evidenced example of the county historian deeply in the grip of an urge to publish in print is of course William Dugdale, and Jan Broadway and others are doing much to illuminate how he operated. In Dugdale's case it is impossible to separate completely the business practice from the intellectual motives in his modus operandi. In his books, the engravings were paid for by subscriptions from the individuals and families he targeted, and provided a cushion against financial disaster as well as financing attractive volumes. Jan's point that in the 1650s county histories provided a rallying point for a wide spectrum of those out of sympathy with republican and Cromwellian regimes is intriguing. The London publishing industry during the 1650s does seem to have taken interesting and perhaps surprising turns. County histories are not the only kinds of Interregnum publication whose underlying themes were towards amity, community or the contemplative life. Isaak Walton's The compleat angler (1653) and John Beale's discourse on Herefordshire cider, Herefordshire orchards: a pattern for all England (1658), can all be included in this category. In this last work, those gentry figures in Herefordshire experimenting with fruit-growing are described as 'admirable contrivers for the public good' from whom the author hopes that 'a worthy patriot will break through the difficulties of an obstructive people' to tackle the county's problems of poverty and godlessness.[6]

To find satisfactory explanations for why certain manuscripts were turned into products in London booksellers we need to consider the links between metropolitan and provincial literate culture which Ian Warren's essay illuminates so helpfully: what he describes as the process of negotiation between metropolitan and local influences and loyalties. Publishing involved a series of business transactions and technical processes in London and hardly anywhere

5.   E.H. Carr, *What is history?* 4th edn (Basingstoke, 2001), p. 17.
6.   J. Beale, *Herefordshire orchards: a pattern for all England* (London, 1658), p. 40.

else, but all the processes involved what Ian describes as a two-way exchange between local and national, urban and rural. John Beale's work on cider is an interesting example of how these processes might operate. The book is advertised as the product of a continuing dialogue between himself and the polymath Samuel Hartlib. It contains some generalised expressions of hope for a 'worthy patriot' from Herefordshire to solve the county's problems. Superficially, the book reads as a rather attractive horticultural manual, with a dash of local piety. Beale's surviving unpublished correspondence with Hartlib, from which the book emerged, reveals him to have been a more sophisticated individual than his book itself would suggest: a man who took a keen and detailed interest in politics, who could discuss in a letter to Hartlib the proposed functions of Richard Cromwell's second chamber in parliament, and refer to its members as 'moral and rational efficients' – not the language of a provincial backwoodsman. Yet it remains primarily a book about cider, with the political messages muted or subliminal.

We need to know more about these provincial writers whose books were not expressly about politics. What were their motives for following the trail to London to get their books published? Jan Broadway detects an upsurge in county history publishing during the rule of the major generals. Was this a response to the clamp-down by the state or to the divisiveness it caused? Or is it rather a commentary on the comparatively liberal approach towards the London publishing industry shown by the Cromwellian regime? County pride was evidently not just about publishing books. Newton Key has located the origins of county feasts, discussed in this volume by David Appleby, to precisely the time when Dugdale and Daniel King were active and when William Lambarde's *Perambulation of Kent* was reissued. Most county feasts were meetings of gentry in London. They were dinners at which charity collections were made, and they were usually, if not invariably, preceded by a sermon. Their historian has attributed the rise of the feasts in the mid-1650s to social anxieties about the rise of Quakers and Ranters, and their format is an illustration both of the metropolitan/provincial relationship Ian Warren discusses and of the importance of the clergy as social commentators.[7]

But to return to Alan Everitt. His book on Kent was not simply arguing that loyalty to one's county was a driving force among those who lived in provincial society. The essentials of his thesis were:

A: the semi-autonomy of counties, which he called 'partially independent states';
B: the particularism of Kent, which he characterised as an insular society;

7.   N.E. Key, 'The political culture and political rhetoric of county feasts and feast sermons, 1654–1714', *Journal of British Studies*, 33 (1994), pp. 223–56; idem, 'The localism of the county feast in late Stuart political culture', *Huntington Library Quarterly*, 58 (1996), pp. 211–37.

C: the primacy of loyalty to local society in political terms, which manifested itself in 1640 as a shallow opposition to Charles I because local society was merely reacting to the king's innovations; shallow support for parliament during the civil war because local society was merely reacting to parliament's innovations; and during the 1650s as a sullen backward-looking enduring, and a longing for old ways.

Everitt's first published work on Kent was the study of the county committee of Kent during the first and second civil wars, published in 1957 as an Occasional Paper by the department of local history in Leicester. It appeared in the same year as the edition of the Staffordshire county committee order book edited by Donald Pennington and Ivan Roots, and both works represent an exposition of the worlds of the county committees that have never really been surpassed. Everitt's paper became Chapter 5 of the larger book and, for me at least, his study of the county committee remains the valuable core of his work because it was based on a detailed study of certain manuscript materials in the National Archives which were then only really beginning to be subject to the scrutiny of scholars. As a study of how a county committee operated it still has much to commend it. The main arguments of the Everitt thesis have fared less well. In particular, the concept of the counties as 'partially independent states' now seems exaggerated and unconvincing, as all the historians writing in this volume would agree.

Jacqueline Eales's essay reminds us of how Everitt's work needs to be located within a strong tradition of writing on Kent. It has to be remembered that Everitt was reacting to the common view of Kent, presented in the seventeenth century as well as the twentieth, as 'largely an offshoot of London'. He was seeking to present Kent as rather more interesting than that. He presented it as a region where partible inheritance still exercised some purchase, and where transhumance, the movement of cattle and sheep from marsh to downs according to the season, was still practised. He sought to present a pattern of 'slow organic growth ... in the hamlets of the Downland, with their small and lonely churches, flint-strewn fields and woods of yew and whitebeam'.[8] In passages like that, in their sensitivity to landscape and its impact on human society, the influence on Everitt of W.G. Hoskins is evident. Hoskins's influence is suggested too in Everitt's characterisation of his own times, the swinging 1960s, as marked by 'laxity and indifferentism'.[9] That could as well be Hoskins as Everitt speaking, and the *obiter dictum* allows a rare insight into Everitt the man. But when the uniqueness of Kent's landscape is granted, and the validity of studying counties as political units is confirmed, the idea that counties were 'partially independent states' will not stand up to serious scrutiny. Even in my research on a county where partible

8.   A. Everitt, *The community of Kent and the Great Rebellion 1640–60* (Leicester, 1966), p. 24.
9.   Ibid., p. 54.

inheritance and transhumance had a far stronger grip on society than they did in Kent, geographically remote Cardiganshire, I was surprised to find how readily the gentry there resorted to the London law courts, got together to socialise in the capital, successfully attracted the royal mint to Aberystwyth during the reign of Charles I and had a good smattering of prominent English incomers such as the Stedmans of Strata Florida and Katherine Phillips, the epistolary poetess, the Matchless Orinda, among their luminaries.[10]

Eales shows us how historians writing after Everitt were able convincingly to criticise the key elements of his argument. Ian Warren, too, points out how Clive Holmes, for example, found plenty of examples of the use of the word 'country' to describe the national political interest rather than the county. We could add another challenge to Everitt's dictum that country meant county. It could also mean region or district or *pays*, to adopt the French word that another distinguished director of the Leicester department, Charles Phythian-Adams, was later able to make much use of in his work on English regional identities.[11] Everitt's handling of the evidence relating to those who were not of the gentry class was somewhat uncertain, as David Appleby shows. He argued with perhaps pardonable hyperbole that Kent society saw itself as 'all one family'.[12] Yet he also presented evidence that the county committeemen, from a lower social rank than those they subjected to sequestration, were diligent, hard-working and committed to the parliament whose diktats they were obeying. He presented evidence that the family histories in Kent of these lesser figures were 'post-Tudor' compared with those of the greater gentry, but the evidence was neither plentiful nor convincing.

As Jacqueline Eales demonstrates in her essay, there is scope for further work on social and political allegiances in Kent. Her discussion of the wave of petitioning in Kent between 1640 and 1642, and again in January 1649, offers a fresh agenda for work on that county. The process by which signatures were harvested for petitions is little understood. Work currently in progress by John Walter is looking at how the 'Protestation' of May 1641, an affirmation of support for parliament in its struggle with the king, was imposed on the country at large. Another kind of list, of potential voters in a parliamentary election, has been published and discussed by Jason Peacey.[13] Sometimes misleadingly called a poll book, the list of freeholders that Sir Roger Twysden thought he could rely upon in his campaign to secure election in the spring election of 1640 provides historians with plenty of potential

10. S.K. Roberts, 'Cardiganshire and the state, 1540–1689', to be published in E.M. White and J.G. Jones (eds), *Cardiganshire county history*, 2, forthcoming.

11. For example, C. Phythian-Adams, *Societies, cultures and kinship, 1580–1850* (Leicester, 1993).

12. Everitt, *The community of Kent*, p. 185.

13. J. Peacey, 'Tactical organization in a contested election: Sir Edward Dering and the spring election at Kent, 1640', in C.R. Kyle (ed.), *Parliament, politics and elections, 1604–48*, Camden Society, 5th series, 17 (2001), pp. 237–72.

for prosopographical (collective biographical) analysis at a level of detail that Everitt was unable to undertake. Jacqueline Eales's point that there was little overlap between the signatures of the petitioners in 1642 and 1649 provides a very promising line for further inquiry. If the signatures on the Kent petitions are anything like those on the petition for better preaching of the gospel in south-east Wales of the same period, there will be many duplicated names and intriguing patterns visible in how the signatures were assembled.

A more detailed study of the clergy will also doubtless yield dividends, as David Appleby implies. Generally, the Church was accorded scant space in the Everitt-influenced county studies, suffering from the dismissals by historians of it as 'an unassuming Anglicanism which minded its own business and only required lip service on Sundays'. Relations between clergy and their lay gentry patrons, the management of Church landed wealth and prosopographical studies of the parish clergy are obvious topics for future enquiry. Should the clergy be considered as a sub-set of the gentry, to whom they often owed their livings and to whom they were often closely related by family links? My impression is that the Devon clergy on the eve of the civil war were predominantly Devonians themselves. For Herefordshire, Devon and Kent, good materials survive for a social history of the clergy. Jacqueline Eales's point that conflict over the conduct of the clergy pre-dated 1640 is a crucial one in any revision of Everitt's notion of political, religious and social harmony in Kent before 1640 being disrupted by the monarchy. One collective biography exercise on Kent has now been completed. The definitive parliamentary history of Kent has now been written – although it is not yet published – by Jason Peacey as a series of articles for the History of Parliament, House of Commons 1640–60 volumes.[14] These articles on the MPs and constituencies of Kent, which together returned as many as 29 men to parliament in the two elections of 1640, leave few walls of Everitt's edifice still standing. Everitt thought that the opposition to Charles I in 1640 was 'more important for its revelation of the social organisation of the county than for its insight into the politics of the nation'.[15]

But, contrary to Everitt's impression of a county which would rather have been left alone than be troubled with national politics, there was stiff competition for seats in 1640 and a high level of informed interest among the electorate. Local interests other than that represented in the county struggled to be heard, notably in the Cinque Port boroughs of Sandwich, New Romney, Dover and Hythe, where the townsmen themselves sought to get their own men in alongside the nominees of the lord warden. Local puritan interests were well-organised, and once MPs reached Westminster their experiences in Kent borough elections fed into the Commons' perceptions and actions on aristocratic influences on the

14. To be published in S.K. Roberts (ed.), *The history of parliament: the House of Commons, 1640–1660*.
15. Everitt, *Community of Kent*, p. 83.

electoral process. The two-way relationship that the writers of the papers in this volume have identified in a number of contexts worked in parliamentary politics too. The local fed into the parliamentary, and vice versa, in ways that defy the simple polarity that underlay much of Everitt's argument. Even so, one significant feature of the picture that he painted of Kent still stands. Of the 29 men returned to Westminster in the two elections of 1640 for the county or the eight boroughs, 21 were men of Kent, even if the roots there of some were more adventitious than those of others. This argues for Everitt's sense of county community. In this respect, it fits the pattern visible in other large counties such as Devon. When the final full picture of constituencies elsewhere emerges, I rather suspect that Kent will probably fit into a very common pattern, rather than be seen as a special case.

The contributors to this volume have suggested some examples of how the research interests of Alan Everitt are being taken forward in new ways. Both David Appleby and Jacqueline Eales flag up the desirability of research on the social and political significance of the clergy and the need to address the issue of political and religious allegiance below the level of gentry. The relationship between metropolitan and provincial culture, over-simplified by Everitt into a clear dichotomy, can be explored further both in relation to material culture broadly defined and more specifically in the areas of print culture and scribal publication, particularly in terms of author motivation. The print and material culture of the 1650s in particular needs further research to illuminate a decade which by Everitt – and by many of his successor 1960s and 1970s county historians – was scooped up and dealt with rather cursorily in one chapter of his and their books.

Beyond the 1650s, David Appleby shows how the Restoration period can be viewed as a 'post-conflict culture' in which the urge towards reconciliation rubbed uneasily against a monarchical government better placed than any predecessor regime to extract loyalty and money from an exhausted political class fearful of further anarchy and bloodshed. Everitt had concluded, in Appleby's words, that after 1660 'a new species of cavalier had now emerged; men more intent on furthering their personal interests by soliciting favours at Whitehall or Westminster than shouldering the mundane responsibilities of the shire.' There are intriguing parallels to be noted between post-Restoration England and sixteenth-century post-union Wales, where, as Lloyd Bowen notes, a 'proliferation of county offices ... opened up new opportunities for honour, prestige and wealth which simply were not available beforehand'. It is clear that the 1530s, at least in Wales, and 1660, in England, Wales and doubtless in Scotland and Ireland too, saw a renegotiation of the relationship between the political or ruling class and the government. The essence of this renegotiation lay in consent, and it was a complex process of cultural assimilation, however quickly it was achieved. Such renegotiations cannot be adequately explained by simplistic notions of localism, and were as much cultural processes as sociological ones.

To conclude, one or two other avenues might be proposed that would repay future research effort by historians wishing to develop the primacy of local experiences which was at the heart of Everitt's work. One is the area of politics at supra-county regional level. Everitt's book was about the civil wars and the way allegiances were shaped before, during and after the conflict. His model of the centralising state intruding on the semi-autonomous counties has been challenged and superseded in many ways, as Jacqueline Eales shows, although comparatively little recent writing on allegiances has been based on any organising principle other than the county. But the operation of the military associations of the civil wars would be a fruitful future avenue for research that sought to investigate further the purchase of the notion of region on loyalties. The associations were the political bodies that supervised the various armies that were raised during the civil wars. As an example, the Association of Gloucester, Worcestershire, Shropshire and Herefordshire was established in October 1642 by Sir Robert Harley, from Herefordshire, and Sir Robert Cooke, from Gloucestershire. Harley's standing in this association entitled him to a place on the committee for Gloucester garrison a year later, where he was friends with the governor, Edward Massie. Because of his links with the Gloucestershire politicians, he initially chaired the Western Association, a parallel association of Gloucestershire, Hampshire, Wiltshire, Somerset, Dorset, Devon and Cornwall. This committee was a vehicle for raising an army for Sir William Waller intended to win the West Country for the parliament. In April 1644 Harley led a restructuring of committees in the west, helped by his allies Waller and Massie. This restructuring in turn led to an extension of committee rule into south-east Wales, where the difficulties of defeating the royalists encouraged the division of the committee into a body based in the House of Commons which supported Gloucester garrison and a flexible body based in the marches of Wales. In October 1644 and the summer of 1645 parliamentarians from Monmouthshire and Glamorgan were added.

Between 1642 and 1645, the story of the interweaving of Harley's parliamentary career with committees in the various counties of western England, in a stepping-stone process, was one of a continuing expansion of his interests and influence. Paradoxically, it was when Hereford fell to parliament in December 1645 that Harley's dominance of his own county was challenged. Hereford was taken by John Birch, a commander out of Harley's sphere of influence and accountable to other committees. A bitter quarrel sprang up between the small Herefordshire county committee (backed by Harley) and Birch, which spread out into a dispute over parliamentary elections in the region, even as far away from Hereford as Cirencester, where a Harley client stood in a by-election in 1647. Other associations whose areas of operation butted up against or overlapped with Harley's Association would be the Western Association, already touched upon, and the Association of Warwickshire, Worcestershire, Staffordshire and Shropshire, under the command originally of Lord Brooke of

Warwick Castle, and then Basil Feilding, second Earl of Denbigh. Other parts of the country threw up comparable patterns. The relationships between powerful political figures like Harley, the county interests both within and between the counties, the military interests and events in parliament are complex, but trying to work out the dynamics of this evolving and often fast-moving set of conflicts and allegiances offers a way forward in civil-war studies that owes much to Everitt in terms of questions posed, if not answers provided.

A final but not least significant interest of Alan Everitt's which could be profitably taken forward is his interest in landscape history, or rather his interest in the relationship between topography, the economy, social structure and political behaviour. We might call this environmental history. None of the county historians of the 1960s, 1970s and 1980s did better than Everitt did in the second chapter of his Kent book to bring out some suggested relationships between these things. It was another historian who has sadly recently died, David Underdown, who in the mid-1980s took this aspect of civil-war history to a new level. He had already published an Everitt-style history of Somerset in the civil wars, but in *Revel, riot and rebellion* Underdown leapt forward to develop a subtle and plausible thesis that in Wiltshire and Somerset the landscape and the economy, the wood-pasture areas and the grain-growing felden areas, contributed towards political allegiance.[16] This was perhaps the boldest and most exciting step forward from Everitt's position that any historian has accomplished, but attempts to develop in turn Underdown's thesis have been unconvincing, tending to founder on questions of evidence. In the English civil wars, what did constitute 'allegiance' to one side or the other?[17] Jacqueline Eales reminds us how signatures on documents can be evidentially problematic. Still more problematic are definitions of allegiance that hang on the petitions of maimed soldiers made years after the war, or the idea that in counties like Devon where, for the most part, the civil wars consisted of garrison rule parishes could be described as consistently and meaningfully either royalist or parliamentarian. We need historians to revisit the links made by historians such as Hoskins, Everitt and Underdown between politics and the environment. It will only be convincingly done by careful examination of the surviving evidence about landownership, demography, material and other forms of culture, and will be difficult. But the reintroduction of what might possibly be called the Leicester approach to issues of political allegiance, motivation and identity during the civil-war period would be proof that Alan Everitt's work on local communities in the 1640s and 1650s can still provide a stimulus to fresh enquiry.

16.   D. Underdown, *Somerset in the civil war and Interregnum* (Newton Abbot, 1973); idem, *Revel, riot and rebellion: popular politics and culture in England* (Oxford, 1985).
17.   R. Weil, 'Thinking about allegiance in the English civil war', *History Workshop Journal*, 61 (2006), pp. 183–91.

Select bibliography

Acheson, E., *A gentry community: Leicestershire in the fifteenth century c.1422–c.1485* (Cambridge, 1992).

Adamson, J., 'Introduction: high roads and blind alleys – the English civil war and its historiography', in J. Adamson (ed.), *The English civil war: conflict and contexts, 1640–1649* (Basingstoke, 2009).

Arvanigian, M., 'A county community or the politics of the nation? Border service and baronial influence in the palatinate of Durham, 1377–1413', *Historical Research*, 82 (2009).

Atherton, I., 'An account of Herefordshire in the first civil war', *Midland History*, 21 (1996).

Barnes, T.G., *Somerset, 1625–1640: a county's government during the 'personal rule'* (Cambridge, MA, 1961).

Bayley, A.R., *The great civil war in Dorset, 1642–1660* (Taunton, 1910).

Bennett, M.J., 'A county community: social cohesion among the Cheshire gentry, 1400–25', *Northern History*, 8 (1973).

Bennett, M.J., *Community, class and careerism: Cheshire and Lancashire society in the age of Gawain and the Green Knight* (Cambridge, 1983).

Binns, J., *Yorkshire in the civil wars: origins, impact and outcome* (Pickering, 2004).

Blackwood, B.G., *The Lancashire gentry and the Great Rebellion, 1640–1660*, Chetham Society, 25 (1978).

Blackwood, B.G., 'Parties and issues in the civil war in Lancashire and East Anglia', *Northern History*, 29 (1993).

Blackwood, B.G., 'The cavalier and roundhead gentry of Norfolk', *The Local Historian*, 26 (1996).

Blackwood, B.G., *Tudor and Stuart Suffolk* (Lancaster, 2001).

Braddick, M., *God's fury, England's fire: a new history of the English civil wars* (London, 2008).

Broadway, J., *William Dugdale and the significance of county history in early Stuart England*, Dugdale Society, occasional papers, 39 (1999).

Broadway, J., '"To equall their virtues": Thomas Habington, recusancy and the gentry of early Stuart Worcestershire', *Midland History*, 29 (2004).

Broadway, J., 'No historie so meete': gentry culture and the development of local history in Elizabethan and early Stuart England (Manchester, 2006).

Broadway, J., 'Aberrant accounts: William Dugdale's handling of two Tudor murders in *The Antiquities of Warwickshire*', *Midland History*, 33 (2008).

Broadway, J., *William Dugdale: a life of the Warwickshire historian and herald* (Gloucester, 2011).

Broxap, E., *The great civil war in Lancashire, 1642–1651* (Manchester, 1910).

Carpenter, C., 'The duke of Clarence and the midlands: a study in the interplay of local and national politics', *Midland History*, 11 (1986).

Carpenter, C., *Locality and polity: a study of Warwickshire landed society, 1401–1499* (Cambridge, 1992).

Carpenter, C., 'Gentry and community in medieval England', *Journal of British Studies*, 33 (1994).

Chalkin, C.W., *Seventeenth-century Kent: a social and economic history* (London, 1965).

Clark, P., *English provincial society from the Reformation to the revolution: religion, politics and society in Kent, 1500–1640* (Hassocks, 1977).

Cliffe, J.T., *The Yorkshire gentry from the Reformation to the civil war* (London, 1969).

Cliffe, J.T., *The puritan gentry: the great puritan families of early Stuart England* (London, 1984).

Cliffe, J.T., *Puritans in conflict: the puritan gentry during and after the civil wars* (London, 1988).

Coate, M., *Cornwall in the great civil war and Interregnum, 1642–1660: a social and political study* (Oxford, 1933; 2nd edn Truro, 1963).

Cogswell, T., *Home divisions: aristocracy, the state and provincial conflict* (Manchester, 1998).

Cogswell, T., Cust, R. and Lake, P. (eds), *Politics, religion and popularity in early Stuart Britain: essays in honour of Conrad Russell* (Cambridge, 2002).

Coleby, A., *Central government and the localities: Hampshire, 1649–1689* (Cambridge, 1987).

Cooper, J.P., 'The counting of manors', *Economic History Review*, 2nd series, 8 (1956).

Cornwall, J., *The county community under Henry VIII: the military survey, 1522, and lay subsidy, 1524–5, for Rutland* (Oakham, 1980).

Cust, R. and Hughes, A. (eds), *Conflict in early Stuart England: studies in religion and politics, 1603–1642* (Harlow, 1989).

Cust, R. and Hughes, A., *The English civil war* (London, 1997).

Cust, R.P., 'News and politics in early seventeenth-century England', *Past and Present*, 112 (1986).

Cust, R.P., 'Honour and politics in early Stuart England: the case of Beaumont v. Hastings', *Past and Present*, 149 (1995).

Cust, R.P., 'Catholicism, antiquarianism and gentry honour: the writings of Sir Thomas Shirley', *Midland History*, 23 (1998).

Duffin, A., *Faction and faith: politics and religion of the Cornish gentry before the civil war* (Exeter, 1996).

Dyer, C. and Richardson, C. (eds), *William Dugdale, historian, 1605–1686: his life, his writings and his county* (Woodbridge, 2009).

Eales, J., *Puritans and roundheads: the Harleys of Brampton Bryan and the outbreak of the English civil war* (Cambridge, 1990).

Eales, J., 'The rise of ideological politics in Kent, 1558–1640', in M. Zell (ed.), *Early modern Kent, 1540–1640* (Woodbridge, 2000).

Eales, J., *Community and disunity: Kent and the English civil wars, 1640–1649: four local history lectures* (Faversham, 2001).

Eales, J., 'Kent and the English civil wars, 1640–1660', in F. Lansberry (ed.), *Government and politics in Kent, 1640–1914* (Woodbridge, 2001).

Eales, J., '"So many sects and schisms": religious diversity in revolutionary Kent, 1640–1660', in C. Durston and J. Maltby (eds), *Religion in revolutionary England* (Manchester, 2006).

Evans, J.T., *Seventeenth-century Norwich: politics, religion and government, 1620–1690* (Oxford, 1979).

Everitt, A.M., *The county committee of Kent in the civil war*, University of Leicester, Department of English Local History, occasional papers, 9 (1957).

Everitt, A. (ed.), *Suffolk and the Great Rebellion, 1640–60*, Suffolk Records Society, 3 (1960).

Everitt, A., *The community of Kent and the Great Rebellion, 1640–60* (Leicester, 1966).

Everitt, A., 'Social mobility in early modern England', *Past and Present*, 33 (1966).

Everitt, A., 'The county community', in E.W. Ives (ed.), *The English revolution, 1600–1660* (London, 1968).

Everitt, A., *The local community and the Great Rebellion*, Historical Association, general series, 70 (London, 1969).

Everitt, A., *Change in the provinces: the seventeenth century*, University of Leicester, occasional papers, 2nd series, 1 (1972).

Everitt, A., 'Country, county and town: patterns of regional evolution in England', *Transactions of the Royal Historical Society*, 5th series, 29 (1979).

Everitt, A., 'The local community and the Great Rebellion', in R.C. Richardson (ed.), *The English civil wars: local aspects* (Stroud, 1997).

Fletcher, A., *A county community in peace and war: Sussex 1600–1660* (London, 1975).

Fletcher, A., *The outbreak of the English civil war* (London, 1981).

Fletcher, A., 'National and local awareness in the county communities', in H. Tomlinson (ed.), *Before the civil war: essays on early Stuart politics and government* (London, 1983).

Fletcher, A., *Reform in the provinces: the government of Tudor and Stuart England* (New Haven, CT, 1986).

Forster, G.C.F., 'Faction and county government in early Stuart Yorkshire', *Northern History*, 11 (1975–6).

Forster, G.C.F., 'Government in provincial England under the later Stuarts', *Transactions of the Royal Historical Society*, 5th series, 33 (1983).

Freeman, J.R., 'Middlesex in the fifteenth century: county community or communities?', in M.A. Hicks (ed.), *Revolution and consumption in late medieval England* (Woodbridge, 2001).

Gladwish, P., 'The Herefordshire clubmen: a reassessment', *Midland History*, 10 (1985).

Godwin, G.N., *The great civil war in Hampshire* (London, 1882).

Gratton, J.M., *The parliamentarian and royalist war effort in Lancashire, 1642–1651*, Chetham Society, 3rd series, 48 (2010).

Heal, F., *Hospitality in early modern England* (Oxford, 1990).

Heal, F. and Holmes, C. (eds), *The gentry in England and Wales, 1500–1700* (Basingstoke, 1994).

Hirst, D., 'The defection of Sir Edward Dering', *Historical Journal*, 15 (1972).

Holmes, C., *The Eastern Association in the English civil war* (Cambridge, 1974).

Holmes, C., 'The county community in Stuart historiography', *Journal of British Studies*, 19 (1980).

Holmes, C., *Seventeenth-century Lincolnshire* (Lincoln, 1980).

Holmes, C., 'The strange case of a misplaced tomb: family honour and the law in late seventeenth-century England', *Midland History*, 31 (2006).

Holmes, C., 'Centre and locality in civil-war England', in J. Adamson (ed.), *The English civil war: conflict and contexts, 1640–1649* (Basingstoke, 2009).

Hughes, A., 'Militancy and localism: Warwickshire politics and Westminster politics, 1643–1647', *Transactions of the Royal Historical Society*, 5th series, 31 (1981).

Hughes, A., 'Warwickshire on the eve of the civil war: a "county community"?', *Midland History*, 7 (1982).

Hughes, A., 'The king, the parliament and the localities during the English civil war', *Journal of British Studies*, 24 (1985).

Hughes, A., *Politics, society and civil war in Warwickshire, 1620–1660* (Cambridge, 1987).

Hughes, A., 'Local history and the origins of civil war', in R. Cust and A. Hughes (eds), *Conflict in early Stuart England: studies in religion and politics, 1603–1642* (London, 1989).

Hunt, W., *The puritan moment: the coming of revolution in an English county* (Cambridge, 1983).

Hutton, R., 'The Worcestershire clubmen in the English civil war', *Midland History*, 5 (1979).

Hutton, R., *Debates in Stuart history* (Basingstoke, 2004).

Jones, N.L. and Woolf, D. (eds), *Local identities in late medieval and early modern England* (Basingstoke, 2007).

Ketton-Cremer, R.W., *Norfolk in the civil war: a portrait of a society in conflict*, 2nd edn (Norwich, 1985).

Key, N., 'The political culture and political rhetoric of county feasts and feast sermons, 1654–1714', *Journal of British Studies*, 33 (1994).

Key, N., 'The localism of the county feast in late Stuart political culture', *Huntington Library Quarterly*, 58 (1996).

Kingston, A., *Hertfordshire during the great civil war* (London, 1894).

Kingston, A., *East Anglia and the civil war* (London, 1897).

Lake, P., 'The "court", the "country" and the Northamptonshire connection: watching the "puritan opposition" think (historically) about politics on the eve of the English civil war', *Midland History*, 35 (2010).

MacCulloch, D., 'Catholic and puritan in Elizabethan Suffolk: a county community polarises', *Archive für Reformationsgeschichte*, 72 (1981).

MacCulloch, D., *Suffolk and the Tudors: politics and religion in an English county, 1500–1600* (Oxford, 1986).

Maddicott, J.R., 'The county community and the making of public opinion in fourteenth-century England', *Transactions of the Royal Historical Society*, 5th series, 28 (1978).

Maddicott, J.R., 'Magna Carta and the local community, 1215–1259', *Past and Present*, 102 (1984).

Moreton, C., *The Townshends and their world: gentry, law and land in Norfolk, c.1450–1551* (Oxford, 1992).

Morgan, V., 'Cambridge University and "the country", 1540–1640', in L. Stone (ed.), *The university in society*, 1 (London, 1975).

Morgan, V., 'The cartographic image of "the country" in early modern England', *Transactions of the Royal Historical Society*, 5th series, 29 (1979).

Morrill, J.S., *Cheshire 1630–1660: county government and society during the English revolution* (Oxford, 1974).

Morrill, J.S., 'The northern gentry and the Great Rebellion', *Northern History*, 15 (1979).

Morrill, J.S. (ed.), *Reactions to the English civil war, 1642–1649* (Basingstoke, 1982).

Morrill, J.S., *Revolt in the provinces: the people of England and the tragedies of war, 1630–1648*, 2nd edn (London, 1999).

Payling, S., *Political society in Lancastrian England: the greater gentry of Nottinghamshire* (Oxford, 1991).

Peacey, J., 'Tactical organization in a contested election: Sir Edward Dering and the spring election at Kent, 1640', in C.R. Kyle (ed.), *Parliament, politics and elections, 1604–1648*, Camden Society, 5th series, 17 (2001).

Peacey, J., 'Sir Edward Dering, popularity and the public, 1640–1644', *Historical Journal*, 54 (2011).

Pennington, D.H., 'County and country: Staffordshire in civil war politics, 1640–4', *North Staffordshire Journal of Field Studies*, 6 (1966).

Pennington, D.H., 'The county community at war', in E.W. Ives (ed.), *The English revolution, 1600–1660* (London, 1968).

Pollard, A.J., *North-eastern England during the War of the Roses: lay society, war and politics, 1450–1500* (Oxford, 1990).

Pollard, A.J., 'The Richmondshire community of gentry in the Wars of the Roses', in C.D. Ross (ed.), *Patronage, pedigree and power in later medieval England* (Gloucester, 1979).

Richardson, R.C., *The debate on the English revolution* (London, 1977).

Richardson, R.C. (ed.), *Town and countryside in the English revolution* (Manchester, 1992).

Richardson, R.C. (ed.), *The English civil wars: local aspects* (Stroud, 1997).

Roberts, S.K., *Recovery and Restoration in an English county: Devon local administration, 1646–1670* (Exeter, 1985).

Roberts, S.K., 'Local government reform in England and Wales during the interregnum: a survey', in I. Roots (ed.), *'Into another mould': aspects of the Interregnum* (Exeter, 1981; 2nd edn Exeter, 1998).

Rollison, D., *Local origins of modern society: Gloucestershire, 1500–1800* (London, 1992).

Roots, I., 'The central government and the local community', in E.W. Ives (ed.), *The English revolution, 1600–1660* (London, 1968).

Saul, N., *Knights and esquires: the Gloucestershire gentry in the fourteenth century* (Oxford, 1981).

Scott, D., 'The Barwis affair: political allegiance and the Scots during the British civil wars', *English Historical Review*, 115 (2000).

Sharpe, K., 'Crown, parliament and locality: government and communication in early Stuart England', *English Historical Review*, 101 (1986).

Simmons, J. (ed.), *English county historians* (Wakefield, 1978).

Smith, A.H., *County and court: government and politics in Norfolk, 1558–1603* (Oxford, 1974).

Smith, B., 'A county community in early fourteenth-century Ireland: the case of Louth', *English Historical Review*, 108 (1993).

Stoyle, M., *Loyalty and locality: popular allegiance in Devon during the English civil war* (Exeter, 1994).

Stoyle, M., *West Britons: Cornish identities and the early modern British state* (Exeter, 2002).

Styles, P., 'Dugdale and the civil war', *Transactions of the Birmingham and Warwickshire Archaeological Society*, 86 (1974).

Tawney, R.H., 'The rise of the gentry, 1558–1640', *Economic History Review*, 11 (1941).

Tawney, R.H., 'The rise of the gentry: a postscript', *Economic History Review*, 2nd series, 7 (1954).

Thomas-Stanford, C., *Sussex in the great civil war and the Interregnum, 1642–1660* (London, 1910).

Underdown, D., *Somerset in the civil war and Interregnum* (Newton Abbot, 1973).

Underdown, D., 'The chalk and the cheese: contrasts among the English clubmen', *Past and Present*, 85 (1979).

Underdown, D., 'Community and class: theories of local politics in the English Revolution', in B.C. Malament (ed.), *After the Reformation: essays in honour of J.H. Hexter* (Manchester, 1980).

Underdown, D., 'The problem of popular allegiance in the English civil war', *Transactions of the Royal Historical Society*, 5th series, 31 (1981).

Underdown, D., *Revel, riot and rebellion: popular politics and culture in England* (Oxford, 1985).

Virgoe, R., 'Aspects of the county community in the fifteenth century', in M.A. Hicks (ed.), *Profit, piety and the professions in later medieval England* (Gloucester, 1990).

Ward, J.C., *The Essex gentry and county community in the fourteenth century* (Chelmsford, 1991).

Warmington, A.R., *Civil war, Interregnum and Restoration in Gloucestershire 1640–1672* (Woodbridge, 1997).

Warren, I., 'London's cultural impact on the English gentry: the case of Worcestershire, c.1580–1680', *Midland History*, 33 (2008).

Wolffe, M., *Gentry leaders in peace and war: the gentry governors of Devon in the early seventeenth century* (Exeter, 1997).

Wood, A.C., *Nottinghamshire in the civil war* (Oxford, 1937).

Woolrych, A., 'Yorkshire's treaty of neutrality', *History Today*, 6 (1956).

Wright, S., *The Derbyshire gentry in the fifteenth century*, Derbyshire Record Society, 8 (1983).

Index

Page numbers in italic refer to illustrations.